INTERPRETING China's Grand Strategy

Past, Present, and Future

Michael D. Swaine • Ashley J. Tellis

Project AIR FORCE | RAND

Prepared for the United States Air Force
Approved for public release; distribution unlimited

The research reported here was sponsored by the United States Air Force under Contract F49642-96-C-0001. Further information may be obtained from the Strategic Planning Division, Directorate of Plans, Hq USAF.

Library of Congress Cataloging-in-Publication Data

Swaine, Michael D.
   Interpreting China's grand strategy / Michael D. Swaine and Ashley J. Tellis.
      p. cm.
   "MR-1121-AF."
   Includes bibliographical references.
   ISBN 0-8330-2815-4 (clothbound)
   ISBN 0-8330-2767-0 (paperback)
   1. China—Military policy. 2. National security—China.
I. Tellis, Ashley J. II. Title.
UA835 .S82 2000
355' .033051—dc21   00-025086

RAND is a nonprofit institution that helps improve policy and decisionmaking through research and analysis. RAND® is a registered trademark. RAND's publications do not necessarily reflect the opinions or policies of its research sponsors.

Cover design by Eileen Delson La Russo

Published 2000 by RAND
1700 Main Street, P.O. Box 2138, Santa Monica, CA 90407-2138
1333 H St., N.W., Washington, D.C. 20005-4707
RAND URL: http://www.rand.org/
To order RAND documents or to obtain additional information, contact Distribution Services: Telephone: (310) 451-7002; Fax: (310) 451-6915; Internet: order@rand.org

This study identifies and analyzes the major factors determining China's grand strategy—past, present, and future—to better understand the motivations behind Chinese strategic behavior and to assess how such behavior might evolve in the future, over both the near and long term. The ultimate purpose of such analysis is to more clearly understand whether, and in what manner, China's grand strategy might pose fundamental challenges to U.S. strategic interests.

The study was conducted as part of a larger, multiyear project on "Chinese Defense Modernization and Its Implications for the U.S. Air Force." Other RAND reports from this project include:

Mark Burles, *Chinese Policy Toward Russia and the Central Asian Republics*, MR-1045-AF, 1999.

Zalmay M. Khalilzad, Abram N. Shulsky, Daniel L. Byman, Roger Cliff, David T. Orletsky, David Shlapak, and Ashley J. Tellis, *The United States and a Rising China: Strategic and Military Implications*, MR-1082-AF, 1999.

Mark Burles and Abram N. Shulsky, *Patterns in China's Use of Force: Evidence from History and Doctrinal Writings*, MR-1160-AF, 2000.

This project is conducted in the Strategy and Doctrine Program of Project AIR FORCE and was sponsored by the Deputy Chief of Staff for Air and Space Operations, Headquarters, U.S. Air Force (AF/XO), and the Director, Intelligence, Surveillance and Reconnaissance,

Headquarters, U.S. Air Force (AF/XOI). Comments are welcome and may be directed to the authors or to the project leader, Dr. Zalmay Khalilzad.

PROJECT AIR FORCE

Project AIR FORCE, a division of RAND, is the Air Force federally funded research and development center (FFRDC) for studies and analysis. It provides the Air Force with independent analyses of policy alternatives affecting the development, employment, combat readiness, and support of current and future aerospace forces. Research is performed in four programs: Aerospace Force Development; Manpower, Personnel, and Training; Resource Management; and Strategy and Doctrine.

CONTENTS

MAPS, FIGURES, AND TABLE

Maps

Figures

Table

Accurately understanding and effectively responding to the rise of China constitutes one of the most important challenges facing the United States in the early 21st century. China has always been an important state in the international system, thanks to its great potential power: large territory, vast resources, and a large population. But its significance for international politics has dramatically increased since 1978 when the market reforms initiated by Deng Xiaoping placed China on a course of action that could rapidly transform its latent potential into actual power. This process is significant not only because it promises the internal transformation of one of the world's oldest civilizations but also because, if concluded successfully, it could result in a dramatic power transition within the international system. The rise of China, consequently, embodies great analytical and policy interest and examining the determinants of China's basic approach to political-military security (i.e., its grand strategy) is critical to any assessment of current and future Chinese security behavior, especially Chinese behavior toward the United States and its allies.

This study examines China's grand strategy from historical and conceptual perspectives, identifies the major features of the strategy and the major factors driving it, and assesses how the strategy will likely evolve in the future.

Despite the fact that China's grand strategy has never been explicitly presented in any comprehensive manner by its rulers, there is little doubt that China, like any other state, has pursued a grand strategy conditioned substantially by its historical experience, its political interests, and its geostrategic environment. China's grand strategy is keyed to the attainment of three interrelated objectives: first and foremost, the preservation of domestic order and well-being in the face of different forms of social strife; second, the defense against persistent external threats to national sovereignty and territory; and third, the attainment and maintenance of geopolitical influence as a major, and perhaps primary, state.

For most of Chinese history, the efforts to attain these objectives have produced a security strategy oriented toward the maintenance, as a first priority, of internal stability and prosperity and the attainment of Chinese preeminence, if not control, along a far-flung and vulnerable geographic periphery. To carry out this strategy, China has relied upon a strong, authoritarian government employing a monolithic, hierarchical value system, the frequent and at times intense application of coercive force, a wide range of diplomatic stratagems of balance and maneuver, and the numerous advantages resulting from the maintenance for centuries of a dominant cultural and economic system throughout most of Central and East Asia. In general, strong, unified Chinese states have sought to control their strategic periphery and assert Chinese primacy by eliciting various forms of deference from periphery peoples, preferably through the establishment of unambiguous suzerainty relations backed, if possible, by superior military force. When faced with various internal and external obstacles to such methods (including domestic resistance to a prolonged, intensive use of force), strong Chinese states have relied upon a variety of noncoercive, suboptimal external security strategies, including appeasement, alliances, culturally based sinocentric patterns of interaction, and various types of personal understandings among rulers, as well as a heavy reliance on static defenses. Weak or declining Chinese states have relied primarily on noncoercive tactics to stave off foreign attacks or maintain stability along the periphery.

During the modern era (from roughly 1850 to the present), China's basic security objectives have remained unchanged. However, significant changes have occurred in China's threat perceptions, definition of the periphery, requisites for periphery control, and internal and external requirements of domestic order and well-being that together have implications for the specific type of security strategies pursued by the Chinese state. The modern era has witnessed the emergence of a hybrid "weak-strong" state security strategy that combines elements of traditional "strong-state" efforts to control the strategic periphery through military and political means with elements of a "weak-state" approach employing a primarily territorial-defense-oriented force structure and a relatively high level of involvement in diplomatic balance and maneuver.

In recent decades, following both the absorption of many former periphery areas into the Chinese state and the emergence of strong industrial powers along China's periphery, China's weak-strong state security approach has produced a "calculative" strategy, characterized by (a) a nonideological policy approach keyed to market-led economic growth and the maintenance of amicable international political relations with all states, especially the major powers; (b) a deliberate restraint in the use of force, whether toward the periphery or against other more distant powers, combined with efforts to modernize and incrementally streamline the Chinese military; and (c) an expanded involvement in regional and global interstate politics and various international, multilateral fora, with an emphasis, through such interactions, on attaining asymmetric gains. Under China's calculative strategy, confrontation or conflict with the United States or its allies in Asia would most likely occur as a result of "normal" disputes between states—especially those disputes arising from perceived threats to China's domestic order and well-being and China's territorial integrity—and not from explicit or implicit great power struggles over control of the international system.

Assuming that no catastrophic revisions of the calculative strategy are forced in the near to mid term, the natural longevity of this strategy then becomes largely a function of long-term economic, military, and domestic political developments. If present trends in these areas hold, it is only by the period 2015–2020 at the very earliest—and more likely 2020–2025—that China might begin an extended transition phase to a new security strategy. This transition phase could last for one or two decades, and its span will be determined largely by how quickly and durably Beijing can consolidate its power capacities relative to other great powers in the international system, including the United States.

Although certainly possible, it is on balance unlikely that China's political, economic, and social order will disintegrate into chaos either during the period of the calculative strategy or during the transition beyond that strategy. It is also unlikely that a more cooperative China will emerge during this period if Beijing's relative power grows to the point where a systemic power transition becomes plausible. Instead, growing Chinese power will most likely result, over the very long term, in a more assertive China. As part of this process, China could reasonably be expected to pursue most, if not all, of the core elements of those assertive grand strategies pursued by major powers in the past. These elements include efforts to augment its military capabilities in a manner commensurate with its increased power; develop a sphere of influence by acquiring new allies and underwriting the protection of others; acquire new or reclaim old territory for China's resources or for symbolic reasons by penalizing, if necessary, any opponents or bystanders who resist such claims; prepare to redress past wrongs it believes it may have suffered; attempt to rewrite the prevailing international "rules of the game" to better reflect its own interests; and, in the most extreme policy choice imaginable, even perhaps ready itself to thwart preventive war or to launch predatory attacks on its foes.

Even if the rise of Chinese power and its associated assertiveness occur, however, both preemptive containment and preemptive appeasement strategies toward a rising China would be counterproductive, for two reasons. First, so long as there is some chance that the predicted outcome of assertiveness may not occur, U.S. strategy ought to neither create the preconditions for its occurrence nor retreat in the expectation that its occurrence is inevitable. Second, if there exists some hope that the worst ravages of future security competition between the United States and China can be avoided, U.S. grand strategists are bound both by the dictates of prudence and by moral sensibility to explore every possibility that reduces the prospects of international turmoil. Hence, a policy that assumes the need to realistically engage China over the course of the calculative strategy is the most optimal approach.

To maximize the desired effects of such engagement however, U.S. policy must

- Orient the concept of engagement to include three related strands of policy: to *pursue*, whenever feasible, the possibilities of cooperation with China aimed at attaining deeper levels of encounter, stronger degrees of mutual trust and confidence, more clearly defined notions of reciprocity or equity, and greater levels of Chinese integration into the international system, and to use the resulting expanded level of cooperation and integration to encourage movement by China toward a democratic form of government; to discourage or, if ultimately necessary, *prevent* acquisition by China of capabilities that could unambiguously threaten the most fundamental core national security interests of the United States in Asia and beyond; and to remain *prepared*, if necessary, to cope with—by means of diplomacy, economic relations, and military instruments—the consequences of a more assertive and militant China with greater capabilities in a variety of political, strategic, and economic issue-areas;

- Clearly appraise the multiple instruments available to support the three central strands of engagement described in the paragraph above and assess the tradeoffs inherent in the use of these instruments;

- Maintain a clear understanding of the ends to which engagement is pursued, by developing a very short list of objectives, preferably centered on China's external security behavior, particularly as manifested in key issue-areas of interest to the United States, such as the U.S. presence and alliance structure in Asia, the open economic order, and the proliferation of weapons of mass destruction;

- Evaluate the range and types of hedging strategies required of the United States and assess how the pursuit of some hedging strategies could either undermine or enhance the success of engagement to begin with. Overall, the development of a more effective engagement policy requires a more thorough understanding of how the operational elements of China's calculative strategy might evolve over time, as China's capabilities change.

Even as this sharper reassessment of engagement is developed, however, it is important to clarify U.S. grand strategy and the objectives to which it aspires: The engagement of China should not be a policy prescription designed to assist the growth of Chinese power so that it may eventually eclipse the United States, even if peacefully. Rather, engagement must be oriented toward encouraging a more cooperative China, whether strong or weak, while also preserving U.S. primacy in geopolitical terms, including in critical military and economic arenas, given the fact that such primacy has provided the conditions for both regional and global order and economic prosperity. Together, the predicates of engagement should also focus on assisting Beijing to recognize that challenging existing U.S. leadership would be both arduous and costly and, hence, not in China's long-term interest.

The U.S. effort in this regard arguably will be facilitated if China becomes a democratic state that is more fully integrated into the international order and less inclined to employ military means. In general, so long as Beijing eschews the use of force and works peacefully to both adjust to and shape the future international system, the most destabilizing consequences of growing Chinese power will be minimized and, if the advocates of the democratic peace are correct, a U.S.-led international order of democratic states of which China is a part might even be able to avoid the worst ravages of security competition. Yet one must also keep in mind that the historical record suggests that the challenges to the attainment of this goal are likely to prove enormous because the structural constraints imposed by competitive international politics will interact with the chaotic domestic processes in both the United States and China to most likely produce pressures toward an antagonistic interaction between these entities at the core of the global system.

ACKNOWLEDGMENTS

This study has benefited greatly from the comments, suggestions, and corrections provided by several friends and colleagues over the course of its development. It was formally reviewed by Professor Edward Dreyer of the University of Miami and Professors Richard Betts and Samuel Kim of Columbia University. We have incorporated as many of their excellent suggestions and comments as possible into the text. Valuable informal written reactions to all or part of various drafts were also provided by Iain Johnston, Lyman Miller, Chas. F. Freeman, Doug Paal, Michel Oksenberg, and Jonathan D. Pollack. James Mulvenon provided essential assistance in tracking down footnotes and composed several of the graphics. Madeline Taylor pulled together the final version of the manuscript and provided all manner of logistical support. Pamela Thompson assisted in drawing the maps. Patricia Bedrosian contributed her excellent editorial expertise.

In the final analysis, however, the information, judgments, and assessments contained in this study are entirely the responsibility of the authors.

ACRONYMS

ASEAN	Association of Southeast Asian Nations
ASM	Air-to-Surface Missile
ASW	Antisubmarine Warfare
AWACS	Airborne Warning and Control System
BMD	Ballistic Missile Defense
BWC	Biological Weapons Convention
CFC	Chlorofluorocarbons
CTBT	Comprehensive Test Ban Treaty
CWC	Chemical Weapons Convention
EW	Electronic Warfare
FDI	Foreign Direct Investment
GATT	General Agreement on Tariffs and Trade
GCI	Ground Control Intercept
GDP	Gross Domestic Product
IMF	International Monetary Fund
JSOF	Japanese Self-Defense Force
MFN	Most Favored Nation
MTCR	Missile Technology Control Regime
MTR	Military-Technical Revolutions

NPT	Non-Proliferation Treaty
OED	Office of Economic Development
PLA	People's Liberation Army
PLAAF	People's Liberation Army Air Force
PLAN	People's Liberation Army Navy
PPP	Purchasing Power Parity
PRC	People's Republic of China
ROC	Republic of China
SSM	Surface-to-Surface Missile
UN	United Nations
WTO	World Trade Organization

CHRONOLOGY OF CHINESE HISTORY[1]

Shang Dynasty, 16th to 11th century B.C.

Zhou Dynasty, 11th to 3rd century B.C.

    Western Zhou Dynasty, 11th century to 771 B.C.

    Eastern Zhou Dynasty, 770 to 256 B.C.

    Spring and Autumn period, 770 to 476 B.C.

    Warring States period, 475 to 221 B.C.

Qin Dynasty, 221 to 207 B.C.

Han Dynasty, 3rd century B.C. to 3rd century A.D.

    Former (or Western) Han Dynasty, 206 B.C. to 24 A.D.

    Later (or Eastern) Han Dynasty, 25 to 220

Three Kingdoms era, 220 to 280

    Wei Dynasty, 220 to 265

    Shu Han Dynasty, 221 to 263

    Wu Dynasty, 222 to 280

Western Jin Dynasty, 265 to 316

Eastern Jin Dynasty, 317 to 420

---

[1]Adapted from *A Chinese-English Dictionary* (1992), p. 972.

Era of North-South Division, 420 to 589

Sui Dynasty, 581 to 618

Tang Dynasty, 618 to 907

Five Dynasties and Ten Kingdoms era, 907 to 960

Song Dynasty, 960 to 1279

    Northern Song Dynasty, 960 to 1127

    Southern Song Dynasty, 1127 to 1279

    Liao Dynasty, 916 to 1125

    Jin Dynasty, 1115 to 1234

Yuan Dynasty (Mongols), 1271 to 1368

Ming Dynasty, 1368 to 1644

Qing Dynasty (Manchus), 1644 to 1911

Republic of China, 1912 to 1949

People's Republic of China, 1949 to present

Chapter One

CHINA AS A NATIONAL SECURITY CONCERN

Managing the rise of China constitutes one of the most important challenges facing the United States in the early 21st century. China has always been one of the most important states in the international system, primarily because of its large territory, vast resources, and large population. Although a relatively weak power throughout the modern era, China's significance for international politics has been dramatically increasing since 1978, when the market reforms initiated by Deng Xiaoping placed it on a course of action that could lead to a rapid transformation of its latent potential into actual power, both within Asia and in the global arena. This process is significant not only because it promises the internal transformation of one of the world's oldest civilizations but also because *if concluded successfully* it could result in a dramatic power transition within the international system. Such power transitions, if the long-cycle theorists of international relations are correct, come about once every 100 years and involve fundamental shifts in the relative power relationships prevailing among the major states of the system. More important, most such shifts have often resulted in "global wars" between those dominant states that provide the vital function of order-maintenance for the international system and rising states that seek to challenge, directly or indirectly, the authority and rules of the system. Such wars usually lead to the emergence of a new pattern of dominant states that control the function of order-maintenance during the following century.[1]

---

[1]The most systematic exposition of this phenomenon can be found in Thompson (1988).

Given these considerations, the rise of China generates great analytical and policy interest, especially for the United States—the primary provider of order-maintenance for the international system since the Second World War. More specifically, China is seen to present a potential national security concern for the United States, for three reasons:

- Its general geostrategic significance and growing national capabilities,

- Its expanding involvement in and influence over the international community, and

- Unique historical and cultural factors that could exacerbate Sino-U.S. tensions over the long term.

China's huge size and geographic position as the only Eurasian continental power directly bordering on Northeast Asia, Southeast Asia, South Asia, Central Asia, and Russia mark it as a major geostrategic player able to critically affect U.S. global and regional interests. Beijing's ability to influence events across Eurasia has increased greatly during the past two decades as a result of booming economic growth and an expanding involvement in the global economic and political order. China's gross domestic product (GDP) has tripled in less than two decades, leading some analysts to conclude that with average growth rates of approximately 8–9 percent per annum over the next 20 years, China's GDP could surpass that of the United States within 10–15 years.[2] The time frame governing such an outcome seems exceedingly optimistic, given recent drops in China's growth rate and the likely long-term adverse consequences of such current events as the Asian financial crisis and China's domestic banking crisis. However, even appreciably lower growth rates, if sustained for many years and higher than those of the United States and other Western countries, would merely delay, rather than eliminate, the possibility of China's GDP overtaking that of the United States in the next century.

China's high growth rate is increasingly driven by rapidly expanding economic and technological links with the outside, especially with

---

[2]For example, see Wolf et al. (1995).

the United States, and with the highly foreign-trade-oriented economies of South Korea, Japan, Taiwan, and Southeast Asia. Largely because of these trends, China is seeking greater influence beyond its borders; it is becoming an active participant in a wide variety of international diplomatic and economic institutions and fora and is increasingly emphasizing maritime Asia in its economic and geostrategic calculations. Such developments pose obvious implications for U.S. global and regional economic and political access and influence.

In addition, China's abandonment in the 1980s of the failed autarkic and centrally planned economic system of the Maoist period and subsequent adoption of a successful, market-driven and outward-oriented reform strategy have permitted significant, albeit largely incremental, increases in aggregate Chinese military power. Of particular significance to the United States is China's nuclear weapons and ballistic missile modernization, its growing capabilities in the areas of space and information operations, and its development of air and naval battlespace denial capabilities along its eastern and southern coastlines. Continued increases in China's GDP will almost certainly translate into further improvements in Chinese military capabilities and a growing maritime strategic orientation, with direct implications for the security position and capabilities of the United States and its allies in East Asia.

The potential negative implications for U.S. security interests of a possible fundamental structural shift in the distribution of economic and military power across Eurasia are increased by several specific historical and cultural features of China's strategic outlook, experience, and behavior. First, throughout most of its long imperial history, China was the predominant political, economic, cultural, and military power of East Asia. Such predominance created a deep-rooted belief in the geopolitical centrality of China to the region. As China's relative power grows, this belief could eventually predispose Beijing to seek to displace the United States as the preeminent power and central provider of security across much of the Asia-Pacific.

Second, China's modern history of defeat, subjugation, and humiliation at the hands of the West and Japan has produced an acute

Chinese desire for international respect as a great power, as well as an enduring commitment to an independent foreign policy separate from the formal collaborative or alliance structures of other major powers, especially the United States. This impulse is exacerbated by a deeply rooted strain of xenophobia in Chinese culture. These features, when combined with the current Chinese government's longstanding and deeply felt suspicion toward the United States, suggest that reaching mutual strategic understanding and accommodation with Beijing as China's capabilities increase could prove to be very difficult.

Third, China holds strong claims to contested territories along its continental borders and its maritime periphery, the most important of which are Taiwan and the Spratly Islands in the South China Sea. These claims, some of which offer potentially enormous economic benefits to Beijing, receive wide support within China because both the elite and an apparently growing segment of the populace favor a state-centric nationalist ideology dedicated to national reunification and the creation of a strong and wealthy state. The usefulness of this nationalist ideology as a means of providing popular legitimacy to China's ideologically discredited communist government, reinforced by the general national pride engendered by China's impressive economic accomplishments, suggests that Beijing could become more assertive in pressing many of its irredentist claims as its overall capabilities increase. Efforts by China to employ military force in this effort would clearly challenge a vital U.S. interest in the continued peace and stability of Asia.

The continued increase in China's relative economic and military capabilities, combined with its growing maritime strategic orientation, if sustained over many years, will almost certainly produce both a redefinition of Beijing's strategic interests and increased efforts to improve Beijing's ability to protect those interests in ways that directly or indirectly challenge many of the existing equities of the United States and its allies. Although this process of geopolitical transformation will inevitably be part of a larger Chinese effort to carve a new place for itself in the international system—an effort that could eventually involve "a transformation of the existing hierarchy of states in the system and the patterns of relations dependent on that hierarchy"[3]—the direct and specific challenges to existing U.S. strategic interests would likely occur in four key areas:

- The U.S. military's freedom of action throughout East Asia,

- U.S. economic access to East Asia and beyond,

- The privileged political relations with most Asian powers enjoyed by the United States, and

- The overall U.S. emphasis on specific formal and informal alliances as a way to ensure peaceful and stable development in Asia.

Alternatively, the reversal or collapse of China's dynamic reform process could lead to growing domestic social and political conflict and the emergence of a weak, insecure, and defensive Chinese regime that would also present major adverse challenges to the interests of the United States and its allies. Although almost certainly less able to challenge the prevailing freedom of action and predominant influence and access of the United States in Asia, such a Chinese regime could become more belligerent and assertive over critical nationalist issues such as Taiwan and less cooperative toward a variety of regional and global issues of concern to the United States, such as arms proliferation, free trade, human rights, and the peaceful resolution of the situation on the Korean peninsula.[4]

To assess China's ability and willingness to pose such fundamental challenges to U.S. strategic interests over the long term, this study systematically identifies and examines a range of critical domestic and international factors influencing Chinese security outlook and behavior. Chapter Two assesses China's basic and longstanding security problem and its resulting general security strategy, derived from both its geopolitical security interests as a continental Asian power and its general historical and cultural approach to security. This leads in Chapter Three to an assessment of China's security behavior historically, especially with respect to the use of force versus diplomacy. This is followed in Chapter Four by a detailed analysis of

---

[3]Gilpin (1988), p. 596.

[4]For a more detailed examination of the likely security stance of a weak, insecure Chinese regime, see Swaine (1995b), pp. 104–109.

China's current "calculative" approach to security, its genesis, its logic, and its manifestations in various issue-areas of international politics. Chapter Five assesses both the natural longevity of the current calculative strategy and the long-term alternatives to that strategy, using theoretical and empirical arguments to speculate about China's future grand strategic trajectories as a rising power in international politics. Finally, Chapter Six presents several concluding comments about the eventual likely emergence of an assertive China, along with several general policy recommendations.

Throughout this study, China's grand strategy is assessed primarily from a power-political perspective, using elements of a realist approach to international relations. Adopting this approach implies that the focus of analysis rests principally on the state as a political entity dedicated to ensuring the internal and external security (i.e., survival and prosperity) of both elite and populace. Material factors such as the country's geographical position, resource endowment, economic size and structure, and military power, as well as the power wielded by senior political leaders, are emphasized as critical determinants of a regime's capability to provide for its security. Moreover, external and internal power relationships and power-oriented behavior among major international entities and key leaders, as measured primarily by such material factors, are stressed as basic elements determining threat perceptions and overall security calculations and actions. Hence, the international system is viewed primarily as a set of interactions among competitive, power-oriented states. At the same time, the approach used in this study acknowledges that various social and elite values and beliefs and the influence of different political systems (e.g., centralized authoritarian versus pluralist or democratic regimes) significantly condition, at times in critical ways, the perceptions of security issues held by political elites, their preferences, and their actions to ensure the security of the state. Indeed, the analysis attempts to assess the manner and degree to which such nonmaterial factors combine with structural factors to shape the formulation and implementation of China's grand strategy.

Although the analysis presented in Chapters Two through Four includes an assessment of both the subjective intentions and the objective structural conditions influencing Chinese security behavior in the past, the assessment of possible future Chinese behavior presented in Chapter Five does not assume that any particular set of Chinese intentions will shape China's future security strategy, other than a continued, general desire to strengthen and preserve economic power and regain geopolitical prominence. The attempt to identify and assess the likelihood of alternative future Chinese grand strategies is based mainly on a discussion of material elements that affect possible changes in Chinese state and national capabilities, as well as inferences drawn from China's historical experience as a unified state over many centuries and the experience of other rising states. In other words, the analysis of future Chinese security behavior presented in this study does not assume the existence or emergence of either malevolent or benevolent intentions on the part of China's leaders or populace. Rather, China's future security stance is seen to arise from primarily structural, systemic, and historical factors. Where historical evidence is available, the analysis incorporates it as appropriate; where historical evidence is inappropriate—as, for example, in the discussion of future Chinese strategic behavior—the analysis uses a mixture of deductive argument supplemented by historical insights relating to the behavior of other great powers.

Any examination of China's grand strategy, such as this, faces particular methodological problems. Clearly, many objections can be leveled against attempts to generalize about the security behavior of the Chinese state across the imperial and modern eras. For example, some China historians argue that each Chinese regime or dynasty possessed a unique set of political, social, and intellectual characteristics that prevent the drawing of any meaningful generalizations about state behavior. Other scholars question the very notion that a Chinese state (as a political and institutional, as opposed to cultural and ideological entity) existed before the modern era. Although it is extremely important to recognize (and incorporate into the analysis) differences in individual regime characteristics and structures, there are arguably sufficient similarities and continuities in the geographic location, ethnic make-up, and political structures and beliefs of the Chinese state to justify attempts to generalize about its security behavior throughout both pre-modern and modern times.

Other objections can be raised against the basic subject of this study, as well as its conceptual approach. Some analysts of China's current and historical approach to security argue that the Chinese state has never consciously and deliberately pursued a grand strategy, of whatever type. Others argue that the imperial Chinese regime was less concerned with protecting its territory and asserting its material power over other political entities than with ensuring its cultural and ideological preeminence through proper ritual and right conduct, and that the modern Chinese nation-state similarly emphasizes status and prestige over state power. Despite the fact that China's grand strategy has never been explicitly presented in any comprehensive manner by its rulers, the historical and contemporaneous analysis presented in this study indicates that China, like any other state, has indeed pursued a grand strategy conditioned substantially by its historical experience, its political interests, and its geostrategic environment. Moreover, although there is no question that a concern with cultural or ideological preeminence has often influenced Chinese security behavior, China's historical record, as well as deductive analysis relating to the behavior of other great powers, together suggest that the ability of the Chinese state to sustain such preeminence ultimately relies greatly on both internal and external material conditions and power relationships.

Chapter Two

CHINA'S SECURITY PROBLEM

China's security strategy is heavily conditioned by four fundamental features of its security environment.

- A long and in many places geographically vulnerable border,

- The presence of many potential threats, both nearby and distant,

- A domestic political system marked by high levels of elite internecine conflict at the apex and weak institutions or processes for mediating and resolving such conflict, and

- A great power self-image.

Even though the total geographic expanse of the areas under the control of the unified Chinese state has repeatedly expanded and contracted throughout China's long history (as discussed in detail in the next chapter), its territorial borders or frontiers have extended, at a minimum, over many thousands of miles. For example, China's present-day land borders extend for well over 10,000 miles.[1] In comparison, the northern boundaries of the Roman Empire at the time of Augustus—from the northwestern tip of Spain in the west to Jerusalem in the east—measured roughly 5,500 miles. Much of the Chinese border crosses relatively open and flat grass and scrublands, deserts, and dry steppes. To the east and south, China's ocean borders abut the Yellow Sea, the East China Sea, and the South China Sea. Such a long, open, and exposed border has presented a major

---

[1]See Map 1.

RAND*MR1121.M1*

Map 1—China and Its Surrounding Areas

challenge to every Chinese government's efforts to maintain an adequate defense against external attack.

The presence, during various periods of Chinese history, of significant numbers of potentially threatening nearby tribes, kingdoms, and states further exacerbates the challenges to territorial defense posed by a long, vulnerable border. During the imperial era, the primary security threat to Chinese territory was posed by an array of nearby nomadic tribes located along China's northern and northwestern continental borders. These peoples, skilled in the tactics and techniques of mounted warfare and desiring Chinese resources to enrich and strengthen their local political and social positions, constantly raided and harassed the Chinese state and frequently formed confederations that challenged and at times overthrew Chinese imperial regimes. A secondary but nonetheless significant threat to Chinese territory was posed, between the 7th and 9th centuries, by a large and expansionist, nonnomadic Tibetan kingdom located along China's western border.[2] Other political entities located in present-day Japan, Taiwan, and Southeast Asia also at times posed security threats to imperial China. Moreover, during the first two-thirds of the modern period (i.e., between approximately 1850 and 1945),[3] major threats or security concerns to China's continental and maritime borders were posed by aggressive imperialist powers such as Russia, Japan, Germany, Great Britain, and France. Since the end of the Second World War, a variety of militarily strong or highly industrialized nation-states such as India, Russia, Japan, and the United States have posed a variety of security threats or concerns to Chinese leaders, including the threat of invasion.

Historically, the Chinese political system has been marked by a highly personalistic pattern of rule at the top in which ultimate authority derives primarily from the power and beliefs of individual leaders, not legal or organizational norms and processes.[4] In such a political structure, senior leadership conflict and succession are resolved and critical policy issues are decided through a largely informal process of contention among complex patron-client alliance networks organized along familial, power, and policy lines[5] and often reinforced by more formal bureaucratic structures. During

---

[2]Tibetans captured the Tang Dynasty capital of Ch'ang-an in 763.

[3]The modern era overlaps slightly with the imperial era, which ended with the collapse of the Qing Dynasty in 1911.

[4]This is not to say that the Chinese polity is not highly bureaucratized. Chinese regimes from imperial times to the modern era have invariably contained complex and intricate bureaucratic organizations and procedures, many of which served to facilitate, constrain, and generally channel a wide range of leadership interactions. However, at the apex of the Chinese political system, such structures and processes served more to support, rather than to define and determine, elite power relations and policy decisions. More important, they did not authoritatively mediate conflict or ensure peaceful leadership succession.

[5]Chapter Three discusses the major policy issues that have historically divided Chinese political leadership groups.

the imperial era, contending political leadership groups consisted of the emperor; related members of the imperial household; imperial retainers or servants such as eunuchs, concubines, and personal advisors; military officers; and an array of Confucian scholar-officials and bureaucrats. During the modern period, dominant party leaders, subordinate contenders for party leadership, military officers, advisors and secretaries, and bureaucratic officials have formed the core of most personal political groupings.

Within such a highly personalized political system, policy content and behavior, including external policy, often become a tool in the domestic power struggle among the senior leadership. As a result, basic shifts in the state's policy content and direction can at times derive from the power calculations of a particular leadership group or may occur because of changes in the balance of power among contending groups or because of the rise or fall of a particular leader. Also, for such a system, periods of internal order and stability often result from the victory of a leadership group or coalition led by a single "strong man" or dominant clique in command of the main coercive instruments of rule (i.e., the military and internal security apparatus). Conversely, political and social disorder and, at times, regime collapse and civil war, can result from prolonged elite strife, corrupt and repressive leadership actions, and the arbitrary, unchecked exercise of power.

Once in power, Chinese leaders have historically sought to retain legitimacy, diffuse internal and external threats, maintain control, and thereby reduce internecine political conflict by frequently invoking widely accepted ethical or ideological norms, beliefs, and processes formulated to justify the authority of the Chinese state and to peacefully regulate state-society relations. Such concepts are contained, to varying degrees, in the traditional corpus of thought associated with Chinese state Confucianism and more recently in the highly state-centric variants of nationalism and communism espoused by the modern Chinese regime.

Despite such stabilizing efforts, China's personality-based pattern of rule has remained highly prone to internecine political conflict, often exacerbated by economic and political corruption, and to broader challenges from both Chinese society and omnipresent foreign threats. Because of these and other factors, the Chinese state has often been plagued by internal political strife, extended periods of disunity, and open internal warfare. Indeed, the Chinese state has been united as a single entity under Chinese rule for only approximately one-half of the period since the end of the Han Dynasty in 220 A.D. During the other half of this period, China has been embroiled in domestic conflict, divided between Chinese and non-Chinese regimes, or entirely ruled by non-Han Chinese invaders. Moreover, throughout Chinese history, periods of domestic weakness and disarray have often been accompanied by instances of foreign invasion and occupation. As a result, China's vulnerable borders and history of repeated foreign incursions have established a strong connection, in the minds of most Chinese, between internal political and social weakness and foreign aggression.

The combination of China's long-standing geopolitical centrality in Asia, its high level of economic self-sufficiency, and its past economic, cultural, and political influence over the many smaller states, tribes, and kingdoms along its periphery have produced a deep-seated belief in China's political, social, and cultural preeminence in Asia. Indeed, throughout most of its long history, the Chinese state, as an organized bureaucratic, political-military institution, confronted no peer competitors. Although confederations of nomadic and semi-nomadic tribes from Inner Asia and Manchuria at times overthrew and displaced the Chinese state, these entities were incapable, organizationally and conceptually, of providing an alternative system of political and military control and social order. Almost invariably during the imperial era, alien occupiers were compelled, to differing degrees, to adopt Chinese administrative structures and procedures to govern the much larger Han Chinese population.[6]

During late imperial times (i.e., since at least the Song Dynasty of 960–1279), the belief in Chinese preeminence among the states and confederations of East Asia was greatly reinforced by the hierarchical and universalistic political-ethical values of Song Neo-Confucianism.

---

[6]This is not to deny that several classic features of the imperial Chinese state and society emerged in part as a result of extensive contact with nomadic peoples. For example, many of the more militant, totalitarian, and coercive aspects of imperial rule, most clearly exemplified in the autocratic and at times despotic power of the emperor (in contrast to the bureaucratic and ideological authority of Confucian civil administrators), derived in large part from nomadic practices. See Fairbank (1992), pp. 110–112.

This belief system asserted that peace and stability within societies and among states resulted from the maintenance of a set of superior-inferior relationships in which each individual or political entity clearly understood and performed its proper role relative to others. Within such a system, proper conduct ideally resulted from self-education in the Confucian classics or the emulation of a virtuous leader who commanded respect and authority through his moral, upright behavior in upholding correct, hierarchical, patterns of human relations. In society, this leadership figure was usually the father or patriarch of an extended lineage-based clan; within the political realm, it was the emperor.[7]

Within the cosmology of imperial interstate relations, China stood at the top of the pecking order, providing an intellectual and bureaucratic model of proper governance for Chinese and non-Chinese alike. Other states or kingdoms beyond the realm of imperial China were normally expected to acknowledge, and thereby validate, the superior position of the emperor in this sinocentric world order. Deference to the authority of the Chinese ruler thus not only affirmed, conceptually, the proper ethical relations among states but also, in the Chinese view, ensured peace and tranquillity in the Chinese world order by removing any ideological challenges to the superior position of the Chinese state. However, the imperial Chinese belief in the virtues of a hierarchical world order does not imply that China's political leaders always treated other political entities as inferiors. Chinese imperial rulers were often highly practical in their approach to statecraft. When confronted with relatively strong potential or actual foes, they at times adopted far less hierarchical practices.[8] Yet the traditional preference was clearly for a sinocentric order.

On the material level, China's great power self-image was also strengthened, throughout most of Chinese history, by the high level of economic self-sufficiency and abundance of resources enjoyed by the imperial state and the resulting significant level of economic influence China exerted over its smaller neighbors. Although many Chinese imperial regimes permitted extensive trade and commercial

---

[7]Fairbank (1992), pp. 51–53, 62–63.

[8]This point is discussed in greater detail in the next chapter.

contact with the outside, such activities were in most instances not essential to the maintenance of domestic order and well-being. In fact, an excessive dependence on foreign economic activities was often seen as a source of regime weakness and vulnerability to foreign manipulation and influence and hence was resisted by many Chinese rulers. Moreover, for most of its history, the Chinese state was far wealthier, and controlled far more resources, than any of the foreign states, kingdoms, or tribal groupings with which it interacted.

The above suggests that China's self-image as a great power during the imperial era derived primarily from the dominant influence China exerted over the Asian region by virtue of the sheer size, longevity, cultural and bureaucratic influence, and economic wealth of the Chinese heartland and the Chinese state that ruled it. China's military might also contributed to its great power self-image. Yet this factor was arguably of secondary importance in the minds of most Chinese. In other words, China's sinocentric world view did not result primarily from nor rely upon an ability to exercise clear military dominance over its neighbors. Indeed, as discussed in the next chapter, strong imperial Chinese states did not always manage to dominate militarily neighboring political entities.

During the modern era, several events have injected a strong element of political equality into Chinese perceptions of interstate relations: Chinese contact with industrialized nation-states operating in a global political arena, the collapse of Neo-Confucianism as China's conceptual framework for the international order, and its subsequent replacement by a state-centric form of nationalism. As a result, since at least the early 20th century, many educated Chinese have stressed the need for China to attain the status, respect, and influence of a major power contending with other major powers in the global arena. That is, they have stressed the need for China to attain equality with, and not necessarily superiority over, other major powers. At the same time, the notion that China should in some sense enjoy a *preeminent* place among *neighboring Asian states* remains relatively strong among both elites and ordinary Chinese citizens. This is true even though the form and basis of Chinese preeminence in the modern era have changed significantly. In particular, the loss of China's cultural preeminence and economic self-sufficiency and the emergence of powerful industrialized nation-states along its borders have resulted in a stronger emphasis on the attainment of great power status through external economic/technological influence and military might. However, it remains unclear as to whether and, if so, to what degree China's aspirations for regional great power status consciously require military dominance over its periphery; it is even less clear whether China's self-image as a great power requires the deliberate attainment of a superior military position on a global scale.[9]

Historically, the combination of extreme geographic vulnerability to attacks from the periphery, state-society volatility, and a deeply rooted great power mentality have produced two fundamental sets of security perceptions among most Chinese: On the one hand, an intense fear of social chaos and political fragmentation or collapse, usually seen as "just-around-the-corner" and often closely associated with aggression and intervention from the outside; on the other hand, a belief that such chaos can be avoided only through the establishment and maintenance of a strong, united, and "just" (i.e., relatively uncorrupt and unabusive) government. From the Chinese perspective, such governmental qualities ideally require the creation and maintenance of a monolithic political order with a single source of power and authority and, until recent decades, a high level of economic self-sufficiency. Moreover, these qualities of government are to be cultivated and protected by the moral rectitude of individual leaders—and in particular by a single, dominant, public-spirited leader—not by an internal structure of institutional checks and balances or the adherence to impartial legal procedures and rulings.[10]

For the Chinese, such a personalistic, concentrated pattern of political power is viewed as necessary to provide domestic order and well-being, deter potential nearby threats to Chinese territory, and gen-

---

[9]This of course is not to deny that material factors associated with a perceived need to protect and advance China's expanding economic and political interests could eventually compel Chinese rulers to seek such military dominance. The details of the evolution of China's self-image as a great power and its implications for Chinese security behavior will be discussed in greater detail below.

[10]The strong belief in the need for a monolithic political order does not imply that Chinese regimes have invariably been led by a single, powerful figure. In many imperial regimes (e.g., during the Qing Dynasty), the power of the supreme leader was severely limited by the practical realities and complexities of elite politics. See, for example, Bartlett (1991); and Oxnam (1975). The authors are indebted to Lyman Miller for drawing our attention to these sources.

erally maintain regional peace and tranquillity. Moreover, for most Chinese, the full attainment of these core security objectives requires not only strong military defenses and economic wealth but also the ability to greatly influence, if not dominate, events on China's periphery, through both military and nonmilitary means. In the modern period, these requirements have also included a strongly felt need to deter aggression from and elicit the respect, if not deference, of more distant, major powers outside the periphery.

The twin security goals of preserving domestic order and well-being and deterring external threats to Chinese territory are closely interrelated, from the Chinese perspective. On the one hand, the maintenance of domestic order and well-being is viewed as the *sine qua non* for the defense of Chinese territory against outside threats. Specifically, a weak, divided and conflictual, or "unjust" (i.e., highly coercive and corrupt) leadership and an impoverished, disgruntled populace are viewed as the primary sources of domestic instability and conflict and invariably lead to a weakening of China's defenses, which in turn invite foreign manipulation and aggression. On the other hand, maintaining a strong defense, eliciting political (and, during the premodern period, cultural) deference from the periphery, preserving the broader goal of Chinese regional centrality, and influencing the actions of more distant powers are seen as absolutely necessary not only to ensure regional order and deter or prevent foreign aggression and territorial dismemberment but also to avert internal social unrest. This is because a state that is unable to control its borders and command the respect of foreign powers is seen as weak and unable to rule its citizenry.

Overall, in the Chinese security calculus, the maintenance of domestic order and well-being usually takes precedence over the preservation of geopolitical centrality and the establishment of influence over the Chinese periphery, for two reasons. First, the latter two goals cannot be reached without the prior attainment of the former objective. Second, historically, domestic order and well-being have often proved to be extremely difficult to achieve and preserve over time, as indicated above, and thus usually require enormous efforts by the state. In contrast, although an inability to maintain adequate material capabilities and resources for internal order poses a direct threat to regime survival, weakened military capabilities vis-à-vis the outside could be compensated for, at least over the short to medium term, through the doctrinal and ritualistic trappings of imperial preeminence or the maintenance of a large, defense-oriented standing army and, most recently, a small nuclear deterrent force.

The central problem arising from China's core security goals and requirements thus was (and remains) how to maintain, first and foremost, the robust level of resources and control features needed to preserve or enhance an often precarious domestic order and well-being and at the same time ensure an adequate defense and external presence keyed primarily to the maintenance of control over or dominant influence along China's periphery to support, ultimately, the attainment or preservation of geopolitical primacy.

Three sets of variables influence the interaction between these external and internal security demands and constraints and thus determine the type of security strategy adopted by the Chinese state at any particular point in time:

- The capability and outlook of the central government, as measured by the unity, integrity, and security priorities of its leadership and the extent of control it exercises over the government bureaucracy and military,

- The level and origin (external or internal) of resources available to the state for national defense versus internal security and social welfare, and

- The capabilities and dispositions of potential foes, particularly those located along China's periphery, as well as more distant major powers.

As discussed in greater detail in the next chapter, throughout most of Chinese history, the largely self-sufficient, internally oriented, and instability-prone Chinese state has been more concerned, when providing for its external security, with controlling or neutralizing direct threats to an established geographic heartland originating from an extensive periphery than with acquiring territory or generally expanding Chinese power and influence far beyond China's borders. During the imperial period, wealthy and powerful Chinese regimes often sought to ensure external security and affirm (or reaffirm) the superiority of the Chinese politico-cultural order by attaining a position of clear dominance over the nearby periphery, preferably through the establishment of unambiguous suzerainty relations backed, when possible, by superior military force. This was particularly evident during the founding or early stages of a regime, when strong, charismatic military figures controlled events. But the ability of a strong regime to implement and sustain such dominance varied greatly, depending upon the capabilities and geostrategic disposition and posture of the foreign state, kingdom, or tribal confederation in question and, to a lesser extent, on the general attitudes and beliefs of later Chinese emperors toward the use of force and the level of civilian elites' opposition to costly and politically disruptive, military-based, coercive security approaches. Often, when faced with both domestic opposition and leadership uncertainty and persistent external pressure, strong imperial Chinese states would discard coercive, offensive military strategies in favor of a variety of pragmatic, noncoercive, suboptimal external security strategies, all carried out under a guise of symbolic deference to "superior" Chinese authority.

In contrast, relatively weak or declining imperial Chinese regimes, usually faced with growing concerns over domestic order and well-being and often unable to elicit even symbolic deference from other states, would rely primarily on noncoercive strategies to stave off foreign attacks or maintain stability along the periphery. When such strategies proved unsuccessful, weak and internally divided regimes would in a few instances resort to desperate military means to defend their security, at times in response to the demands of dominant, conservative domestic leadership groups. Such resistance invariably met with little success, however, and a severely weakened regime, or the wholesale collapse of a regime, would result in major reductions in Chinese control over the periphery and sometimes also in the loss of Chinese territory to foreigners. Yet strong, unified Chinese regimes would eventually reemerge and seek to regain such losses. Hence, the dynamic interaction among changing foreign and domestic capabilities and domestic elite attitudes and behavior created a repetitive, cyclical pattern of expansion, consolidation, and contraction of Chinese control over the periphery that coincided with the rise, maintenance, and fall of imperial Chinese regimes.

During the modern period, China's security problem and resulting strategy has continued to center on efforts to preserve a fragile degree of domestic order and well-being as a first priority, and to consolidate control over the periphery as a primary means of external defense. However, these efforts have taken place largely within an environment of generally limited but increasing resources and capabilities. Moreover, as discussed in greater detail in the next chapter, the modern era has precipitated some major shifts in China's overall security environment and leadership outlook, leading to changes in threat perceptions, the definition of the periphery and requisites for periphery control, the internal and external requirements of domestic order and well-being, and hence the specific type of security strategies pursued by the Chinese state. The key question that China's basic security problem presents for the future is the extent to which these changing requirements for domestic order and periphery control, combined with China's increasing capabilities, will alter or reaffirm past historical patterns of strong state behavior, especially regarding the use of force rather than diplomacy. To answer this question, the historical record concerning China's security behavior will first be examined more closely. Following that, the study examines the specific features of China's present security strategy, assesses its longevity, and identifies what might replace it over the long term.

Chapter Three

THE HISTORICAL CONTEXT

Chinese security behavior since the emergence and maturation of the unified Chinese state well over 1,000 years ago has contained five core features, each significant to both current and future security policy:

- Efforts to protect the Chinese heartland through border defense and control over a large and long-standing strategic periphery whose outer geographic limits remained relatively constant over time.

- Periodic expansion and contraction of periphery control and regime boundaries, primarily as a result of fluctuations in state capacity; the eventual reemergence of a unified state, often despite long periods of fragmentation and civil war.

- The frequent yet limited use of force against external entities, primarily for heartland defense and periphery control, and often on the basis of pragmatic calculations of relative power and effect.

- A heavy reliance on noncoercive security strategies to control or pacify the periphery when the state is relatively weak, unable to dominate the periphery through military means, or regards the use of force as unnecessary or excessively costly.

- A strong, albeit sporadic, susceptibility to the influence of domestic leadership politics, through both the largely idiosyncratic effect of charismatic leaders and elite strife and the more regular influence of recurring leadership debates over autonomy and the use of force.

21

This chapter describes and analyzes each of these features, thus providing the historical context for presenting and evaluating China's current and possible future strategic orientation and behavior, contained in Chapters Four and Five, respectively.

BORDER DEFENSE AND PERIPHERY CONTROL

For over 1,000 years, China's external security behavior has been keyed to the defense of a Chinese cultural, geographic, and sociopolitical heartland. This area largely comprises present-day North and South China Proper, which encompasses a mosaic of rich agricultural plains, interspersed with small and medium-sized mountain ranges, centered on the tributaries and floodplains of the Yellow River in the north and the Yangtze River in the south. The eastern, southern, and southwestern boundaries of the Chinese heartland are defined primarily by geographical barriers (the Yellow Sea, the East China Sea, the South China Sea, and the mountains, jungles, and high plateaus of the west and southwest). In the north, however, the boundaries of the Chinese heartland were determined by a combination of both geographic and human factors: the enormous expanse of the arid steppes and deserts of the north and northwest, which resisted the establishment of the sedentary, intensive agricultural settlements of the south, and the fierce resistance presented by nomadic tribes that occupied the entire northern frontier. Map 2 highlights the approximate area of the Chinese heartland.

Demographically, over 90 percent of the occupants of the Chinese heartland are ethnic Han Chinese or descendants of mixed Han-nomadic or Han-Southeast Asian peoples.[1] These people constitute a highly homogeneous culture distinguished by a single written language, a tight-knit, lineage- and clan-based pattern of social organization, and a common set of social beliefs drawn largely from the humanistic and ethical doctrine of Confucianism.

---

[1]The Han Chinese have not remained separate from other cultures in Asia. They have absorbed many of the political and social customs and beliefs of nearby peoples throughout their long occupation of the Chinese heartland. Indeed, prolonged interaction between Han Chinese and Inner Asian peoples in particular significantly influenced the structure and behavior of the imperial Chinese state, as discussed below.

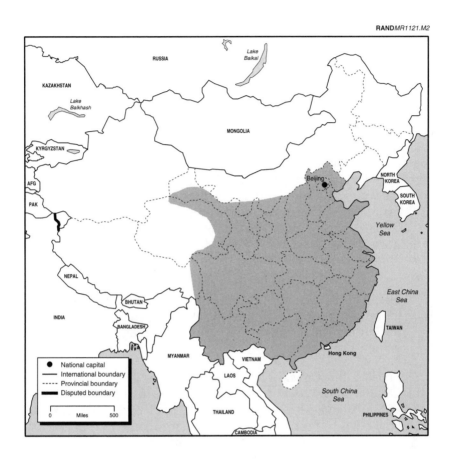

RAND*MR1121.M2*

Map 2—China's Heartland

The Chinese heartland emerged over 1,000 years ago largely as a result of four historical developments:

- The creation of a single, unified Chinese state (the short-lived Qin Dynasty) in 221 B.C., through a protracted process of warfare and diplomatic maneuver among many rival feudal kingdoms. This first Chinese state encompassed much of present-day North China south of the Great Wall.

- The emergence of the major institutional and conceptual features of the imperial Chinese state during the Former Han Dynasty (206 B.C.–24 A.D.), the refinement and extension of those features over the next several centuries, and the concurrent extension of the Chinese regime's centralized political and military control over most of the heartland region described above.[2]

- The subsequent occupation and settlement of the entire heartland region, through the gradual migration of northern Chinese peoples southward, eastward, and southwestward to the ocean, the high plateaus of Central Asia, and the jungles of Southeast Asia. Much of North and Central China Proper had been settled by the end of the Later Han Dynasty (220 A.D.), although parts of the southwest and South China Proper were not fully, and permanently, settled until centuries later, during the Tang Dynasty (618–907), the Song Dynasty (960–1279), and, in the case of present-day Yunnan Province, during the early decades of the Ming Dynasty (1368–1644).

- The gradual acceptance by the entire populace of the heartland region of the fundamental precepts of Confucianism as a basis for ordering relations within society; this process began during the Former Han Dynasty and continued through at least the end of the Tang Dynasty.

Historically, the defense of this Chinese heartland required efforts by the Chinese state to directly or indirectly control, influence, or neutralize a very large periphery surrounding it.[3] For virtually the entire imperial era (i.e., from the Han Dynasty until the mid 19th century, when the late Qing Dynasty came into contact with many Western imperialist powers), this periphery region primarily encompassed large tracts of land along the northern and northwestern frontiers,

---

[2]Although the Qin had conquered and absorbed its rivals, abolished many of the social and economic foundations of the previous feudal order, and established a centralized bureaucratic polity across North China, its rulers governed by rigid and despotic laws and harsh punishments. Thus it did not survive long past the death of its founder. In its place eventually emerged a more sophisticated regime that combined elements of its autocratic predecessor with a more enlightened political and social system led by civilian government administrators and scholar-officials educated in Confucian precepts that stressed the maintenance of political and social order through the broad acceptance of explicit hierarchical roles and ethical values.

[3]The central importance of the concepts of core and periphery to Chinese security policy are also stressed by Michael H. Hunt, whose work has influenced our overall understanding of this complex subject. See in particular, Hunt (1996).

i.e., modern-day Xinjiang, Outer and Inner Mongolia, Tibet, and northeast China (i.e., former Manchuria). The northern part of present-day Southeast Asia and the Korean Peninsula were only intermittently regarded as a part of China's strategic periphery during the imperial era, whereas ocean regions adjacent to China's eastern and southern coastline, Hainan Island, Taiwan, Japan, and the Russian Far East first took on a strategic value only at the end of the imperial era, during the Qing Dynasty.[4] In other words, for most of the imperial era, China's strategic periphery consisted primarily of inland regions adjoining its continental borders. During the modern era (i.e., since the mid 19th century), China's strategic periphery has expanded to fully encompass both continental and maritime regions. Map 3 shows the approximate extent of China's historical periphery.

Throughout most of Chinese history, the pacification or control of this periphery was usually regarded as essential to prevent attacks on the heartland and, during various periods of the imperial era, to secure Chinese dominance over significant nearby inland (and, to a much lesser extent, maritime) trade routes. The establishment of Chinese control or influence over the periphery, whether actual (as in the form of military dominance or various specific types of lucrative economic and political arrangements) or largely symbolic (as reflected in the more ritualistic aspects of China's tributary relations with periphery "vassal" states and kingdoms), was also considered extremely important during most of the imperial era as a means of affirming the hierarchical, sinocentric, Confucian international order. Even when periphery areas did not pose a significant security threat to the Chinese heartland, or during times of relative Chinese

---

[4]The period of the Southern Song Dynasty (1127–1279) constitutes a partial exception to this general statement. As explained in greater detail below, at that time, the imperial Chinese state was forced, by the loss of North China to nomadic powers, to defend increasingly important maritime trade and transport routes along the southern coastline and to ensure the security of China's rivers and tributaries. During the final years of the Song, the growing Mongol threat to China's rivers, lakes, and seacoast prompted a significant expansion of the Song navy. Swanson (1982), p. 59. For the vast majority of the imperial era, however, inland-oriented Chinese rulers did not view the oceanic regions adjoining China's coastline as a strategic periphery to be controlled through the maintenance of a superior green or blue water naval force.

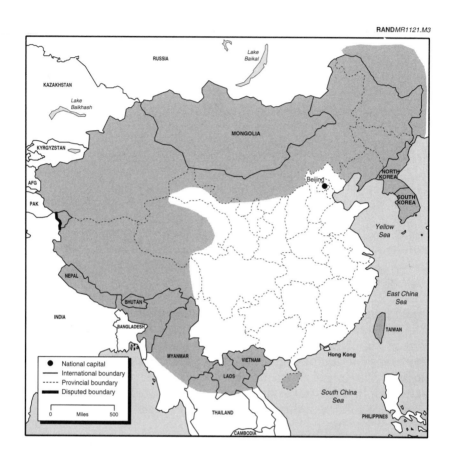

Map 3—China's Periphery

weakness, the symbolic maintenance of a sinocentric order nonetheless remained an important objective of the Chinese state, to sustain the political legitimacy and authority of the Chinese order and, it was hoped, to deter potential adversaries.

In addition to seeking control or influence over the strategic periphery, the Chinese state also frequently employed a more passive means of defending the heartland—various types of static defenses along China's territorial frontier and coastline. These defenses usually consisted of military garrisons and fortifications. The foremost example of the latter was, of course, the famous Great Wall, constructed along a major portion of China's northern frontier to protect against nomadic attacks. The Chinese also at times built fortifications and garrisons at various points along China's southern maritime borders, primarily to defend against attacks by pirates.[5] Such attacks at times constituted significant security threats to the Chinese heartland.[6] Although sometimes serving as mutually reinforcing strategies for the defense of the heartland, sharp debates often occurred within China's ruling circles over whether to rely primarily on static defenses along China's more turbulent northern and northwestern frontier or to launch more costly military expeditions to control the periphery beyond. These debates are discussed in greater detail at the end of this chapter.

During the first part of the modern era (i.e., the late 19th and early 20th centuries), most of the northern and western parts of China's long-standing strategic periphery were directly and formally incorporated into the Chinese heartland, either by military force and occupation (in the case of Tibet and Xinjiang) or by the sinicization of the region through cultural assimilation and acceptance of Han Chinese migration and settlement (in the case of Inner Mongolia and Manchuria). (Mongolia itself, however, thanks to its prior status as a client of the Soviet Union, escaped this process.) As a result of this assimilation, the territorial boundaries of the Chinese state attained their maximum extent, reaching the borders of established states that had emerged in the modern era. Although marking an unprecedented increase in the aggregate territorial size of the Chinese state, this expansion did not greatly increase the overall size of those combined heartland and periphery areas that had historically fallen under Chinese rule or influence. In other words, after incorporating

---

[5]As Swanson (1982, p. 55) asserts, imperial Chinese maritime strategy centered on the largely shore-based defense of river approaches, major harbors, and large offshore islands.

[6]During the Ming, pirates repeatedly attacked the seacoasts of East Asia, from Korea to Indochina. They threatened some of the most fertile and prosperous areas of imperial China and at times struck far inland to seize and plunder important towns and cities. Between 1552 and 1559, for example, pirate attacks spread to areas north and south of the Yangtze delta, extended into modern Jiangsu and Anhui Provinces, and threatened urban centers such as Nanjing, Suzhou, and Yangzhou—the original base of Ming power, the location of the founder's grave, and a political center next in importance to the Beijing area. Such attacks accelerated the decline of the Ming. So (1975), pp. 3–7.

most of its traditional northern and western strategic periphery, the Chinese state in the early modern era (i.e., during the late Qing and nationalist periods) did not immediately seek to control or dominate a new, more distant strategic periphery beyond Tibet, Xinjiang, Inner Mongolia, and Manchuria. This was most likely because the state at that point was either materially unable to establish such control or did not see the need to do so. The communist regime has also thus far generally eschewed efforts to control a new, larger strategic periphery.

The geographical delineation of the Chinese heartland and the extensive periphery beyond it remained relatively constant into the modern era for several reasons: First, major geographical formations (i.e., oceans, mountains, high plateaus, arid steppes, deserts, and jungles) largely determined the outer limits of the heartland in the pre-modern era. Such major physical boundaries prevented, for both geographic and practical economic/administrative[7] reasons, more distant migration and permanent settlement by the largely sedentary Han Chinese agricultural population and the accompanying establishment of those stable governing institutions found within the heartland.

Second, the periphery areas along China's continental border were occupied by marauding tribes and kingdoms of the northeast, north, northwest, and southwest. These included, in early times, the Xiongnu and Xianbi of the north and northeast steppes, and, later, the Jurchens and Manchus of the northeast, the Mongols of the north, and the Turkic and Tibetan peoples of the northwest and southwest desert and plateau areas.[8] During the imperial era, these peoples posed the primary security threat to the Chinese state and heartland and resisted efforts by Chinese rulers to control or domi-

---

[7]Lattimore (1979), pp. 274–275, and Lattimore (1962), pp 88–89. Lattimore argues that very practical cost-benefit calculations of military and administrative expense versus local tax revenue income often determined the limits of Chinese imperial expansion. For a similar argument, see Sheperd (1993). Sheperd states that, because of limited fiscal capacity, "the Chinese state only found direct rule of frontier territories attractive when a jurisdiction's economic development ensured that local tax revenues would cover the costs of administration or when strategic concerns dictated an administrative presence (that might have to be subsidized by the central government) despite low revenue potential" (p. 401). Also see Hucker (1975), pp. 61–62.

[8]Barfield (1989).

nate their lands. Although many fewer in number than the Han Chinese and generally lacking political and social institutions suitable for administering the settled agricultural population of the Chinese heartland, these largely pastoral nomadic and semi-nomadic[9] tribes, kingdoms, and confederations constantly harassed and encroached upon the inland continental boundaries of the Chinese state, frequently controlled large portions of Chinese territory,[10] and twice conquered the entire Chinese heartland.[11] In fact, non-Chinese ruled all or part of the Chinese empire for considerably more than one-half of the period between 1000 and 1911.[12]

The threat posed by nomadic warriors was largely due to their superior warfighting capabilities and high mobility. Expert horsemen skilled in the use of the bow and sword, they could quickly concentrate overwhelming forces at a single point and thus overwhelm China's usually static defenses. They were also usually able to evade pursuit and destruction by much larger, yet slower, infantry-based and heavily armored Chinese forces. Such forces were often hard to deploy in sufficient numbers at critical points along the border, difficult to provision in barren frontier areas, and constrained in their movement and length of time in the field by a heavy reliance on long supply trains.[13]

Third, throughout the imperial period, no other major power centers beyond the Chinese state were positioned either to threaten China or

---

[9]Semi-nomadic peoples included tribes from areas that contained both settled farming and pastoral nomadic communities. These were found primarily in parts of Manchuria and Turkestan. One major power that threatened the imperial Chinese state was not nomadic: the Tibetan Empire.

[10]Most notable were the regimes established in North China by the Liao (916–1125) and the Jin (1115–1234), when parts of South China were ruled by the Han Chinese Song Dynasty (960–1279).

[11]The Yuan Dynasty (1264–1368) was established by the Mongols and the Qing Dynasty (1644–1911) was established by the Manchus, both non-Han Chinese nomadic or semi-nomadic peoples. For a brief overview of the origin and nature of these non-Chinese regimes, see Hucker (1975), pp. 122–133, 144–157, and Fairbank (1992), pp. 112–118, 143–162.

[12]Oxnam (1975), p. 4.

[13]For further details on nomadic military prowess and the problems confronting most imperial Chinese forces that operated in northern and northwestern periphery areas, see Barfield (1989), pp. 55–56; Hucker (1975), pp. 122–123; and Jagchid and Symons (1989), pp. 52–53.

to provide allies against nearby threats. Contemporaneous empires centered in modern-day European Russia, India, and Italy were geographically distant or extremely difficult to reach and largely uninterested in the affairs of an empire located at the far end of the Eurasian continent, remote from most critical pre-modern maritime and land-based lines of communication and trade. As a result, the Chinese state was not compelled to expand beyond its historical periphery to balance or counter distant threats from other established powers. It persisted as the dominant civilization and political power within Central and East Asia until the mid 19th century.

Fourth, and closely related to the previous point, the relatively fixed extent of the Chinese heartland and periphery also resulted from the general economic and political self-sufficiency of the Chinese state. Although at times engaged quite extensively in trade and cultural contact with other lands, and while absorbing and adapting an array of foreign religious and ethnic beliefs and practices, the imperial Chinese state generally remained self-sufficient (and, at times even insular) as an economic and political entity. Specifically, unlike smaller states or larger maritime empires, the Chinese state did not rely on external sources of raw materials, commodities, or know-how to prosper or survive; nor, during most of the imperial era, did it highly value or depend upon external political or military support, in the form of explicit, long-standing alliances, for its existence, although it certainly cooperated at times with foreign entities to counter major threats.

External economic interests played a notable, but highly limited, role in imperial Chinese security calculations primarily in four ways. First, the Chinese desire to protect trade routes through Central Asia to the Middle East and beyond (e.g., the famous Silk Road) gave added impetus to Beijing's efforts to control or dominate parts of Chinese Turkestan (Xinjiang). Second, the imperial court's interest in pearls, ivory, and other precious materials spurred efforts to subjugate parts of Southeast Asia, especially Vietnam. Third, the Chinese need to secure tax revenues from seaborne commerce prompted the Southern Song Dynasty to build a notable coastal naval presence.

Fourth, the later Ming Dynasty constructed a major blue water naval force in part to expand China's tributary trade relations.[14]

However, none of these economic factors was absolutely critical to external Chinese security behavior, or persisted over long periods of time. The extension of imperial Chinese control far into modern-day Xinjiang was primarily strategic and reactive, i.e., intended to outflank nomadic and semi-nomadic tribes to the north and northeast and to deny them the resources of that area. The expansion of Chinese influence into northern parts of modern-day Southeast Asia was part of the larger southward migration of Han Chinese populations and culture mentioned above and also at times occurred in response to various security threats, discussed below. The significance of seaborne commerce during the Song Dynasty was only a temporary phenomenon, reflecting the fact that the Song regime had been pushed out of North China by nomadic peoples and was forced to augment its declining land tax revenues by levying taxes on seaborne trade. This situation did not persist long after the collapse of the Song, however, as the Mongol Yuan Dynasty (1271–1368) was able to establish control over the entire Chinese heartland and resume the traditional reliance of the Chinese imperial state on land taxes and internal grain transport. The subsequent development of a major blue water naval force under the early Ming emperors partly reflected the desire to increase significantly imperial coffers after the devastation wrought by the Mongol Yuan Dynasty and the costs of establishing the Ming Dynasty, and did not survive the death of its strongest patron, the Emperor Ming Yongle.[15]

Politically, for most of the imperial era, the Confucian institutions and beliefs of the Chinese state and the parochial interests of various leadership groups usually led to a stress on internal order over development and the maintenance of domestic harmony, stability, and prosperity over the conquest and absorption of foreign territories,

---

[14]Zheng He undertook seven voyages between 1405 and 1433 as commander of the Ming fleet under Emperor Ming Yongle. His fleet visited Southeast Asia, Ceylon, India, the Persian Gulf, and East Africa.

[15]Hucker (1975), pp. 59–61; Fitzgerald (1972), pp. 90–93, 185–186; Levathes (1994); Wolters (1970), pp. 156–157; and Thomas Barfield, personal correspondence. The significance of the Ming fleet in relation to the Chinese use of force will be discussed in some detail below.

especially those areas *beyond the periphery.*[16] During various periods of imperial Chinese history, military incursions into the known periphery and more ambitious efforts to expand China's political, economic, and military reach beyond the existing periphery were often strongly resisted by Confucian civilian bureaucrats and imperial advisors, for both selfish individual/bureaucratic reasons and broader conceptual reasons.[17] Moreover, although certain foreign beliefs such as Buddhism were clearly regarded by some Chinese rulers as threats to the harmony and stability of the Confucian Chinese state and society, such intellectual threats almost invariably prompted defensive reactions from the Chinese state (i.e., sporadic efforts to stamp out the offending ideas domestically or insulate Chinese society from further such intrusions) rather than offensive (and expensive) forays far from home to destroy the source of the ideas.

During the modern era, contact with industrialized nation-states, the related demise of Confucian concepts of state authority and inter-state relations, and the overall increasing demands of economic and military modernization have compelled the Chinese state to significantly alter the means by which it seeks to control its periphery, while also limiting its ability to do so. However, these developments have *thus far* not resulted in a major expansion of China's strategic periphery beyond its historical limits. This might largely be because the security challenge posed by Western industrial states and Japan has taken place during a weak state era covering the decline of the Qing Dynasty in the late 19th and early 20th centuries, a subsequent period of internal political fragmentation in the early to mid 20th century, and the emergence, under communist leadership, of a unified yet still relatively weak Chinese nation-state in 1949. During these periods, the Chinese state has been almost entirely preoccupied with reestablishing domestic order, ensuring domestic well-being, and strengthening China's control over traditional frontier areas, in part through the incorporation of past periphery regions into the heartland. Only very recently (i.e., since the mid 1980s) have *some* Chinese strategists and leaders begun to speak about the need to expand and in some cases redefine China's strategic frontiers to

---

[16]For various views on the primarily non-expansionist outlook of imperial Chinese rulers, see Kierman and Fairbank (1974).

[17]More on this point below.

include regions well beyond China's present territorial boundaries and entirely new areas such as outer space and cyberspace.[18] Whether a stronger China will formally adopt an expanded definition of its strategic periphery and use more assertive policies to defend it will be discussed in Chapters Five and Six.

FLUCTUATIONS IN PERIPHERY CONTROL AND REGIME BOUNDARIES

Historically, virtually every Chinese regime (both Han Chinese and non-Han Chinese alike) has at various times sought to maximize its control or influence over the strategic periphery described above and thus set regime boundaries at the maximum level permitted by geographic, economic-administrative, and military-political constraints. However, such efforts usually depended upon the prior establishment of domestic order and well-being, which in turn depended upon the existence of a relatively strong and unified state. Hence, a pattern of peripheral (and territorial) expansion and contraction emerged that coincided with the rise and decline of individual Chinese regimes.[19]

For most major regimes of the imperial era (e.g., during the Han, Tang, Ming, and Qing Dynasties), attempts to assert control or influence over the periphery usually occurred *after* an initial period of internal regime formation and consolidation. Throughout this early period, which sometimes lasted for several decades, the energies of China's new political leadership were devoted to eliminating any remaining domestic resistance and reestablishing internal order and control. As a result, external security policy during these times was usually keyed to the establishment of static defenses along those territorial boundaries inherited from the previous regime and the pursuit of noncoercive measures (such as various appeasement or divide-and-conquer tactics, discussed below) designed to placate or neutralize nearby potential threats.

---

[18]Nan (1997); and Godwin (1997).

[19]The following overview of the general pattern of periphery expansion and contraction relies upon several sources, including Barfield (1989); Fairbank (1992); Hucker (1975); Huang (1997); Hunt (1984); Harding (1984); Spence (1990); Kierman and Fairbank (1974); and O'Neill (1987).

Major exceptions to this pattern of behavior during the imperial era were presented by the Qin (221–207 B.C.) and Sui (581–618) Dynasties. Both regimes united China by force after long periods of political division and warfare and subsequently adopted and sustained highly aggressive, coercive policies toward the periphery from their earliest years, as they did in the domestic realm. Yet such excessively militant policies contributed greatly to the early demise of both regimes and arguably provided a negative lesson for later dynasties (and particularly for the Han and Tang Dynasties that immediately followed the Qin and Sui, respectively).

Once internal order had been established and a regime's unity and authority had been assured, most Chinese regimes (both imperial and modern) would undertake efforts to assert (or reassert) direct control over the periphery and consolidate the territorial boundaries of the Chinese state at their maximum historical limits. During the imperial era, such undertakings would sometimes cover several generations and were usually carried out by a series of early or "founding" emperors possessing extensive experience or interest in military affairs and the motivation and resources necessary for such a costly effort. The foremost examples of imperial "founding" efforts to subdue or dominate periphery peoples occurred during the Han Dynasty, under Emperor Han Wudi (against present-day Xinjiang, South China, Southeast Asia, and parts of southern Manchuria and northern Korea), the Tang Dynasty, under Emperor Tang Taizong (against Central Asia, Mongolia, Tibet, northeast India, and northern Korea), the Ming Dynasty, under Emperors Ming Hongwu and Ming Yongle (against southern Manchuria, Central Asia, Mongolia, Burma, northern Korea, and Vietnam), and the Qing Dynasty, under Emperors Kang Xi and Qianlong (against Taiwan, southeast Siberia, Mongolia, Central Asia, Tibet, and Nepal). Such efforts were not always successful. For example, the early Ming attempt to reincorporate much of present-day Vietnam into China failed after the death of its major proponent, Ming Yongle.[20]

During the modern era, both the Republican and Communist governments undertook similar "founding" efforts to reestablish and then consolidate Chinese influence along the periphery. In both

---

[20]See below for more on imperial Chinese security policy toward Southeast Asia.

cases, however, this occurred largely despite the absence of a prior period of regime formation and consolidation.

Nationalist China sought to capitalize on prior Qing successes in absorbing most periphery territories into the Chinese empire. On February 15, 1912, the former prime minister of the defunct Qing court (Yuan Shikai) proclaimed, in the articles of abdication of the last Qing emperor (Emperor Pu Yi), that all former periphery territories acknowledging Qing suzerainty or nominally under Qing rule were to be considered part of the new Republic of China (ROC). These included Mongolia, Xinjiang, Manchuria, and Tibet.[21] In the decades before the announcement of the abdication document, Xinjiang and Manchuria had already been formally incorporated as Chinese provinces (in 1884 and 1903, respectively) but had been subsequently ruled by local warlords as quasi-independent states. Tibet had acknowledged Qing suzerainty during most of the Qing Dynasty (usually under duress) but subsequently rejected the nationalist claim to the kingdom. Inner and Outer Mongolia, which had also been vassal states of the Qing, also rejected the nationalist claim. Nationalist Chinese leaders subsequently sought to confirm their claim to Tibet and Mongolia by sending military forces into both areas soon after the establishment of the ROC.[22] These efforts were not successful, however, largely because of the weakness of the ROC regime. Taiwan was not included in Yuan Shikai's proclamation of 1912 because it had been formally incorporated into China centuries earlier and had become a part of the Chinese heartland through extensive Han Chinese migration.[23]

The communist regime moved to reaffirm or consolidate Chinese control over virtually all the above periphery areas (including Taiwan, but excluding Outer Mongolia) within the first decade of its establishment in 1949, through a combination of political and military means. These efforts resulted in the formal incorporation of each

---

[21]O'Neill (1987), pp. 57, 214.

[22]Goldstein (1989), pp. 65–66, 83; and Paine (1996), pp. 317–318.

[23]Taiwan became a prefecture of Fujian Province from 1684, the date of the establishment of undisputed Qing control over Chinese settlements on the West coast of the islands. It then became a Qing province in 1887, largely in response to foreign aggression from Japan and France. For further details, see Sheperd (1993), especially pp. 106–107, 397.

area into the People's Republic of China as either a province (in the case of Xinjiang, former Manchuria, and Inner Mongolia) or an autonomous region (in the case of Tibet), with the sole exception of Taiwan, which was prevented from being absorbed into the PRC by the intervention of the United States in 1950.

Throughout history, attempts to consolidate Chinese control over the periphery served three specific purposes: (a) to eliminate existing or potential threats to Chinese frontiers and trade routes posed by nearby tribes, kingdoms, or foreign states; (b) to intimidate or persuade neighboring states, kingdoms, and peoples along the periphery into accepting Chinese suzerainty and thereby acknowledging China's sinocentric world view; and generally (c) to reinforce, among the Chinese populace, the personal authority of the new regime and its leaders. These purposes all derived, in turn, from the fundamental desire of the Chinese state (both imperial and modern) to affirm its legitimacy, authority, and status with regard to both domestic and foreign audiences and to defend the heartland from attack.

During virtually the entire imperial era, security concerns arguably constituted the primary motive for efforts to control or influence the periphery along China's turbulent northern and northwestern borders, whereas legitimacy and status concerns, although important, were usually of secondary importance. In contrast, policy toward China's southern and southwestern periphery was arguably motivated primarily by regime legitimacy and status concerns throughout most of the imperial era, although security issues were clearly involved in several instances, especially in relations between the Tang Dynasty and both Tibet and the Tibeto-Burman Nan-chao kingdom. These became increasingly important during the Ming and Qing periods as southern and southwestern borderlands became increasingly unstable. During the modern era, security concerns have come to dominate Chinese calculations toward the entire periphery, whereas legitimacy and status concerns have become far less significant, given the collapse of the Confucian world view.[24]

---

[24]The difference in emphasis on security versus nonsecurity concerns in China's policy toward the periphery is further discussed below, in the context of the use of coercive versus noncoercive security measures.

From the time of the Han Dynasty, when the Chinese state had expanded to occupy, if not entirely control, virtually the entire heartland described above, efforts to control or influence China's strategic
periphery have been largely limited to the reestablishment of the
level of dominance that was lost during previous periods of regime
decline and/or fragmentation. In other words, periphery expansion
has been primarily defensive in nature, intended to eliminate persistent external security threats and bolster or reestablish regime authority within the established periphery and heartland, not to extend
regime power and influence significantly beyond the known
periphery described above.

The sole major exception to this general pattern of limited expansion
during the imperial era was presented by the Mongol Yuan Dynasty.
This regime sought, with varying degrees of success, to extend its direct control beyond China's traditional periphery to include India,
the entire Korean peninsula, Japan, Burma, and Java. This effort occurred largely because the conquest of China was only one part of
the overall Mongol conquest and occupation of the Eurasian continent—a conquest that ultimately extended from eastern Germany to
Korea and from the Arctic Ocean to Turkey and the Persian Gulf. In
other words, the Mongols treated the Chinese heartland as one of
many conquered territories and as a stepping stone to further con-
quests; this was highly atypical of Chinese regime behavior toward
the periphery.[25] In contrast, other nomadic occupiers of the Chinese
heartland generally undertook efforts to control or dominate only the
existing periphery. The one partial exception was the Manchu Qing
Dynasty, which established stronger controls over larger expanses of
territory along many inland peripheral areas and also for the first
time began to treat certain offshore, maritime areas in a strategic
manner.

For example, Taiwan was first considered a strategic territory and
hence regarded as part of China's strategic periphery during the Qing

---

[25]The Mongols were also extremely atypical in their approach to domestic government. They were the only nomadic occupiers of the Chinese heartland who did not
generally adopt Chinese methods of administration and did not extensively intermarry
with Han Chinese. The Mongol presence in China was essentially a military occupation designed to keep the Chinese subdued and to exploit Chinese resources. For further information on the origins and nature of the Mongol occupation of China, see
Barfield (1989), pp. 187–228. Also see Wang (1968), p. 49.

era. The Qing rulers came to view Taiwan as a potential security threat, for three reasons: First, it had served for many years as a strategic haven for the Ming loyalist Zheng Chenggong (Koxinga) and his heirs, who had harassed the Qing regime for decades after the establishment of the dynasty in 1644. Second, it had been occupied and partly colonized in the last years of the Ming by representatives of what was at that time a formidable imperialist power—the Dutch East India Company. Third, it was viewed as a potential staging area for attacks on the Mainland by pirates (a major problem during the Ming, as indicated above) and by domestic rebels.[26]

The contraction of central state control over China's traditional periphery occurred primarily during the latter one-third of a regime's existence, as a result of accelerating systemic decline. During each dynastic regime, imperial revenues would gradually decrease, and government effectiveness decline, because of a combination of several factors, including (a) the progressive withdrawal of land from taxation to benefit the ruling class; (b) the increasing inefficiency of the ruling house resulting from protracted struggles among imperial relatives, retainers, and concubines; and (c) the general decline in leadership capability and bureaucratic capacity resulting from growing corruption, factional intrigue, and the emergence, over time, of greater numbers of weak or dissolute emperors. This process would continually increase the burden of taxation on the common peasantry and eventually precipitate peasant unrest, which in turn would produce greater demands within leadership circles for a larger amount of shrinking resources to be spent on the maintenance of domestic order and well-being. As a result, each Chinese regime suffered a steady reduction in the level of state resources and leadership attention available for periphery defense and control.[27]

Most imperial regimes would initially attempt to compensate for declining central capabilities by relying on quasi-independent regional military forces or on various noncoercive measures, such as

---

[26]Sheperd (1993), pp. 1, 106, 142; and Kessler (1976), p. 90. As Sheperd states, for the Qing, Taiwan was not a neglected frontier, but rather "a strategic periphery that frequently commanded central government attention" (p. 3).

[27]Descriptions of the process of dynastic decline and regime weakening can be found in Fairbank (1992); Hucker (1975); and Huang (1997). Also see Sheperd (1993), pp. 400–406.

gifts, subsidies, the ritual trappings of imperial prestige, and various diplomatic maneuvers (discussed in greater detail below) to ensure the quiescence of periphery peoples. Eventually, however, growing state incapacity would force a withdrawal from the periphery or at least a major reduction in effective central control over periphery areas and borderlands, especially those areas along the northern and northwestern border. This process of periphery contraction usually occurred in the face of mounting nomadic incursions, internal peasant uprisings, and increasing signs of independence among regional military leaders and officials. Overall, such developments would also produce a prolonged interregnum of domestic unrest and eventually lead to either the wholesale collapse of the central state or its displacement from a large part of the Chinese heartland.

In some instances, this decline would result in the prolonged division of the heartland among several competing states, often both Han Chinese and nomadic in origin.[28] In other cases, the disintegration or contraction of the central state would soon be followed by the emergence of a new, unified regime, usually by a successful leader of peasant rebellion, a formerly loyal regional military leader, or sometimes by a nomadic invader.[29] Regardless of the length of time and severity of political conflict and division involved, however, a new, unified regime would eventually reemerge from the ashes of the previous regime. And once established, the new regime would again seek to assert control over the entire Chinese heartland and periphery. If successful, this would lead to a new cycle of expansion and subsequent decline and contraction.

This pattern has continued into the modern era. Both the nationalist and communist regimes sought to reestablish a unified political-social order and expand and consolidate control over China's longstanding periphery areas after the collapse or defeat of the preceding regime (i.e., the Qing and the Republic of China, respectively). However, the entire process of regime establishment, consolidation, mat-

---

[28]The foremost examples of these periods of political disunity include the era of North-South Division (420–589), the Five Dynasties and Ten Kingdoms era (907–960), and the Song-Liao-Jin Dynasties era (960–1234).

[29]The most notable examples of a relatively rapid process of regime reemergence after the collapse of the previous regime are the Ming Dynasty (which emerged from the Yuan) and the Qing Dynasty (which emerged from the Ming).

uration, and decline and the associated pattern of periphery expansion and contraction did not run its full course in either case. The nationalist regime never managed to fully reestablish domestic order and recover territories lost to foreign imperialists or domestic insurgents before it was severely damaged by Japanese militarists and toppled by the communists.[30] The communist regime achieved both of these key objectives but is still evolving toward an uncertain future.

The general expansion and contraction of Chinese state control over periphery (and sometimes heartland) areas is illustrated by Maps 4a–h.[31]

The impetus to reunify the Chinese state and regain control over the periphery, rather than permit the Chinese heartland to be permanently divided into separate warring states, reflects the influence of deep-seated material and cultural factors. Perhaps most important is the existence, among the peoples of the Chinese heartland, of a highly homogeneous culture and civilization incorporating a common set of political and social beliefs about the organizational and procedural requirements for stability, peace, and prosperity in an often chaos-prone environment. During imperial times, these beliefs centered, as outlined above, on the notion of a harmony-oriented Confucian-Legalist order enforced by a single imperial bureaucracy and sustained by a broad stratum of educated scholar-officials who served as both government administrators and social/intellectual elites across the entire Chinese heartland. During the modern era, the commitment to a unified regime rests upon a popular belief in the historical longevity and persistence of a single Chinese state and a single Chinese culture and, most recently, a less traditional, state-

---

[30]From this perspective, the era of the nationalist Chinese state, spanning the relatively short period between the collapse of the Qing Dynasty in 1911 and the rise to power of the communists in 1949, should most appropriately be viewed as an interregnum of internal disunity separating two eras ruled by unified Chinese regimes.

[31]These maps were adapted from Barraclough (1993), pp. 80–81, 124–125, 164–165, and 228, and Huang (1997), pp. 50, 71, 101, 176, and 215. They do not depict the exact boundaries of the imperial Chinese state, as the actual extent of imperial control along the periphery and within the heartland was indeterminate over many periods and varied in administrative type (e.g., military versus civilian control). The purpose is to show the general fluctuation that occurred in the extent of Chinese control over heartland and periphery areas between early and late regime periods.

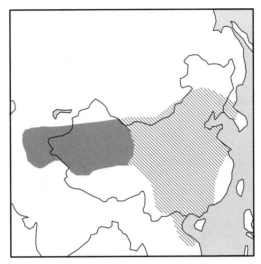

▨ Chinese presence was primarily military

Map 4a—Early Han Dynasty

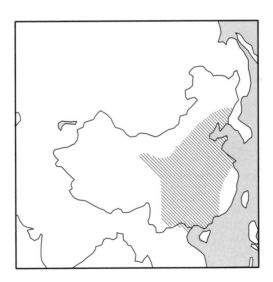

Map 4b—Late Han Dynasty

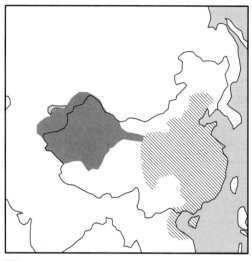

■ Chinese presence was primarily military

Map 4c—Early Tang Dynasty

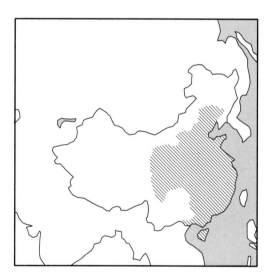

Map 4d—Late Tang Dynasty

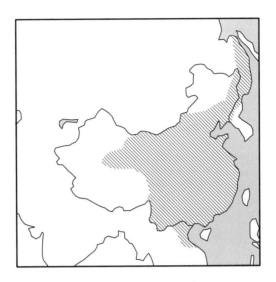

Map 4e—Early Ming Dynasty

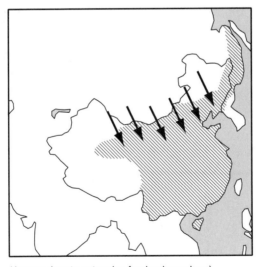

(Arrows denote extensive foreign incursions)

Map 4f—Late Ming Dynasty

Map 4g—Early Qing Dynasty

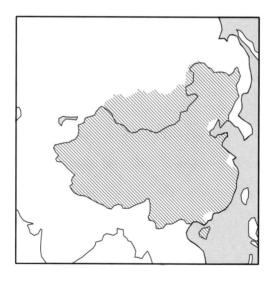

Map 4h—Late Qing Dynasty

centric form of Han nationalism centered upon a putative "alliance" between ethnic Han Chinese, other mixed Han and non-Han peoples of the heartland, and the minority peoples of the traditional periphery.[32] Overall, for both pre-modern and modern Chinese regimes, the unity of the Chinese nation is strongly associated with peace and plenty, whereas disunity means civil war, insecurity, and disaster for elite and commoners alike.[33]

THE USE OF FORCE

Many students of China's strategic history (including many Chinese scholars) argue that Chinese rulers and military leaders generally denigrate the role of violence in preserving external (or internal) state security, preferring instead to subdue or persuade an opponent through nonviolent stratagems involving subterfuge, maneuver, accommodation, and moral suasion or force of example. For such observers, warfare is viewed by the Chinese as a last resort. This argument often derives from the belief that (a) Chinese philosophers and military theorists such as Confucius, Mencius, and Sunzi generally eschewed violence in favor of accommodation, moral suasion, or stratagem; and (b) the views of these highly esteemed thinkers determined the beliefs and actions of Chinese practitioners of statecraft and warfare regarding when and how to employ force.[34]

A closer examination of the above thinkers' writings and of the historical record does not generally confirm this viewpoint, however. First, one must clearly distinguish between the beliefs of Confucius and Mencius, who were primarily concerned with how to create and maintain proper civilian government and, to those ends, emphasized the importance of moral suasion and imperial virtue (*de*) over coer-

---

[32]This concept was enshrined in the nationalist Chinese definition of the state at the time of the formation of the ROC in 1912., when the Chinese regime was said to include five races: Han Chinese, Manchu, Mongol, Tibetan, and Hui (Muslim, largely located in Xinjiang). This concept was subsequently repeated by Chiang Kai-shek (1943). O'Neill (1987), p. 214; Hunt (1984), p. 17; and Gladney (1991).

[33]Fairbank (1978a), p. 22.

[34]For a representative example of the argument that Chinese historically and culturally "disesteem violence," see Fairbank (1974), pp. 1–26. For a broader summary of the secondary literature in support of this argument, see Johnston (1995), pp. 63–65, 117–123, and Johnston (1998), pp. 6–8.

cion,[35] and the views of Sunzi, who was primarily concerned with how to win military campaigns. Moreover, Sunzi's emphasis on the use of stratagems over simple coercion related more often to the *tactics* of military campaigns than to the larger *strategic* question of whether to deploy armies against an opponent. In other words, Sunzi was primarily concerned with how a military leader could vanquish his opponent without relying extensively on brute force, once the decision had been made to use military measures. He did not advocate shirking from the use of force when it was deemed necessary and effective. Thus, Sunzi was far more willing to apply coercion against a foreign power than were either Confucius or Mencius.[36]

Second, even though the pacifistic views of Confucius and Mencius as espoused by the practitioners of Confucian statecraft have at times influenced strategic decisions concerning whether, and to what degree, force should be employed, a cursory examination of the security behavior of the Chinese state suggests that Chinese rulers have frequently resorted to violence to attain their national security objectives. In fact, one could argue that the use of force has been endemic in Chinese history. According to one Chinese military source, China engaged in a total of 3,790 recorded internal and external historical wars from 1100 B.C. (Western Zhou) to 1911 (end of the Qing Dynasty). These included both violent internal conflicts during periods of internal division and conflicts with non-Chinese powers. Moreover, in the Ming alone, China engaged in an average of 1.12 *external* wars per year through the entire dynasty.[37] The overall extent of state-sanctioned violence against both internal and external foes is broadly indicated by Figure 1.

Figure 2 shows the degree to which imperial and modern Chinese[38] regimes have used violent methods *against periphery peoples or along the periphery*. As the figure indicates, most major external military campaigns carried out by the unified Chinese state occurred

---

[35]Of the two philosophers, Mencius arguably placed a greater stress on the importance of moral suasion over coercion. Confucius was more willing to permit the use of force to punish wrongdoing and to educate the wayward subject or foreign leader.

[36]See, for example, Boylan (1982), especially pp. 343–345.

[37]For all of these figures, see Johnston (1995), p. 27.

[38]Information on the Mongol Yuan regime is not included in Figure 2 because it is not considered to be a Chinese or highly sinicized regime.

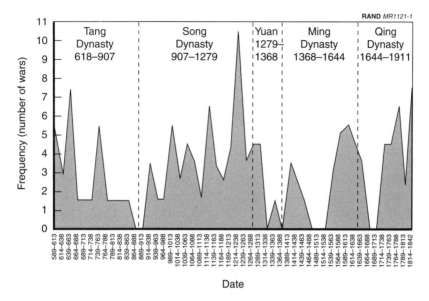

SOURCE: Adapted from Lee (1988), p. 362.

Figure 1—War Frequency in Imperial China

during the first one-third of a regime's existence (a period that lasted in some cases as long as 100 years) and were directed almost exclusively against peoples of the periphery. This general pattern also seems to hold for the most recent era. Iain Johnston shows that the use of force by the Chinese communist regime against external foes has been relatively frequent and intense as compared with other major powers of the modern era, occurred more often during the early years of the communist regime (i.e., the 1950s and 1960s), and has been primarily directed at the resolution of territorial issues along the periphery.[39]

In addition, the use of force by the Chinese state has involved relatively large numbers of soldiers, during both the imperial and modern periods, and has often resulted in significant numbers of

---

[39]Johnston (1998), pp. 27–29.

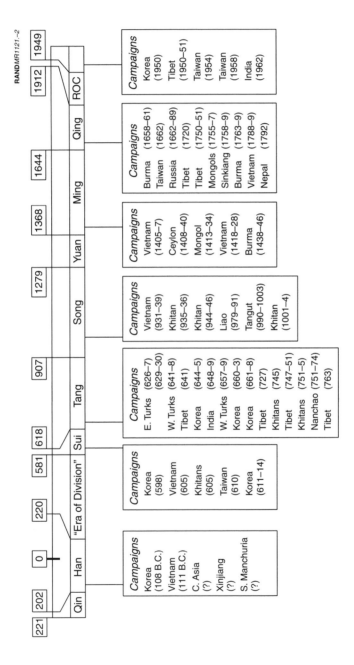

SOURCE: Compiled primarily from information contained in O'Neill (1987), and Barraclough (1993).

Figure 2—Major Chinese Campaigns Against the Periphery, 221 B.C. to the Present

casualties. One scholar has estimated that imperial Chinese armies on average mobilized approximately 100,000 soldiers for combat, and in some cases fielded armies in excess of a million men out of a total population of less than 50 million.[40] Modern Chinese standing armies have also totaled over a million soldiers. By comparison, the armies of feudal Europe rarely exceeded 50,000 men, and modern Western armies could approach or exceed a million soldiers only under conditions of total war mobilization.

Iain Johnston attributes the Chinese state's reliance on violence to the workings of a hard realpolitik strategic culture that prefers the complete elimination of security threats through force over less coercive methods. According to Johnston, this viewpoint, which is not only reflected in the behavior of Chinese civilian and military rulers but also contained in many overlooked classical writings on statecraft and warfare, views war as a relatively constant element in state affairs, regards the stakes involved in interstate behavior in zero-sum terms, often views pure violence as highly efficacious, and yet is also highly sensitive to relative material capabilities and tends to show absolute flexibility (*quan bian*) in the application of force. As a result, according to Johnston, the Chinese state will usually choose to eliminate an opponent through offensive force over static defense or accommodation when it clearly enjoys a superior military position and confronts minimal political or economic repercussions.[41]

The broad historical assessment of Chinese security behavior presented in this chapter tends to support this observation. Unlike Johnston, however, our assessment also suggests that such Chinese behavior has derived more from the material or structural conditions confronting the Chinese regime than from cultural factors. That is, there appears to be a general correlation, over broad periods of Chinese regime history, between decisions to employ various types of coercive and noncoercive measures on the one hand and, on the other hand, shifts in relative power relations with foreign entities, calculations of the relative economic and social cost to the Chinese

---

[40]Lee (1988), pp. 210–212. Lee also concludes that the severity of wars involving the imperial Chinese state, as measured by the estimated number of deaths, was at least as severe as those in Europe, and probably far more so (p. 224).

[41]Johnston (1995), pp. 148–152, 249.

regime of using various measures, and changes in the structure of an often unstable domestic and external security environment. Moreover, the historical record strongly suggests that China's past use of force *against outsiders* has been largely limited to efforts to regain heartland territories lost to foreigners and to generally control or pacify periphery areas.

During the imperial era, every unified Chinese regime resorted to violence against outsiders[42] at various times throughout its existence—from its initial formation through its eventual decline and collapse.[43] However, the external use of violence was especially evident during the early stage of an imperial regime's existence, after domestic rule was consolidated, and was employed to reclaim lost territories or to increase Chinese control or influence over the periphery. Violence was also relied upon, secondarily, during the long middle stages of a regime's existence before its decline, largely in response to armed incursions from the periphery or in an effort to "punish" or "chasten" nearby peoples for affronts to the emperor or "the people" of China. Violence against foreign entities was least evident during the last stages of a regime's existence, when the leadership was often internally divided and largely preoccupied with the suppression of internal revolts.

Almost without exception, once imperial rule had been consolidated internally, the early rulers of an imperial Chinese regime would embark on military campaigns in an attempt to absorb adjacent territories into the Chinese heartland, forcibly retake parts of the heartland lost during the decline of the previous regime, or simply to assert (or reassert) dominant influence over periphery areas by defeating them militarily. Efforts undertaken by Chinese "founding" emperors to reestablish imperial Chinese influence along the periphery were almost exclusively military, and often occurred during the early years

---

[42]Obviously, the greatest aggregate levels of state violence occurred when China was internally divided, as a major component of often prolonged struggles among groups or regimes contending with one another to reestablish unified central control over the heartland. However, this study is concerned primarily with the use of violence by the unified Chinese state against non-Chinese political entities.

[43]The following broad characterization of the conditions under which the Chinese state has employed force against external foes is drawn from Barfield (1989); Fairbank (1992); Hucker (1975); Huang (1997); Hunt (1984); O'Neill (1987); and Lee (1988).

of a regime's existence. These campaigns would sometimes extend over many decades (and in some instances persist sporadically for over a century), largely because of the tenacity and high military capabilities of China's opponents.

The majority of these military forays were directed against nomadic or semi-nomadic peoples along China's northern and northwestern borders and consisted largely of efforts to retake lost territory within the heartland or to reestablish Chinese preeminence along the largely fixed periphery.[44] The use of offensive coercive measures during the early life of an imperial regime was far less prevalent along China's eastern, southern, and southwestern maritime and continental borders. This was largely because most outside powers along those borders were either too distant to pose a serious threat to the Chinese heartland (as in the case of Japan[45]), did not possess formidable military forces, or did not repeatedly encroach upon China to acquire the resources needed to maintain or expand their local power position, as did most nearby inner Asian nomadic and semi-nomadic tribes and kingdoms (more on this point below).

The few cases of major military actions taken against China's eastern, southern, or southwestern neighbors during the early life of an imperial regime usually occurred as part of an effort to expand Chinese territory or to acquire resources. The most notable example of such behavior consisted of attacks against the ancestors of present-day Vietnamese or other minority tribes residing in present-day southwest China during the Qin, Han, Song, and Ming Dynasties.[46] In

---

[44]Efforts to absorb inner Asian territories into the Chinese heartland were usually unsuccessful and therefore less frequently attempted. The most notable exception to this general pattern occurred during the early Tang, when Turkish troops under the Tang banner extended China's borders (although not Chinese settlements) deep into Central Asia. See Barfield (1989), p. 145.

[45]Japan became a security concern to the imperial Chinese state only during the Ming, when Japanese warlord Toyotomi Hideyoshi attacked Korea and tried to conquer China in the 1590s. However, this threat ended with his death in 1598. O'Neill (1987), p. 203.

[46]The founder of the Qin Dynasty, Qin Shih Huang Di, conquered the Vietnamese state of Nan-Yueh (then occupying parts of present-day southwest China and northern Vietnam) in 214 B.C., but the Vietnamese soon regained their independence and were recognized as a vassal state until 111 B.C., when Emperor Han Wudi retook Nan-Yueh and divided it into nine counties. From 111 B.C.–543 A.D., Nan-Yueh was the Chinese province of Chiao-chih. It was administered at senior levels by Chinese offi-

addition, many early rulers of Chinese imperial regimes also attempted at various times to absorb militarily parts of present-day Korea.[47]

The one instance in which maritime military power was applied in the early period of a regime against southern and southwestern periphery areas (and beyond) occurred during the early years of the Ming Dynasty. In addition to fulfilling the specific economic purposes noted above, the large blue water naval force assembled under Emperor Ming Yongle was intended to help complete the unification of the new Ming regime, pacify maritime sea routes, establish or reinforce political relations, support Yongle's effort to conquer Vietnam, and generally assert Chinese influence in areas to the west of the South China Sea, especially as part of a larger strategy aimed at countering the growing influence of Muslim power in Central Asia. Hence, various naval forces and expeditions (which usually contained hundreds of ships and tens of thousands of soldiers) fought and defeated Mongol navies, eliminated local pirates, and defended

---

cials, adopted many Chinese political institutions, and employed Chinese scholars and officials. Strong Vietnamese resistance to Chinese absorption resulted in separation from direct Chinese rule. This eventually led, during the Tang, to the establishment of Vietnam as a protectorate. With the demise of the Tang, a more independent Vietnamese polity emerged: the Ly Dynasty. Modeled after Chinese imperial regimes, the Ly attempted to establish a position as an entirely separate and equal entity to the Chinese court—the seat of the "southern emperor." Resulting frictions led to a failed effort during the Song to reconquer Vietnam and the emergence of a tributary relationship as the only alternative to confrontation and war. In the first decade of the 1400s, early Ming Emperor Ming Yongle reconquered Vietnam (then known as Dai Viet) and attempted to reabsorb it into the Chinese empire as a province under direct Chinese rule. But this effort eventually failed, thus again forcing China to accept a far less intrusive tributary relationship with Vietnam. Chen (1969), pp. 1–9; SarDesai (1998), pp. 13–35; and Taylor (1992), pp. 137–150. As Taylor states: "The lesson for the Chinese of their effort to occupy Vietnam was that tributary relations represented a higher wisdom than did a policy of conquest and assimilation" (p. 150).

[47]Han Wudi incorporated Korea into the Chinese empire in 108 B.C. However, Chinese control was soon limited to the northern part of Korea and thrown off altogether in 313 A.D. The short-lived Sui Dynasty attempted three times to conquer and absorb Korea, without success. The "vigorous warrior kings" of the early Tang had occupied northern Korea by the 660s but were also unable to absorb the kingdom politically. Korea maintained less-intrusive tributary relations with the more distant Song (which did not occupy most of northern China and hence could not pressure Korea), whereas early Ming and Qing rulers were content to employ military, economic, and cultural "persuasion" to establish a more intrusive form of suzerainty over Korea, which became a virtual protectorate. O'Neill (1987), pp. 2, 145, 303–304; Barraclough (1993), pp. 81, 124; Hucker (1975), pp. 88–89, 133–134; Fairbank (1992), p. 114.

those local kings who had offered tribute and gifts to the emperor from armed challenges by usurpers or rebels. They also conferred tributary status on many local leaders and spent considerable time ensuring the security of the Malacca Strait, an important early Ming trade route and entrepôt linking East Asia and the Indian Ocean. However, with the exception of Ceylon, the Zheng He naval expeditions rarely, if ever, used force in dealing with coastal states west of Sumatra.[48] Moreover, as suggested above, this entire episode was exceedingly brief, having been prompted by the pressures (and opportunities) confronting the early Ming and sustained by the energies of Emperor Ming Yongle and his supporters. It came to an abrupt end following the death of the emperor and the decline of his supporters' influence at court.[49]

Military incursions into periphery areas or armed displays would often be accompanied by the establishment of Chinese military garrisons and the construction of fortifications, both within periphery areas and at the outermost limits of the Chinese heartland. These defenses were intended both to protect the heartland from direct attack and to ensure the long-term obedience of the inhabitants of the periphery by providing a quasi-permanent Chinese military presence among them.[50]

Imperial Chinese regimes also resorted to force at various times during the often extended middle period of a regime's existence, before the onset of dynastic decline. During this period, force was most often used in response to external provocations or incursions directed against the Chinese heartland or periphery, or generally to punish and chastise disrespectful statements and behavior or other perceived transgressions against Chinese authority committed by periphery states. In particular, strong, unified Chinese imperial regimes periodically employed force against both nomadic confederations and, to a lesser extent, more established southwestern or

---

[48]Swanson (1982), pp. 32–33, 39–40; Wang (1968), pp. 55–56; and Wolters (1970), pp. 36, 206 (footnote 128), 155–157. Edward Dreyer, personal correspondence.

[49]The Zheng He expeditions also ended because Ming attention and resources became focused increasingly on coping with the challenges posed by a growing Mongol threat from the north and intensifying pirate attacks along China's southern coastline, which led to efforts to fortify land defenses. Swanson (1982), pp. 40–43.

[50]Barfield (1989); Hunt (1984); and Hucker (1975).

southern powers when such entities violated the sinocentric hierarchical structure of the tributary relationship and demanded to be treated *explicitly and formally* as an equal to the Chinese emperor,[51] persistently levied excessively onerous tributary requests, or repeatedly attacked Chinese territory or frontier areas. The Xiongnu nomadic tribes of the Han Dynasty period were perhaps the worst offenders in their demand for formal equality with the Chinese emperor. Unable to accept this affront, the Han rulers frequently employed force against them.[52] Similar Chinese responses occurred at the height of the Tang, which was plagued by military incursions into present-day Siquan and Yunnan Provinces by the Tibetan Kingdom and the Tibeto-Burman Nan-chao Kingdom.[53] And numerous nomadic leaders along the northern and northwestern frontiers provoked an armed response from strong Chinese regimes through their repeated and escalating attacks and demands.[54]

However, strong Chinese imperial regimes generally did not employ force to enforce peace or to extend their influence or direct control beyond the established periphery. Even the famous, far-ranging Zheng He naval expeditions of the Ming era did not employ force against distant peoples or to conquer distant lands. Moreover, imperial Chinese regimes did not routinely use force to separate or subdue warring periphery states or confederations unless such conflict directly threatened Chinese territory or posed the prospect of lowering or removing Chinese influence along the periphery. Thus, imperial regimes would sometimes intervene militarily when an established and loyal vassal ruler was challenged by internal rebellion or attacked by a nonvassal regime but would not generally do so to enforce peace throughout all periphery areas or beyond. Such limited interventions arguably occurred most often in the case of the more sedentary states or kingdoms near China's eastern and south-

---

[51]The Chinese state's demand for ritualistic deference was by no means absolute, however. Weak Chinese regimes often ignored the traditional sinocentric hierarchical approach to interstate relations when state security demanded it.

[52]Barfield (1989), pp. 53–54, 59–67.

[53]Backus (1981). Also see Beckwith (1987), pp. 99–100; and Twitchett and Wright (1973), p. 8.

[54]For a general discussion of the use of force in response to excessive pressures and attacks from nomadic peoples, see Jagchid and Symons (1989), pp. 59, 65; and Barfield (1989).

ern borders, such as Korea and Vietnam.[55] In these instances, expectations of military support usually derived from the overall tribu-
tary-suzerain relationship, which in some cases exchanged a formal
acknowledgment by the vassal of Chinese preeminence for a Chinese
obligation to protect the vassal when attacked.[56]

The use of force against outsiders was least evident during the final
stages of an imperial regime.[57] Rather than rely on highly expensive
and often inconclusive military forays against the northern and
northwestern periphery, weak indigenous Chinese dynasties usually
chose to increase tributary payments to potentially threatening
nomads to keep them quiescent.[58] Such weak regimes would also
usually avoid the use of force in support of periphery vassal states of
whatever type, as suggested above. Moreover, by the later stages of a
dynasty's existence, domestic unrest usually posed a far greater and
more urgent security threat to the regime than external aggression.
In fact, in some instances, large nomadic confederations would
actually assist the Chinese court in fending off internal challenges,
primarily to maintain the lucrative tributary relationship.[59]

A severely weak, declining imperial Chinese regime would usually
resort to force against foreigners out of desperation, or as a consequence of domestic political pressures and machinations. The
former use of force most often consisted of intense (and almost
invariably unsuccessful) armed responses initiated in response to

---

[55]The most famous example of this type of behavior was China's successful military
defense of Korea against Japanese invasion during the Ming Dynasty.

[56]For a general reference to Chinese military support on behalf of vassal states, see
Hunt (1984), p. 15. Also see Lam (1968), p. 178; Swanson (1982), p. 15; and Chen
(1969), p. 8. This was by no means a hard and fast rule, however. Some tributary relationships did not imply Chinese protection of any kind. Moreover, even when such
security assurances had been provided, imperial regimes such as the Qing would at
times invoke the concept of "impartial benevolence" (*i-shi tong-jen*) to disclaim any
responsibility to protect the state or kingdom in question. This would usually occur
during periods of regime decline, however. Fletcher (1978), p. 105.

[57]Again, military campaigns against internal rebellions by central armies or regional
military supporters of the Chinese state are not included in this assessment, which examines the behavior of the unified Chinese state against foreign powers.

[58]Thomas Barfield, personal correspondence. This point is discussed in greater detail
below.

[59]For example, the Uighurs propped up the late Tang to keep tributary payments
coming. Barfield (1989), p. 131.

persistent and major external attacks on the Chinese heartland, along with various types of military bluff to intimidate potential foreign foes. The protracted armed defense of the Southern Song against Mongol invaders and the military actions undertaken against foreign imperialist powers in the mid 19th century by the Qing rulers were particularly notable examples of weak regime defensive military behavior.[60]

Chinese imperial regimes were by no means always successful in applying force against periphery peoples and generally did not persist in the use of force when its disadvantages came to outweigh its advantages. Thomas Barfield has shown that most Han Chinese imperial regimes were largely unable to militarily defeat and subjugate the nomadic tribes and confederations along China's Inner Asian borders, often despite concerted and costly efforts to do so. This was partly because, with few exceptions, Han Chinese rulers, unlike most foreign-originated dynasties, did not fully understand, and hence could not fully exploit, the internal organizational and social strengths and weaknesses of their nomadic opponents.[61] As a result, most unified Chinese regimes often relied on relatively unsophisticated measures to pacify the northern and northwestern periphery, primarily massive military campaigns. Most of these campaigns were either entirely unsuccessful or, when initially successful, did not achieve lasting results. As highly mobile, skilled warriors, nomadic soldiers were generally able to evade decisive defeat by the slower, primarily infantry-based Chinese forces deployed against them.[62] In addition, Chinese forces were unable to subdue Inner Asian peoples

---

[60]For examples, see Hucker (1975), pp. 121–122; Rossabi (1983); Spence (1990), pp. 152–158, 221–223; Hsu (1970), pp. 183–269, 376–422; Wakeman (1978); Fairbank (1978b), pp. 243–249, 252–257; and Liu and Smith (1980), pp. 269–273.

[61]Although many Chinese frontier commanders understood well their nomadic foes, the Chinese court rarely attempted to understand them. The one major exception to this was early Tang Emperor Tang Taizong, who was part Turkish and well versed in the ways of nomadic warfare. But his highly effective, and largely coercive, strategy against nomadic peoples was opposed by Confucian officials and soon ended. Barfield (1989), p. 122.

[62]The Chinese eventually incorporated cavalry units into the forces they deployed against the nomads on the steppe. However, these units had only a limited effect because the Chinese had to buy horses at high prices and could not easily replace their losses, whereas the nomads raised their own horses in large numbers. Hence, the Chinese often lacked sufficient horses to sustain mounted steppe campaigns for prolonged periods. Thomas Barfield, personal correspondence.

by depriving them of subsistence. Pastoral nomadic communities could retreat in the face of Chinese invasions and return to their lands after the Chinese had departed. In contrast, Chinese forces depended upon the food and materials provided by fixed agricultural areas; yet such areas could not be established in significant numbers on the arid steppe. As a result, Chinese forces were dependent upon a long logistical train that originated in the heartland and would thus usually remain in periphery areas for only a few months at a time. Even when they were able to defeat nomadic forces, Chinese armies were eventually forced to return to the Chinese heartland, leaving behind isolated and largely ineffective garrisons. Eventually, nomadic communities and their warriors would reappear, and the strategic balance along the periphery would remain largely unchanged.[63]

The more sedentary, sinitic states or kingdoms near China's eastern and southern borders (such as Korea and Vietnam and parts of Tibet east of the Tibetan plateau[64]) did not enjoy the advantages of terrain and mobility possessed by the Inner Asian peoples. Hence, a strong Chinese state could more effectively bring its superior military forces to bear against these powers or areas and thereby at times establish a clearly dominant position over them. In such instances, the tributary and trade relations established and maintained with strong Chinese regimes were thus ultimately founded on a genuinely hierarchical power structure involving the potential threat of military coercion. However, strong imperial Chinese regimes did not always achieve a sustained, or undisputed, position of military dominance over such powers. This was especially true in the case of Vietnam, as suggested above. At such times, Chinese regimes would again adopt a pragmatic approach and accept from the vassal the symbolic forms of obeisance of the hierarchical tributary relationship, thereby agreeing

---

[63]Barfield (1989) and Jagchid and Symons (1989).

[64]During the Han Dynasty, the Tibetan border with China was not far from present-day Ch'ang-an, far to the east of the present-day border between the Tibet Autonomous Region and China Proper. Hence, eastern Tibet at that time encompassed significant agricultural lands, upon which the Chinese subsequently encroached. As a result of such Chinese expansion, the Sino-Tibetan border moved progressively west, with the intervening territory coming under direct Chinese rule and subject to extensive Han Chinese migration. Later dynasties eventually extended their political influence into the Tibetan plateau itself, which the Chinese were unable to settle. The authors are indebted to Thomas Barfield for this observation.

to what was in effect an armed truce, marked by trade and reasonably amicable political relations. As in the case of nomadic peoples, this would usually remain in effect as long as the power in question did not attack Chinese territory or make excessive demands on the court.[65]

The use of force against the periphery by both Han Chinese and highly sinicized non-Han regimes was also limited by domestic political considerations. Confucian civilian officials and advisors often resisted costly, prolonged military campaigns against nomadic tribes and confederations because such actions weakened their power and influence by diverting resources from domestic civil administration, served to increase the power of military leaders, merchants, and imperial retainers at their expense, and in general increased the personal power of the emperor over the officialdom. Some Confucian officials also opposed the use of force against external foes because, in their eyes, the very application of massive force undermined the authority and legitimacy of the imperial order as a whole. For them, proper rule and order derived from the observance of Confucian benevolence and virtue, not compulsion through the use of arms.[66] The influence of domestic leadership factors on the use of force is discussed in greater detail at the end of this chapter.

It is possible that at least some Han Chinese regimes before the unprecedented occupation of the entire Chinese heartland by the Mongol Yuan Dynasty did not persist in the use of force against the northern and northwestern periphery because they did not believe that nomadic tribes and confederations posed a mortal threat to the Chinese state. This is at least suggested by the fact that most nomadic leaders did not want to conquer and occupy China. Their main intent was to extort from Chinese rulers the riches and materials needed to establish and maintain internal nomadic alliances. Indeed, large nomadic confederations emerged only when a united

---

[65]This is not to imply that tributary relations between sinitic states and imperial Chinese regimes were based solely on calculations of relative military prowess. See below for a more detailed discussion of the advantages of the tributary relationship to both sides.

[66]This argument is especially stressed in Barfield (1989), and in personal correspondence. Also see Jagchid and Symons (1989), pp. 52–62; and O'Neill (1987), pp. 202, 208.

and relatively strong imperial Chinese state existed to provide nomadic leaders with essential resources. Nomadic or semi-nomadic
peoples conquered parts or all of the Chinese heartland usually after
the Chinese state had been severely weakened from within, or had
collapsed altogether and was unable to provide the necessary tribute,
or when parts of China had fallen under the control of non-Chinese
nomadic groups that strongly resisted a strategy of appeasement toward their nomadic neighbors. The first situation largely applies to
the Manchurian conquest of part or all of China, whereas the last led
to the Mongol conquest.[67]

Such experiences tended to confirm the widespread view among
traditional (and modern) Chinese elites that internal weakness invites foreign aggression. However, there is little direct proof that pre-
Ming Chinese rulers did not persist in using force against northern
and northwestern peoples primarily because they did not fear a mortal threat from them. Some of the most successful emperors and military leaders of imperial Chinese regimes were part-nomadic and
hence presumably understood that nomadic tribes had the potential
to do much more harm militarily than merely plunder and raid frontier areas. More important, whether because of internal weakness or
nomadic military prowess, from earliest times, nomadic or semi-
nomadic peoples frequently made major inroads into and at times
occupied large parts of the Chinese heartland (these included, most
notably, various Xiongnu, proto-Tibetan and proto-Mongol Xianbi
tribes during the Later Han and the Manchurian-based Liao and Jin
(Qin) regimes during the Song).[68]

Therefore, on balance, it is more likely that Han Chinese imperial
regimes did not persist in the use of force against the northern and
northwestern periphery for reasons more closely associated with the
military, economic, and domestic political factors mentioned above.
Eventually, the relative ineffectiveness of force against northern and
western nomadic and semi-nomadic opponents, combined with its
enormous financial cost and domestic political divisiveness, often

[67]Barfield (1989), pp. 9–10, 197–198. For similar arguments, see Suzuki (1968).

[68]Hucker (1975), p. 79; O'Neill (1987), p. 316. Fairbank states that the Liao, Jin, and
Yuan regimes "form a connected sequence of incursions of Inner Asian military power
into China and must be viewed as a single, if sporadic, process" (1992, pp. 118–119).

prompted both strong and weak imperial Han Chinese regimes to discard coercive methods in favor of a variety of noncoercive security strategies. As discussed in greater detail below, these strategies usually employed various forms of thinly disguised appeasement, diplomatic maneuver, and a greater reliance on a static military defense.

In contrast to the experience of Han Chinese regimes, dynasties of nomadic or semi-nomadic origin were more successful in subduing periphery peoples by force. Such regimes better understood the complex tribal and personal relationships and internal structures and social beliefs of nomadic tribes as well as the dynamics of con-federation formation. Thus, they would often intervene militarily at crucial points to disrupt and weaken nomadic groups. Moreover, such regimes maintained military forces—especially large cavalry units—that were more able to conduct protracted warfare on the arid steppe.[69] Arguably the most successful practitioners of force against the periphery were the Mongol Yuan and the Manchu Qing leaders. Unlike other imperial regimes, the Yuan conquered areas far beyond the periphery, largely as part of the overall Mongol conquest and oc-cupation of the Eurasian continent. As a result of this and other fac-tors associated with its non-Chinese approach to domestic rule, the Yuan is thus not considered typical of Chinese regimes. In contrast, the highly sinicized Manchu Qing rulers limited their external mili-tary forays largely to the traditional periphery. However, the Qing pursued a particularly aggressive, and generally successful, policy toward the periphery and as a result managed to extend imperial in-fluence and control beyond the limits achieved by earlier regimes. Specifically, using a strong, hybrid military that combined both no-madic and Han Chinese elements, the Qing secured and largely re-tained Korea, Tibet, and both Inner and Outer Mongolia as vassal states, successfully invaded Burma and Nepal (the latter largely in defense of Tibet), advanced China's border well north of the Amur River (in response to Russian settlement in the Siberian Far East), and incorporated Chinese Turkestan (Xinjiang) and Taiwan into the empire as provinces. Moreover, under the Qing, the Mongols and other nomadic peoples were essentially eliminated as a threat to the

---

[69]Barfield (1989), pp. 112–113, 122, 275–276.

Chinese heartland.[70]   These successes provided the basis for the subsequent claims to sovereignty over Xinjiang, Manchuria, Mongolia, Tibet, and Taiwan made by both the nationalist and communist regimes.

However, the Qing did not at first encourage Chinese immigration into any of these areas, preferring instead to maintain them as stable buffers against more distant centers of power, i.e., India, France, Japan, Russia, Great Britain, and, in the case of Taiwan during the 1700s, the Dutch.[71]   Hence, although these regions were administratively incorporated into the Qing empire, they did not become part of the Han Chinese heartland until subsequent Han migration had occurred, often despite restrictions, or they had been formally annexed by the nationalist regime.[72]   Also, the original Qing effort to administratively and militarily incorporate Tibet, Mongolia, and Xinjiang began in the 1700s, well before the imperialist Western threat became serious.   In particular, a Lamaist Buddhist-based religious and political connection between Tibet and Mongolia, established during the Ming, made it necessary for the Qing to conquer Tibet to secure their control of Mongolia and Xinjiang.[73]

The major exceptions to the above pragmatic approach to the use of force by Han Chinese regimes occurred during the Qin (221–207 B.C.), Sui (581–618), and Ming (1368–1644) Dynasties. The first two regimes persisted in the use of force against the periphery throughout their relatively short existence.   Both dynasties united China after centuries of disunity and conflict and then embarked on sustained (and sometimes highly successful) efforts to forcibly

---

[70]For further details on Qing military successes against the periphery, see O'Neill (1987), pp. 45, 139; and Hucker (1975), pp. 150–152. Also Fletcher (1978).

[71]The Chinese also believed that permanent Chinese immigration into periphery areas would be very costly and would exacerbate social unrest by significantly upsetting the ethnic status quo and facilitating the use of such areas by pirates, rebels, and other antigovernment elements. See, for example, Sheperd (1993), pp. 142–145.

[72]O'Neill (1987), pp. 322–323. For example, the Qing were eventually forced in the late 19th century to admit Han Chinese into most of Qing Central Asia and to regularize its provincial administration, in large part to keep Russia at bay.   The authors are indebted to Edward Dreyer for this observation.

[73]Edward Dreyer, personal correspondence.

subjugate nomadic groups.[74] However, the enormous economic and social costs of such an unremittingly militant approach arguably accelerated the decline of both regimes and served as a negative lesson for subsequent Chinese rulers.

The Ming was the only long-lived Han Chinese imperial regime that shunned the appeasement policies of earlier dynasties for most of its existence, at least with regard to threats along China's northern and western borders. Instead, early Ming emperors persisted in largely unsuccessful efforts to subdue militarily the nomadic tribes to the north, and middle and late Ming rulers adopted a siege mentality marked by an emphasis on strong static defenses and reduced contact with the outside. As a result of this largely noncooperative strategy, the Ming experienced incessant raiding along the northern frontier throughout much of its existence. Moreover, the number and intensity of such raids grew over time and continually sapped the strength of the Ming regime both economically and militarily.[75] This largely military-based policy (which had its domestic correlate in a more autocratic form of government[76]) emerged to a great extent because of China's experience at the hands of the uniquely rapacious and destructive Mongol Yuan Dynasty that preceded the Ming. That experience made Ming leaders acutely sensitive to the threat posed to the Chinese heartland by nomadic groups.[77] Eventually, the Ming leadership was compelled, as their power declined, to purchase security by adopting the tributary "pay-off" stratagem

---

[74]O'Neill (1987), pp. 298–300; Hucker (1975), pp. 87–88; Barfield (1989), pp. 32–33, and personal correspondence. We should point out that the Sui was not an entirely Han Chinese regime. It was led by rulers of mixed Chinese-nomadic blood, which probably explains some of its successes against northern periphery peoples.

[75]Barfield (1989), pp. 230–231.

[76]Dardess (1983), p. 253; Barraclough (1993), p.165; Hucker (1975), pp. 134–135.

[77]Barfield (1989), pp. 248–249, and personal correspondence. Also see Wang (1968), pp. 49, 53. In addition, Ming sensitivity was probably increased by the fact that Emperor Ming Yongle (1403–1424) had moved the capital from Nanjing to Beijing in 1421, thus placing it closer to the northern border. If the capital had been far to the south, then even a Mongol invasion that overran the Beijing area would be embarrassing but no real threat to the dynasty, since its economic and population center was in the south. A final factor that explains the greater Ming reliance on military measures is the advent of firearms. This made a wall-building strategy more plausible and gave Ming armies a distinct advantage in the field against the horse archer-style of warfare practiced by the nomads. The authors are indebted to Edward Dreyer and Thomas Barfield for these observations. Also, see Waldron (1990).

used by previous Chinese regimes. Yet Ming arguments in favor of accommodation almost invariably depicted such a strategy as a stop-gap measure designed to allow Ming power to strengthen and thus to improve the effectiveness of offensive uses of power when conditions were ripe.[78]

During the modern era, regime formation and maintenance have similarly involved a frequent yet limited use of violence toward the periphery, although the requirements for establishing and maintaining periphery control (and, indeed, for ensuring China's overall security) have changed considerably in modern times. The newly formed Republic of China undertook military actions against Mongolia, Xinjiang, and Tibet between 1911–1935, largely in an effort to establish strong buffers against continuing (and unprecedented) security threats posed by imperialist powers, especially Russia and Great Britain. These efforts met with only limited success, however, given the general weakness of the nationalist regime and the more pressing security challenges presented by communist insurrection and the Japanese invasion.[79] Ultimately, the nationalist regime was more effective in using diplomatic measures to reduce foreign influence along the periphery during the 1920s and 1930s, even though it did not actually manage to assert full control over most of these areas.[80]

During its formative years (i.e., the 1950s and early 1960s), the People's Republic of China undertook similar military campaigns against the periphery from a decidedly stronger position. These actions subsequently confirmed the earlier formal incorporation into the Chinese state of all periphery regions (i.e., Tibet, Xinjiang, Manchuria, and Mongolia, minus Outer Mongolia) that had taken place during the Qing and early Republican periods.[81] The PRC established an unprecedented level of direct control over periphery territories as a result of such military actions (which were in some instances helped

---

[78]The authors are indebted to Iain Johnston for this last point, personal correspondence.

[79]O'Neill (1987), pp. 214, 322–324; Hunt (1996), p. 16; Forbes (1986), especially pp. 163–170; Goldstein (1989), pp. 83, 222–224, 298.

[80]Kirby (1997), pp. 437–439.

[81]Hunt (1984), p. 18; and Hunt (1996), pp. 222–225.

by support from communist Russia),[82] greatly exceeding the level of control exercised by past Han Chinese regimes such as the Han, Tang, or Ming. In addition, during its early years, the PRC also deployed military forces to counter or deter incursions into or perceived threats against both nearby periphery areas (such as Korea, Tibet, and Nepal) and heartland borders from major industrial powers such as the United States and Great Britain. The PRC leadership also planned to use military force to reestablish direct Chinese control over Taiwan, which had been formally incorporated into the Chinese heartland during the early Qing Dynasty but had remained outside Beijing's sphere of influence since the late 19th century. These latter efforts did not meet with complete success, however, because of the superior military strength of the adversaries involved.[83]

Since the mid 1960s, the PRC has resorted to force less often than during its early years. However, one should not conclude from this apparent decrease in the use of force that the communist regime is entirely satisfied with its level of control over the Chinese periphery. Although having incorporated many traditional periphery areas directly into the Chinese nation-state, the Chinese communist regime remains relatively weak compared with those major industrial powers capable of deploying forces along its borders (e.g., the United States, Japan, and Russia) and, more important, has continued to be plagued by an assortment of domestic ills. As a result, it has not fully restored the level of influence over periphery areas enjoyed by the early Qing rulers, as a result of their highly successful military exploits. This is not to say, however, that the Chinese regime today necessarily seeks to replicate the level and type of control over the periphery enjoyed by strong imperial Chinese regimes, nor that it seeks to expand significantly the geographic expanse of the traditional periphery to encompass, for example, parts of the Russian Far East, Central and Southwest Asia, or the Western Pacific. The influence of mixed weak-strong state capabilities on near-term Chinese security behavior toward the industrial powers and nearby states, and the implications of the emergence of a much stronger China

---

[82]Stalin essentially permitted the PRC to regain control over Manchuria and Xinjiang.

[83]For excellent discussions of PRC security policy and military behavior toward Korea, Nepal, Tibet, and Taiwan, see Hunt (1996), pp. 13–17, 159–200; Christensen (1996b); Chen (1994); Grunfeld (1996); Smith (1998); and Goldstein (1989).

over the longer term for Chinese security policy and behavior will be discussed in greater detail in the next chapter.

To sum up, the historical record suggests that the Chinese state has frequently employed force against foreign powers but generally followed a pragmatic and limited approach to the use of such force. Specifically, it has employed force against foreigners primarily to influence, control, or pacify its strategic periphery and generally has done so when it possessed relative superiority over its potential adversaries on the periphery. In these instances, force was most often used in attempts to establish (or reestablish) relations of deference toward China by periphery powers, to absorb nearby areas such as Vietnam and Korea, or to deter or end attacks from the periphery by either nearby or (in the modern era) more distant powers. However, an inability to establish a material position of superiority over the periphery through military force—or strong levels of domestic opposition to the use of such force—often led to the adoption by the state of noncoercive methods, usually involving appeasement and passive defenses, which frequently provided long periods of security from attack. This suggests that security during much of Chinese history did not require unambiguous military dominance by the Chinese state over periphery areas. In particular, as will be discussed in the next section, when military control over the periphery could not be established or maintained without threatening internal order and prosperity, or the interests of key elites, the Chinese state usually opted for political arrangements that provided some measure of security from attack while often, although not always, preserving some symbol of deference to Chinese authority.

THE USE OF NONCOERCIVE SECURITY STRATEGIES

Despite a frequent reliance on force to eliminate internal opposition, reestablish the strategic periphery, chasten disrespectful foreign powers, and quell or intimidate potential external threats, the rulers of most Chinese regimes (both modern and pre-modern) have sought to employ a variety of noncoercive military, economic, and diplomatic measures to ensure China's security (or maintain China's preeminence) over extended periods. These measures have variously included the construction of passive defenses, policies of appeasement and cooptation, cessation of contact with outsiders, the assertion or maintenance of hierarchical, sinocentric diplomatic relations, or the acceptance of more equal interactions using political balance, tactical alliance, and maneuver. Often, such measures were generally shown to be more effective and deemed less costly and less controversial domestically than offensive, military-centered security policies, and permitted the regime to focus greater energies and resources on the maintenance of domestic order and well-being. The specific precipitant, form, and timing of each noncoercive measure used by the Chinese state varied considerably, however, largely depending on structural factors relating to the relative strength and internal unity[84] of the Chinese regime and the general historical period under examination (i.e., imperial or modern).

During the imperial era, relatively weak Chinese states confronted by internal problems associated with regime formation or decline (e.g., the elimination of remaining resistance to a new imperial order or the suppression of rising domestic rebellion) would rely most often on a combination of static defenses, appeasement, and, at times, cultural-ideological efforts to coopt or indoctrinate foreigners into the sinocentric world view through the ritual trappings of the hierarchical suzerain-vassal tributary relationship.[85] Taken as a whole, these measures were intended to provide the regime with a respite from external attacks and thereby permit a greater concentration on the primary task of establishing (or reestablishing) internal order and well-being.

Toward relatively more dangerous nomadic and semi-nomadic peoples, a weak Chinese state would rely most heavily on a combination of appeasement via trade, subsidies, payments, lavish gifts, and, when possible, static defenses.[86] Toward those ordinarily less-dangerous sinitic powers on its eastern and southern borders, weak Chinese regimes would tend to emphasize the culturally based, hierarchical aspects of the tributary relationship to elicit or maintain

---

[84]The influence of internal political factors on Chinese security strategies will be discussed in the next section.

[85]Fairbank (1968a), pp. 11–12.

[86]Strong imperial regimes were also compelled to employ appeasement policies on occasion. This point is discussed in greater detail below.

deference, while permitting increasingly generous trade relation-ships.[87] Such stratagems were also initially applied during the late Qing period (a decidedly weak state era) to the imperialist powers. In particular, Qing rulers initially attempted to pressure or persuade foreign traders and dignitaries to perform and accept traditional hi-erarchical, tributary-based rituals and trade relations.[88]

During periods of regime decline, such strategies of appeasement and symbolic dominance could not long conceal the weakness of a declining Chinese regime or indefinitely buy off growing external threats, however. In virtually every case, they would soon be aug-mented, if not replaced altogether, by strategies keyed to diplomatic balancing, maneuver, cooptation, collaboration, and largely tactical alliance. This was especially true in the case of imperial China's re-lations with nomadic and semi-nomadic entities, and with regard to late Qing policies toward the imperialist powers from approximately 1880 onward. Such measures reflected a clear recognition of the need for a weak China to become extensively involved in the affairs of the outside world, to play stronger powers off against one another to maximize strategic leverage and flexibility.[89] (This does not mean that strong imperial Chinese regimes did not also engage in diplo-matic balance and maneuver. In fact, they frequently did so, but primarily as an adjunct to more hierarchical, tributary-centered strategies discussed below.)

Elements of this "weak regime" strategy of appeasement and diplo-matic maneuver were also evident during extended periods of inter-nal political fragmentation. During such times, the imperial Chinese state frequently relinquished even the symbolic forms of the hierar-chical tributary relationship and treated potential adversaries as po-litical equals. The foremost example of this type of regime was the

---

[87]This is not intended to imply that weak imperial regimes did not use the ritualistic trappings of the tributary relationship toward nomadic peoples, nor that such regimes would entirely shun efforts at outright appeasement and static defenses toward southern and eastern peoples. An emphasis on one or more strategies over others was largely a matter of degree.

[88]Fairbank (1992), pp. 198–199; Spence (1990), pp. 117–119; and Hao and Wang (1980).

[89]Fairbank (1992), p. 61; for the Qing period, see Hunt (1996), pp. 32–39; Hsu (1980).

Song Dynasty (960–1279).[90] During the life of this dynasty, control over the Chinese heartland was divided between a Han Chinese imperial state and several large nomadic regimes (the Liao, the Xi Xia, and the Jin). In this precarious security environment, the Song rulers kept their potential nomadic adversaries at bay over a very long period of time through policies that combined strong military defenses (by the middle of the 11th century, the Song army numbered well over a million soldiers), diplomatic maneuver, appeasement, alliance behavior, and occasionally (albeit often unsuccessfully[91]) offensive warfare. The Song relied in particular upon an appeasement policy marked by very large, and increasing, subsidy payments to nomadic states. The regime was eventually defeated by the Mongols after a fierce resistance, and largely because Song power had been greatly eroded internally as a result of the influence of weak emperors, domineering chief councilors, and wrangling careerist officials.[92]

In general, strong imperial Chinese regimes would also employ a wide variety of noncoercive measures to ensure peace and stability along the periphery. Once domestic power was consolidated and China's territorial borders secured, most regimes sought largely to maintain order and elicit deference from periphery states and peoples. This normally did not require continuous military coercion or conquest. On the contrary, most established, strong Han Chinese regimes were primarily oriented toward system maintenance and hence took a relatively non-militant approach to security issues.[93] In particular, when not provoked to the use of force by excessively disrespectful or aggressive periphery powers, such regimes would usually rely primarily on a combination of static defenses and tributary/trade relations to attain their security objectives. Along the northern and northwestern frontiers, these measures would also frequently be combined with efforts to "play barbarians off against one

---

[90]See the contributions to Rossabi (1983), for various excellent analyses of Song foreign relations.

[91]The Song was for the most part successful in the use of offensive force only against the more sedentary areas to the south. It conquered and reunified all of the Chinese heartland south of the Yellow River. Fairbank (1992), p. 114.

[92]Rossabi (1983); Shiba (1983), pp. 98–101; O'Neill (1987), pp. 303–304; Fairbank (1992), p. 114; Hucker (1975), pp. 120–121.

[93]For a more detailed discussion of this point, see Wills (1968), pp. 252–254.

another" (*yi-yi-zhi-yi*) in various forms of alliance and maneuver and to control nomads through the regulation of trade contacts and privileges.

For a strong imperial state, the traditional tributary relationship served many practical, political, economic, and cultural purposes: It reaffirmed the applicability to Chinese and non-Chinese alike of China's hierarchical and sinocentric system of political and social values and thereby legitimized the entire Confucian order, it provided an avenue for regular diplomatic communication between the Chinese court and foreign rulers, and it served as a convenient and durable basis for mutually beneficial economic relations between China and foreign states, thereby increasing, in many instances, China's leverage over those states.[94] In addition, tributary relations also gave recipient periphery states important legitimacy, status, and leverage within their own subregion, by providing significant economic benefits and a form of political recognition by the dominant power in East Asia. Moreover, tributary status often, although not always, implied Chinese diplomatic and military protection of the vassal state against domestic usurpers or foreign nontributary states, as noted above.[95]

When possible, strong Chinese imperial regimes generally sought to ground the tributary and trade relationship in a genuinely hierarchical power structure based on a clear position of military superiority.[96] Under such circumstances, periphery powers were often pressured, enticed, or coerced by strong and wealthy imperial Chinese regimes to accept a more clearly defined status as Chinese vassals that involved specific reciprocal benefits and obligations. Local leaders were usually allowed to retain their positions and rule their lands as they wished, provided they "kept the peace, accepted symbols of [Chinese] overlordship, and assisted [Chinese] armies when

---

[94]One of the best summaries of the tribute system is in Fairbank (1964), pp. 23–38. Also see Fairbank (1978a), p. 30; and Wills (1968), p. 254.

[95]Hunt (1984), p. 15.

[96]Sheperd argues that practitioners of Confucian government understood that normative persuasion usually required the threat of coercion to provide effective control (1993, p. 185). Also see Lam (1968), pp. 178–179; and Suzuki (1968), pp. 183–186.

called on."[97] They would also often receive generous gifts, subsidies, and trade concessions from the Chinese court, ostensibly as an expression of the benevolence and generosity of the emperor, but more accurately to ensure continued loyalty and support.[98] Such gifts and concessions (along with various diplomatic ploys) were often used by a strong regime to foment hostilities among nomadic groups and to prevent the formation of nomadic confederations.[99] In some instances, and particularly during the early period of contact with imperialist powers in the mid 19th century, a compliant vassal state (such as Korea at that time) would also agree to avoid foreign relations with states other than China.[100] In return, the Chinese state often assumed a level of responsibility for the security of the vassal, especially against external attack.

This type of more genuine vassal-suzerain relationship was easier to establish and maintain among the more sedentary, sinitic regimes of the eastern, southern, and southwestern periphery, which were culturally more receptive to the hierarchical, sinocentric impulses of Chinese diplomacy,[101] generally less aggressive, and far more vulnerable to military pressure than the nomadic and semi-nomadic peoples to the north and northwest. Indeed, many of these regimes had strong political and economic incentives to maintain a cooperative relationship with China. For example, some regimes used the bene-

---

[97]Hucker (1975), pp. 61–62. Also see O'Neill (1987), p. 327; and Fairbank (1992), pp. 112–113.

[98]Barfield (1989), pp. 64–67, 112. Occasionally, this strategy also included more coercive measures designed to ensure local compliance. Chinese forces were often garrisoned within periphery areas, as a deterrence to attack and a symbol of imperial authority. Moreover, the sons of rulers were often sent to the Chinese capital to receive education in Chinese culture and also to serve as hostages to ensure their father's loyalty, and Chinese noblewomen were given in marriage to local leaders. These more sophisticated practices were more often implemented by non-Han Chinese or partly nomadic imperial regimes against nomadic areas. See O'Neill (1987), p. 313.

[99]Jagchid and Symons (1989), p. 56. Such practices would at times prompt aggressive responses and eventually lead to the breakdown of tributary relations and military conflict along the northern and northwestern frontiers.

[100]O'Neill (1987), pp. 145–146. Also see Lee (1996), p. 2.

[101]For most of the Qing Dynasty, contacts with the more sinitic southern and southeastern states were handled by the Ministry of Rituals, reflecting the common sinitic culture of these peoples. Inner Asian peoples were handled by the Office of Border Affairs. Kirby (1994), p. 17; Hsu (1970), pp. 62–65; and Spence (1990), pp. 117–119.

ficial, tributary-based trade relationship with strong and unified Chinese regimes to establish wealthy trading states, such as the Shrivijaya during the Tang and the Malacca during the Ming.[102] It is thus no surprise that, as a rule, imperial Chinese rulers were more willing and able to employ noncoercive measures, centered on the tributary relationship, toward sinitic periphery states. Such entities were explicitly regarded by several emperors as far less of a threat to the security and stability of the heartland than the nomadic and semi-nomadic peoples of the north and northwest.[103] In fact, many Chinese rulers eventually came to believe, however incorrectly, that the maintenance of peace along the southern, southwestern, and eastern periphery could be explained by the persuasive and attracting power of Chinese culture, as symbolically expressed in the tributary relationship, and not simply by material considerations such as military and economic power relationships.[104]

Among the more threatening and less-submissive nomadic peoples of Inner Asia, the tributary relationship, combined with other noncoercive measures such as frontier trade and markets, intermarriage between nomadic leaders and Chinese maidens, and other gifts and bestowals, often became (as in the case of weak Chinese states) an elaborate form of pay-off, albeit one couched in the guise of deference to Chinese authority. In other words, as long as strong nomadic powers performed ritual obeisance to the Chinese emperor, even strong Chinese states were usually content to purchase peace along the periphery, especially when such powers proved difficult to subdue through military means. And the rulers of such regimes paid tribute not out of a genuine recognition of the superior virtue of the Chinese emperor but because they gained politically and economically from the exchange.[105]

The advent of the modern era witnessed the emergence of several new, or partly new, factors that affected the security environment and outlook of the Chinese state and its leaders. These factors have

---

[102]Wolters (1970), pp. 28–29, 37–38, 155.

[103]Wolters (1970), pp. 31–32, 36, 50. Also see Wang (1968), p. 53.

[104]Wolters (1970), p. 36.

[105]This is a major inference drawn from Barfield (1989). It is also argued by Jagchid and Symons (1989), pp. 52–54, 174; and Suzuki (1968), pp. 183–184.

altered the specific form and application of China's noncoercive security strategies in important ways, although they have not changed the basically pragmatic approach used in the application of such strategies to protect the periphery. Five fundamental factors are of particular importance.

First, the emergence of significant security threats to the heartland from distant, powerful nation-states meant that the Chinese state could no longer protect itself from external attack by merely controlling or dominating, through various types of suzerainty relationships, those areas immediately adjacent to the heartland. By necessity, efforts to control the periphery became intimately bound up in larger strategies to counter actual or potential threats from both near and distant industrial powers. To deal with such threats, the Chinese state would eventually need to establish more direct forms of control over the traditional periphery, where possible, and sustain a highly sophisticated level of diplomatic skills to influence events both regionally and globally.

Second, the superior organizational, material, and ideological capabilities and qualities of the modern nation-state fatally undermined the past attractiveness of the imperial Confucian-Legalist political-cultural order as a basis for defining the heartland and as a means of establishing and maintaining a unified and prosperous Chinese regime. In its place arose a statist, multi-ethnically based definition of Chinese nationalism centered on (a) a putative "alliance" between Han Chinese and the minority peoples of the traditional periphery, and (b) the totalitarian institutions of a monolithic, Leninist bureaucratic state with a strong military component. Thus, Chinese cultural universalism gave way to a stress on national essence and the defense of China's "unique" culture and people. On the organizational level, a centralized, authoritarian, usually status-quo-oriented, and bureaucratic state structure staffed by educated scholar-officials and led by an imperial family and its retainers was replaced by an even more totalitarian and bureaucratic structure of rule staffed by often poorly educated cadres motivated by an ideology of social transformation and control and led by charismatic figures with extensive military experience.

As a result of the above two developments, the geographical scope of the Chinese heartland was broadened and the power and authority of the Chinese state over Chinese society was strengthened and deepened.

Third, closely related to the previous factor, the decline of Chinese cultural preeminence and the rise of a more egalitarian international system of modern nation-states eventually forced the Chinese state to discard the hierarchical, culturally oriented tributary relationship of the imperial era and adopt many of the concepts and practices of the European interstate system (e.g., the use of international law and interstate treaties between legally equal and sovereign powers). In this context, the long-standing Chinese sensitivity to relative material capabilities that often influenced traditional political, cultural, and military relations with the outside world became even more important than during the imperial period and resulted in a primary stress on the relative economic and military capabilities of the major powers and their shifting relationships with one another and with China. At the same time, traditional sinocentric attitudes toward international relations were expressed, at least partly, in an emphasis on China as an exemplary model of a nonhegemonic, nonpredatory, progressive state concerned with the plight of other underdeveloped states.

Fourth, a deep-seated "victim mentality" among both the elite and the populace first emerged in the imperial period[106] but came to full prominence in the modern era as a result of China's humiliation and subjugation by foreign imperialist states. In the context of the previous three factors, this victim mentality has intensified the long-standing Chinese sensitivity to foreign threats and territorial incursions and accentuated the strong commitment to the creation of a powerful and respected Chinese nation-state able to redress past wrongs (e.g., the seizure of Chinese territories such as Taiwan) committed by stronger imperialist states; defend Chinese state sovereignty, national interests, and regime status in a larger international arena dominated by the great powers; and protect Chinese society against foreign "cultural contamination" and threats to domestic order and stability.

---

[106]The Chinese notion of victimization by foreigners has been a long-standing theme in Chinese history, deriving from earlier periods of conquest by nomadic invaders such as the Mongols and Manchus, which exposed Han Chinese internal weakness. The authors are indebted to Thomas Barfield for this observation.

Fifth, the primary challenge of maintaining domestic order and well-being was made worse during the modern era by huge increases in China's population and, until recent decades, by significant declines in productivity per farm laborer. China's population approximately doubled during the last 150 years of the Qing Dynasty and then doubled again after the communist victory in 1949, following a slight decline in population in the late 19th and early 20th centuries, as a result of military conflicts and economic disasters. In large part as a result of such massive population increases and resulting hunger for land, the man-land ratio per household dropped considerably and both agricultural and industrial production slowed.[107] These pressures added greatly to the existing sense of vulnerability of the Chinese state and society to domestic chaos and hence strengthened the perceived need to devote enormous energies to assuring internal order and well-being.

Together, these developments meant that not only the form of diplomatic relations with the outside world but also the substance of China's security policy have changed significantly in the modern era, even though the basic security problem[108] has generally remained the same. To ensure domestic order and establish and maintain control over its periphery, the Chinese state now needed to acquire the sophisticated organizational, material, and conceptual capabilities and practices of an industrialized nation-state. Moreover, to survive, the Chinese state would need to develop such abilities in relation to both nearby periphery states and more distant industrial powers, as part of both regional and global security strategies.

However, the acquisition of these abilities would take a considerable period of time, given the vastly superior capabilities of Western industrialized states, the depth of China's internal problems, and the degree of conceptual and organizational transformation required of Chinese political and military leaders. Indeed, for most of the modern era, and despite its reconstitution by highly disciplined and determined nationalist and communist elites, the Chinese state has

---

[107]Fairbank (1992), pp. 167–173.

[108]That is, a primary emphasis on the maintenance of domestic order and well-being, combined with efforts to dominate or neutralize the periphery and attain geopolitical preeminence in an overall environment of changing resources.

remained relatively weak in comparison with its major actual and potential adversaries, even though it has become significantly stronger than many of the states on its immediate periphery.

Chinese elites in the early modern era did not immediately realize the magnitude of the security challenge that confronted them. Late Qing rulers initially attempted to deal with the security threat posed by imperialist powers through the use of hierarchical tributary-based interactions, trade restrictions and concessions, and usually ill-timed efforts at armed resistance. These actions resulted in disastrous military defeats and a belated recognition of the need to protect the Chinese heartland by a combination of both "strong-state" military efforts to reestablish control over the periphery where possible and prolonged "weak state" diplomatic strategies against the industrialized powers that used much of the language and logic of the European nation-state system. Thus, both late Qing and especially early nationalist rulers relied on external balancing, cooperative relationships, and appeals to international law to fend off imperialist aggression while also undertaking efforts to build a modern military and consolidate direct control over long-standing periphery areas such as Tibet, Mongolia, Manchuria, and Xinjiang.[109]

The reunification of the Chinese heartland and the subsequent establishment of a Chinese communist regime in 1949 brought further modifications in the hybrid "weak-strong" state security strategy of the modern era. The People's Republic of China attained a relatively high level of state capacity, especially compared to the much weaker nationalist regime, which had existed during a period of domestic political division and extreme social disarray. As a result of its greater strength and control over the heartland, and its political affiliation with communist Russia, the PRC was able to successfully incorporate three long-standing periphery areas (Inner Mongolia, Xinjiang, and Tibet) into the Chinese nation. However, despite such successes, the economic and military capabilities of the communist Chinese state remained greatly inferior to those of the advanced industrial states, partly because of the legacy of underdevelopment of the Qing and republican periods, and partly because of the disas-

---

[109]This pattern of behavior is well summarized in Hunt (1996), pp. 31–50; Kirby (1994), pp. 16–19; Kirby (1997), pp. 443–445; Hsu (1970), pp. 317–342; Hao and Wang (1980), pp. 161–172; and O'Neill (1987), pp. 322–323.

trous effects of Maoist and Stalinist socioeconomic policies. Hence, efforts by the Chinese leadership to establish a stronger presence along the entire periphery and to protect the Chinese heartland from direct attack were checked or complicated by the presence of a major continental industrial power to the north and west (the Soviet Union) and a major maritime industrial power to the east and south (the United States), as well as other smaller nearby powers.[110]

In response to this unprecedented situation, the Chinese state has continued to pursue a version of the past "weak-state" security strategy of extensive diplomatic balance and maneuver throughout most of the communist period.[111] Toward the major powers, this strategy has involved Chinese efforts to establish formal or informal alliances or strategic understandings with, first, the Soviet Union, and, then the United States, as the third, and weakest, player in a complex strategic triangle. It has also at times included, as an important corollary to the larger "great power" strategic game, extensive efforts to court lesser industrial states such as Great Britain, Japan, France, and Germany, as well as secondary efforts to elicit support from newly emergent Asian and African states along China's periphery and beyond, through political or ideological appeals to third world or socialist solidarity.[112] Such appeals have frequently included attempts to present China as a model of a peace-loving, nonpredatory, progressive developing state deserving emulation by other developing nations.[113] This was often conveyed through the enunciation of various "principles" that ostensibly guide China's international behavior (e.g., nonintervention in the internal affairs of other countries,

---

[110]Specifically, after 1949, the PRC was prevented from reestablishing direct control over Taiwan, and a position of suzerainty over Korea, Nepal, and possibly Vietnam, by the military and political resistance of the United States, India, and France. It was also unable to reestablish a position of dominance over all of Mongolia and areas north of former Manchuria, because of the presence of the Soviet Union.

[111]One major exception to this approach occurred during the 1960s, when the Chinese state adopted a variant of a "strong state" autonomous strategy, for largely domestic reasons to be discussed below.

[112]Useful summaries of communist China's strategic interactions since 1949 are provided by Barnett (1977); Pollack (1984); Tow (1994); and Yahuda (1994).

[113]This approach was often accompanied, during much of the 1950s and 1960s, by more assertive policies for enhancing Chinese influence that sought to foment Maoist-style revolutions in third world countries. Armstrong (1977).

the rejection of aggressive hegemonic ambitions, and a commitment to a "no first use" nuclear weapons doctrine).

Such moral posturing, which continues to the present day, resonates with traditional Chinese impulses toward cultural preeminence and thus reflects a continuing desire for China to attain and hold a position of prominence within the international community. It also to some extent derives from a genuine desire to reject the supposed predatory motives and actions of major powers in the nation-state era, born of China's perceived victimization by such powers. Perhaps more important, however, it also serves the interests of a weak state by generating support among lesser powers while hopefully deflecting aggressive behavior by stronger powers. Moreover, China's attempt to present itself as a totally nonaggressive state has also been used, at times, to reduce international criticism of its military forays against the periphery.[114]

To successfully pursue the above strategy of balance and maneuver between two militarily and economically superior industrial powers, the Chinese communist state needed to augment its diplomatic capabilities with a level of military prowess sufficient to deter direct attacks by the superpowers and to generally justify China's participation in a great power strategic triangle, albeit as a "junior partner." Hence, the Chinese state maintained, from the pre-1949 era, a massive standing army (with even more massive reserves) trained to wear down a technologically superior opponent through the fluid tactics of infantry envelopment and guerrilla warfare. By the end of the 1960s, the PRC had also acquired a small, crude nuclear weapons capability and, by the early 1980s, an intermediate and long-range nuclear ballistic missile force capable of mounting a credible retaliatory strike against a small number of key Soviet and U.S. cities and nearby military bases. In addition, China's ability to withstand a major attack from either superpower was increased, in the 1960s and 1970s, by the dispersal of major industrial facilities across the

---

[114]For example, as reflected in China's use of the term "self-defense counterattack" to describe its limited military invasion of Vietnam in 1979.

heartland, from the northeast (former Manchuria) to the interior southwest.[115]

In sum, Chinese leaders in the 20th century have generally pursued a hybrid "weak-strong" state security strategy. This strategy includes a variant of the traditional "strong-state" effort to control the strategic periphery (in this case by directly incorporating peripheral areas claimed by the Qing regime into the Chinese heartland, whenever possible) as well as elements of a "weak-state" approach combining a relatively unsophisticated, territorial defense-oriented military force with an extensive level of involvement in diplomatic balance and maneuver, especially in relation to the superpowers. Since the establishment of the communist regime in 1949 and until the decline of the Soviet Union in the late 1980s, the Chinese state relied for the most part upon a security strategy keyed to external balancing through shifting strategic relationships with the United States and Soviet Union (rather than internal balancing through a crash program of military modernization), combined with the maintenance of a strong yet technologically unsophisticated defensive force designed to deter attacks on Chinese territory, not to project Chinese influence and presence beyond the heartland.[116] Thus, in many respects, the overall security approach of the Chinese state in the 20th century has resembled a modern-day variant of the imperial Song security strategy, combining the construction of strong military defenses (and occasional defensive warfare along the periphery) with extensive involvement in diplomatic maneuver and alliance behavior.

In recent decades, a second set of modernizing changes have further altered China's security environment and brought about even greater changes in its security strategy. These developments have resulted in a further adaptation of the existing "weak-strong" state security approach of the modern era toward a highly "calculative" security strategy emphasizing market-led and outward-oriented eco-

---

[115]For overviews of China's defense strategy and force structure during the 1950s, 1960s, and 1970s, see Whitson (1972); Gittings (1967); Pollack (1972); and Pollack (1979).

[116]However, such a defensive force would almost certainly have been sufficient to reestablish dominant influence or control over former periphery areas such as Taiwan, Korea, and Mongolia if the United States and the Soviet Union had not directly or indirectly prevented such actions.

nomic growth, amicable external relations with all states (in contrast to the past emphasis on external balancing), relative restraint in the use of force combined with greater efforts to create a more modern military, and a continued search for asymmetric gains internationally. Unlike the policies of domestic social transformation and autarkic development of the ideologically charged Maoist era, this security strategy is specifically designed to provide for long-term domestic social stability and to generate the means to construct a strong and prosperous nation better able to interact with and influence the international community.

These developments inevitably prompt the question, Will an increasingly capable China eventually resort to a modern-day variant of a purely "strong-state" security strategy that involves efforts to expand geographically its security periphery and dominate that periphery in ways that threaten U.S. interests and potentially undermine the stability of the Asia-Pacific region? The factors shaping China's current calculative security strategy, the major features of that strategy, and its implications for the future will be examined in further detail in the following two chapters.

THE INFLUENCE OF DOMESTIC LEADERSHIP POLITICS

The Chinese state has generally pursued a pragmatic approach to security policy, largely responding to shifts in relative external capabilities and the lessons learned through a long history of border defense to control or influence the periphery. However, domestic factors have at times exerted a critical, and sometimes irrational, influence over the strategic calculations and behavior of the Chinese state. The most important domestic influences on Chinese security policy have been associated with leadership personalities and leadership politics, including leadership strife resulting from the personalized nature of the Chinese political system.

Chinese history is replete with instances of political leadership groups seeking to use both domestic and foreign policies to outmaneuver opponents. In the struggle to amass and maintain individual and bureaucratic power in a highly personalistic system of rule, Chinese leaders have initiated, modified, or completely distorted policy measures in efforts to mobilize supporters, weaken the position of individual opponents, defend/attack vested bureaucratic interests and beliefs, or simply to place a personal stamp on events.

Understandably, the influence of elite power struggles and individual leadership personalities on security policy has generally been greatest when the Chinese regime has been either immersed in intense conflict or led by a particularly charismatic, powerful figure. For example, vigorous, charismatic leaders have occasionally opted for or persisted in policies of external aggression when objective conditions suggested a more cautious, prudent approach. In the modern era, such behavior has often been motivated by a desire to build domestic political support by stimulating deep-rooted anti-foreign attitudes among the populace through the creation or intensification of a foreign threat.[117] Strong Chinese leaders have also pursued aggressive or ideological foreign policies as part of a more rational strategy designed to build domestic political support for approaches that they believe are essential to national security and necessitated by external "objective" factors, not just by domestic elite conflict.[118] In addition, dominant leaders have at times squandered scarce resources instead of using them to strengthen the security of the Chinese state in times of need.[119]

In general, the effect of personalities and power struggles on policy content and direction has been highly idiosyncratic, reflecting the personal whims or predilections of individual leaders and the vagaries of the power contest. Although the effect of such machinations on a particular policy can be profound, it is virtually impossible to measure or predict how or when policy might be thus affected.

Some analysts of the relationship between Chinese domestic politics and foreign policy argue that the frequent use of force by the Chinese state can be largely attributed to the influence of domestic leadership conflict and competition in a political process lacking strong legal and institutional norms. Hence, for these observers, the emergence

---

[117]Liao (1976); and Liao (1984).

[118]Christensen (1996b). This point is discussed in greater detail below.

[119]Perhaps the most notable example of such behavior is the Empress Dowager's decision to reconstruct the Summer Palace using large sums appropriated to build a modern naval force. Partly as a result of this decision, China's navy was unprepared for the Sino-Japanese War of 1894–95. O'Neill (1987), p. 84.

of a less-personalized political order in which elite conflict and leadership succession are mediated by stable institutions, more predictable processes, and commonly recognized legal structures will inevitably produce a more cooperative, less-aggressive pattern of Chinese security behavior.[120]   Although a more institutionalized political process will likely reduce the propensity to use security policy as a tool in the power struggle and also restrain the arbitrary influence on policy exerted by strong leaders, other factors such as relative material capabilities, the structure of the international order, and domestic competition over alternative policy approaches (discussed below) will probably continue to exert a decisive influence on China's use of force, as they have in the past.

Security policy has been affected by domestic politics in a more regular and predictable manner as a result of the formation of leadership groups around enduring alternative policy approaches, each reflecting the influence of long-standing and conflicting philosophical and bureaucratic interests. Historically, the two most important policy debates affecting China's security behavior have been over (a) autonomy or self-reliance (i.e., internal balancing) versus close involvement with or dependence upon other powers (external balancing), and (b) the prolonged use of coercive strategies centered on offensive military force against the periphery versus a policy centered on noncoercive strategies involving static defense. These two policy debates are sometimes closely related: Arguments in favor of autonomy or self-reliance have often stressed a reliance on static defense over offensive force, whereas proponents of extensive involvement with other powers frequently emphasize security approaches centered on the use of offensive military capabilities. However, the two debates are not identical, e.g., a regime can seek to maintain its autonomy through a primary reliance on offensive force.

Throughout much of Chinese history, and particularly in the modern era, exposure to foreign contacts and ideas has generated a deep-seated tension among China's leadership, and within Chinese society, between those who fear excessive involvement in and dependence upon the outside world and those who support extensive interaction with outsiders, and the introduction of foreign ideas, as a

---

[120]For example, Waldron (1990).

necessary way to increase the capabilities of the Chinese state and to develop Chinese society.[121] This highly contentious debate, relevant to policies affecting both domestic development and external security, is of course present in every developing society. But it exerts a particularly strong influence in China. The combination of China's geographical vulnerability to external attack from a variety of near and distant states, the related belief that domestic unrest invites foreign aggression, the historical economic self-sufficiency of the Chinese state, and China's past cultural preeminence within East Asia have together created a strong belief among Chinese elites in the advantages of relying on China's own resources and hence in maintaining autonomy and independence from foreign social, economic, and political contacts and influence. Within Chinese society as a whole, this belief has contributed greatly to the existence of an undercurrent of extreme xenophobia that continues to the present.[122]

During the imperial era, support for an autonomous approach toward both domestic development and foreign security strategies was often expressed, in the political realm, by Confucian advisors and scholar-officials. These individuals argued that extensive diplomatic and economic contact and involvement with foreign "barbarians" (i.e., those outside the Chinese heartland who did not acknowledge or practice the manifestly superior tenets of Confucian political and social organization) would weaken the Confucian-Legalist order, demoralize the population, create economic disruption and lawlessness, and thereby threaten domestic tranquillity, harmony, and stability.[123] On a more practical (and parochial) level, Confucian bureaucrats also generally opposed extensive foreign contacts and involvement with foreign entities because such actions tended to divert resources from internal civil administration and strengthened the political influence and power of their rivals at court (usually imperial retainers and members of the imperial family), merchants, and, in some instances, military leaders. These factors led many

---

[121]This argument is explicitly applied to the modern era in Hunt (1996), pp. 20–25, 31–50. It is less explicitly presented in Barfield (1989).

[122]The virulent, anti-Western reaction of the Chinese government and society to the accidental bombing by U.S.-led NATO forces of the Chinese embassy in Belgrade, Yugoslavia, during the Kosovo conflict of 1998–1999 is at least partly attributable to such xenophobic attitudes.

[123]Hunt (1996), pp. 20–21. Also see Hao (1980).

officials to oppose extensive levels of foreign trade and foreign ventures such as the above-mentioned maritime expeditions of the early Ming Dynasty.[124] Such views and interests thus contributed significantly to the overall limitations on imperial China's activities beyond the periphery.

Opposition among Chinese elites to extensive involvement with, and dependence upon, the outside world has continued during the modern period, although the specific argument against such involvement has changed significantly since the collapse of the Confucian-Legalist order. In addition, sensitivities to extensive political and military involvement with foreigners, and especially with major powers, has arguably been strengthened by the intensely negative experience of Chinese defeat and subjugation at the hands of Western industrial nations and Japan during the imperialist era[125] and, during the communist period, by the collapse of China's alliance with the Soviet Union.[126]

Both nationalist and communist political leaders and intellectuals criticize the negative influence upon the Chinese nation and society wrought by predatory economic imperialism and supposedly decadent and disruptive Western cultural, political, and social ideas. In particular, they point to the alleged damage done to China's economic development by corrupt and rapacious businessmen operating in China; the general threat of "cultural contamination and subversion" posed by Western religious and philosophical beliefs and popular culture and by Western concepts of social, political, and economic pluralism; the egoistic search for profits above all else; a legal system centered on protecting the rights of the individual above

---

[124]Levathes (1994), pp. 72, 163–165, 175–177; Fairbank (1992), pp. 137–139; and O'Neill (1987), p. 37.

[125]This experience included the failure of efforts by late Qing rulers to establish alliances with specific imperialist states (e.g., Russia) to defend against other imperialist states (e.g., Japan), the perceived betrayal of Chinese interests at the Versailles Conference and again at the Yalta Conference, and the general problems encountered during the entire modern era with allegedly exploitative and culturally subversive foreign businessmen and Western missionaries. See Hsu (1970) and Spence (1990).

[126]Hsu (1970), pp. 761–762; Hunt (1996), pp. 24–25; and Hunt (1984), pp. 30–31. The sudden withdrawal of Soviet economic and military assistance to China in the late 1950s and early 1960s seriously damaged China's economic development and defense efforts. For a brief overview of this episode, see Barnett (1977), pp. 36–42.

the group; and other assumed features of industrialized Western society. Such ideas and practices are viewed as detrimental to China's effort to construct a wealthy and powerful nation-state, corrosive to the self-sacrificing collectivist and nationalist beliefs that modern Chinese leaders have sought to cultivate among ordinary citizens and, more broadly, are seen as a threat to the national and cultural identity of the Chinese people. Moreover, some contemporary Chinese leaders and intellectuals argue that Western, and especially U.S., ideas and institutions should also be rejected by the Chinese people because they serve as instruments of U.S. dominance over the international system. Hence, if adopted, such ideas and institutions will allegedly perpetuate China's subservience to the United States in the regional and global arenas. If China is to become a major power in the modern era, proponents of this viewpoint argue, it must therefore reject U.S. influence and develop its own uniquely Chinese developmental forms. Taken as a whole, these attitudes have thus created a highly exaggerated belief, among some leaders and many ordinary citizens, that China's modern-day social, economic, and political development problems have been and will continue to be greatly aggravated, if not completely caused, by extensive contact with or emulation of the West.[127]

To remain secure from foreign material and cultural threats, these leaders argue, as their imperial Confucian predecessors did using a different logic, China must depend primarily, if not solely, on the genius, industry, and patriotism of the Chinese people. Any significant opening of the Chinese heartland to foreign ideas and practices will inevitably erode social order and fatally threaten the stability and security of the Chinese nation and its ability to achieve great power status, they insist. Thus, regarding the realm of interstate relations, such leaders maintain that China must avoid "entangling alliances" or other forms of extensive international diplomatic or political involvement (and especially involvement with superior industrial powers) that limit the freedom and autonomy of the Chinese state or expose Chinese society to extensive foreign political, economic, or social influences. They also argue that China must ultimately ensure

---

[127]Many of the themes mentioned in this paragraph are discussed in Spence (1990); Hsu (1970); Hsu (1980); Hao and Wang (1980); Hunt (1996); and Fairbank (1992). See also Robinson and Shambaugh (1994); and Dittmer and Kim (1993).

its security by building a strong, modern military unencumbered by the limitations inherent in multilateral security structures or defense pacts.[128]

Opponents of this antiforeign, pro-autonomy viewpoint generally fall into one of two broad categories. The first, and more widely accepted, opposition viewpoint has been evident, in various cultural and political forms, during both the imperial and modern eras, but became particularly pronounced during the final decades of the Qing Dynasty, and has emerged again in recent decades as part of the economic reform movement. Its proponents accept the above arguments of the "neo-isolationists" regarding Chinese vulnerability to foreign threats and intrusions that potentially undermine domestic political and social stability and development. However, such individuals also argue that a relatively weak China (especially as compared to the major powers) must adopt and modify foreign attitudes, technologies, and methods and become more deeply involved in the international system to survive and prosper as a strong and independent state in an increasingly interactive, rapidly developing, and often dangerous world. These individuals argue that a weak China cannot maintain true independence and security if it does not locate reliable outside support and, when necessary, draw on appropriate foreign developmental models, beliefs, and technologies while retaining fundamental Chinese moral and philosophical values.[129]

The second opposition viewpoint first emerged during the 20th century and thus far constitutes a minority (but perhaps a growing minority) among those advocating involvement with the outside world. It presents a liberal and western-oriented critique of both the antiforeign, pro-autonomy viewpoint and the views of those advocating the highly limited and instrumental use of Western techniques by a weak Chinese state. Adherents of this viewpoint argue that

---

[128]Kirby (1994); and Hunt (1996), pp. 20–22.

[129]One version of this argument became especially strong in the later years of the Qing Dynasty, during the self-strengthening (*ziqiang*) movement of the latter half of the 19th century. Proponents of this movement argued that China's modernization effort must seek to retain the essential (*t'i*) moral, philosophical, and organizational elements of Chinese state and society while accepting from the West only what is of practical use (*yong*). Wright (1962); Hunt (1996), pp. 21–22, 31–35; Spence (1990), pp. 225–226; Hsu (1970), pp. 333–352; Hsu (1980); Hao and Wang (1980), p. 201; and Fairbank (1992), p. 258.

modernity ultimately requires the permanent adoption and acceptance, as the *core* elements of Chinese state and society, of a wide variety of western-originated or western-supported institutions and ideas, including the centrality of legal norms and procedures and codified institutional processes over subjective, personal bases of authority; formal political and economic limits on the power of the central government; the construction of quasi-autonomous political, judicial, and social spheres; and support for various international and multilateral regimes and fora.[130]   Hence, proponents of this viewpoint insist that to sustain domestic order and well-being, deter external threats to Chinese territory and national interests, and ultimately attain great power status, China must maintain extensive involvement with the outside world and participate in the shaping of the international community not only when it is weak, but also (and especially) after it becomes strong and prosperous.[131]

The debate between these two general positions has grown particularly intense during periods of regime weakness or decline, when the Chinese state has become heavily involved in diplomatic machinations and at times permitted an expanded level of foreign access to Chinese society. Such extensive involvement in foreign affairs, usually accompanied by growing political and social corruption, state incapacity, and economic collapse, often bolstered the position of those opposed to extensive foreign contacts. These individuals blamed China's ills on excessive collaboration with foreigners and demanded the adoption of strategies keyed to political and economic autonomy and self-reliance. This argument resulted in often highly inappropriate Chinese external strategies (including at times the use

---

[130]A recognition of the need for China to adopt Western ideas and practices, not just technologies, was basic to the (often radical, socialist) views espoused by early 20th century Chinese political intellectuals such as Hu Shi, Chen Duxiu, Lu Xun, Liang Qichao, and Sun Yat-sen. However, arguments in favor of many of the fundamental features of Western capitalist democracies have become notable only during the reform period of the 1970s, 1980s, and 1990s. See Nathan (1990); Schell (1988); and Hamrin (1990). Adherents of this viewpoint argue that such a transformation does not require the wholesale rejection of all indigenous Chinese institutions and ideas but rather their modification and adaptation to the universal requirements of modernity, as has occurred, for example, in Japan.

[131]Contemporary Chinese proponents of post-1978 economic and social reform policies and the opening to the outside world include individuals from both of the above "anti-isolationist" schools of thought.

of offensive force) that accelerated the decline of the state and ultimately weakened its overall security.

The two most notable examples of such policy interventions have occurred in the modern era (i.e., since the latter half of the 19th century). During the final years of the Qing Dynasty, the continued inability of the Chinese state to adequately defend the heartland against imperialist pressures through a heightened weak-state policy of diplomatic appeasement, accommodation, and alliance resulted in an abrupt shift toward a policy of total autonomy and armed resistance to all foreigners. This took the form of the so-called Boxer Uprising of 1898–1901. Those who supported the Boxers among the Chinese leadership cited the social corruption and decline resulting from excessive exposure to the West, the pure nativist qualities and fighting capabilities of the Boxers,[132] and the general inability of China's weak-state strategy to protect China against further incursions to justify the adoption of an autonomous, force-based strategy to deal with the foreign threat. However, this strategy merely led to further humiliations and defeat and even greater inroads on Chinese sovereignty by the imperialist powers.[133]

During the 1960s, the communist regime adopted a largely autarkic security strategy of opposition to both superpowers. This occurred despite the continued relative military inferiority of the Chinese state and signs of growing threats from both the Soviet Union and the United States, and largely because of the dominant influence over policy exerted by Mao Zedong.[134] Although the logic of this situation would have suggested the adoption of a weak-state strategy of accommodation or alliance at that time (in fact there is some evidence that certain Chinese leaders wished to improve relations with the Soviets in the mid 1960s—and especially after Nikita

---

[132]The Boxers were originally both anti-Manchu and anti-foreign Han Chinese believers in the power of traditional stylized exercises, martial arts, and magic.

[133]Hunt (1996), pp. 37–38. For a general overview of the Boxer Uprising, see Fairbank (1992), pp. 230–232; Spence (1990), pp. 231–235; and Wakeman (1975), pp. 216–221.

[134]The emergence of a major dispute with the Soviet Union following the collapse of the Sino-Soviet alliance in the late 1950s, and the growing threat posed by the United States as a result of the intervention of the United States in Vietnam, the expansion of the U.S. intercontinental ballistic missile and long-range bomber force, and U.S. unwillingness to consider a "no first use" nuclear doctrine, resulted in the emergence of a dual threat to China.

Khrushchev's ouster in 1964—to strengthen China's strategic leverage and ease its economic problems), the Chinese state instead adopted a "dual adversary" approach and eventually, during the Cultural Revolution of the late 1960s, an isolationist foreign policy. This policy was pushed and justified by Mao Zedong in part on the basis of a strategy of autarkic social and economic development and military defense. Mao argued that foreign ideas and practices, in the form of, on the one hand, Soviet-led "social-imperialism" and its system of repressive, elitist bureaucratic party control and, on the other hand, U.S.-led imperialism and its aggressive predatory system of exploitative capitalism, together threatened the unity, independence, and vitality of Chinese society and stifled Chinese growth. In reaction to these threats, he espoused a policy of self-reliance and ideologically motivated mass mobilization that drew on a theory of the innate "revolutionary" qualities of the Chinese people to innovate, cooperate, and overcome material obstacles to development. This approach arguably weakened China's security and led to confrontations with both superpowers and ultimately a military clash with the Soviet Union in 1969.[135]

The internal leadership debate over whether to use offensive force or less-coercive measures (such as static defense) in Chinese security policy has invoked many of the same arguments outlined above. During the imperial period, a heavy and persistent reliance on offensive force was often resisted by Confucian civilian officials and advisors, for many of the same political and cultural reasons that such individuals opposed extensive involvement with foreigners. In particular, a reliance on offensive force was seen to divert resources from domestic administration (often without producing clear-cut victories) and to augment the power and influence of non-Confucian elites, such as military leaders, merchants, and imperial retainers. More broadly, a sustained preference for coercive over noncoercive measures also tended to increase the personal, often arbitrary power of the emperor over the authority of Confucian officials. This in-

---

[135]Mao also advocated this autarkic, populist approach to domestic development and national defense to weaken the power and influence of his rivals within the senior party apparatus, who tended to support Soviet-style Leninist and Stalinist policies and party structures of rule. For overviews of the origins and evolution of the "dual adversary" foreign policy, see Barnett (1977); Gittings (1974); Harding (1994a); Goldstein (1994); Yahuda (1978); and Hinton (1970).

creasingly became an issue from the late Tang onward, when Chinese emperors became more autocratic and the functions of government administration and military defense became increasingly lodged in separate elites.[136] In addition, for many Confucian officials, the influence of certain core Confucian beliefs such as "rule by virtuous example" or *de* [137] was weakened by a heavy reliance on coercive security strategies, which allegedly debased human nature and led to an increasing dependence on punitive central controls, state monopolies, heavy taxation, and widespread conscription. These practices, whether applied to Chinese or foreigners, were all in theory anti-Confucian and were seen to undermine the dominant belief system and hence the social status and authority of Confucian scholars and officials.[138]

Political and ideological resistance to the excessive use of force, combined with the opposition to extensive involvement with foreigners, often led to a preference among many Confucian officials for a security strategy centered on a strong, static border defense and those diplomatic and economic approaches that minimized or regulated contact with the outside; foremost among the latter were the cooptation and appeasement practices basic to the traditional tributary relationship, as well as the use of frontier trade and markets. Confucian officials generally did not oppose the payment of even extremely high tributary "gifts" to nomadic leaders as long as the latter performed symbolic acts of deference to the imperial order and refrained from attacking the heartland. Even at their highest, the tributary "gifts" demanded by nomadic leaders were much less expensive than the costs of any prolonged military campaign. Also, the most sizeable payments usually tended to come at those times when

---

[136]Fairbank (1992), p. 111.

[137]As Fairbank states, "The central myth of the Confucian state was that the ruler's exemplary and benevolent conduct manifesting his personal virtue (de) drew the people to him and gave him the Mandate [to rule]" (1992, p. 111). This concept was applied to both residents of China and foreign "barbarians."

[138]Fairbank (1992), pp. 62, 111, 138–139; O'Neill (1987), pp. 202, 208, 355; and Barfield (1989), pp. 91, 131, and personal correspondence. One of the most eloquent and energetic advocates of "rule by virtue" over the use of force was Wei Cheng, the leading scholar-advisor to Emperor Tang Taizong of the Tang Dynasty. See Wolters (1970), pp. 28–33. For a particularly good overview of Confucian arguments against the use of force when dealing with nomadic and semi-nomadic peoples, see Jagchid and Symons (1989), pp. 54, 61–62.

the imperial state was weakest and thus willing to buy peace at any price to preserve itself.[139]

However, Confucian officials were not entirely opposed to the use of force and did not invariably shun extensive involvement with foreigners. Theoretically, in the view of such officials, there was no fundamental contradiction between virtue and the use of force as long as the force was applied by a ruler who possessed virtue, as measured by a *primary* reliance on noncoercive measures and the maintenance of a stable and harmonious society.[140] Indeed, some Confucian officials strongly favored aggressive military measures to chastise and subdue periphery people. In particular, they could be very demanding of military punishment for what they viewed as symbolic insults to the doctrinal authority of the imperial order, such as the refusal by foreign leaders to pay ritual homage to the superior position of the emperor in the tributary relationship.[141] In the early modern era, some Confucian officials during the final years of the Qing Dynasty also supported the use of force against imperialist powers in a desperate effort to limit or eliminate foreign influences on Chinese society, as discussed above in the case of the Boxer Rebellion. At the same time, however, more pragmatic Confucian officials also recognized that extensive diplomatic involvement in the affairs of other powers was at times required for the survival of the Chinese state. As a general principle, therefore, Confucian officials opposed an *excessive or prolonged* reliance on such practices as corrosive of their political position and the existing political and social order.

Opposition to the Confucian preference for noncoercive security measures was most often expressed by military figures, including hereditary military nobles and defense commanders and "warrior" founding emperors. At times, political opponents to Confucian officials at court, such as members of the imperial household, non-Confucian imperial advisors, and imperial retainers, would also

---

[139]The authors are indebted to Thomas Barfield for these observations.

[140]Wang (1968), p. 49.

[141]Confucian officials of the Han Dynasty were strong advocates of force against the nomadic Xiongnu tribes for precisely this reason. Barfield (1989), pp. 53–54. Such examples can also be found in later dynasties.

advocate the use of force, including both extensive military campaigns against periphery powers and, more rarely, efforts to extend China's territorial borders. Such advocacy derived from both narrow political motives (i.e., a desire to undermine the influence of Confucian officials) and a more principled belief that the maintenance of Chinese centrality and the preeminence of the emperor, both domestically and internationally, required relatively frequent displays of the military superiority of the imperial regime.

The balance of power between advocates of force and advocates of noncoercive measures would usually depend on both the material circumstances confronting a particular regime (especially its relative strength or weakness compared to periphery states or regimes, as discussed above) and the origins and internal leadership makeup and outlook of a regime. In general, strong, militant (or militarily experienced), and actively engaged emperors would usually tilt the balance decidedly in favor of pro-force advocates. This especially occurred during the early decades of a regime, and often despite vigorous protests by Confucian officials. As suggested above, advocates of force would also tend to prevail when aggression by periphery peoples was especially persistent and accompanied by insulting behavior, in part because such actions would permit an alliance between Confucian and non-Confucian elites. Conversely, advocates of noncoercive approaches would tend to exert a greater influence on policy toward powers along the southern and southwestern periphery, especially given the reduced threat posed by such entities and the fact that such states were highly receptive to core Chinese political and social beliefs.

The use of force against outsiders became a subject of intense debate within senior leadership circles at numerous times in the history of imperial China. In many instances the outcome could have gone either way; at times, such conflict would produce paralysis or highly erratic behavior.[142] However, as a general rule, the influence of Confucian officialdom, as the carrier of China's core political and cultural norms, increased significantly over time during each dynasty and became especially dominant during the middle stages of a long-

---

[142]Jagchid and Symons (1989), pp. 65, 178; Taylor (1992), pp. 144–145; Struve (1984), pp. 36–37; Waldron (1990), Chapters Seven and Ten; Beckwith (1987), pp. 99–100; and Wolters (1970), p. 30.

lasting regime. In many instances, this trend would reinforce the general tendency during those times to prefer noncoercive measures and, when employing force, to avoid prolonged and expansionist wars. This would be far less true for the non-Han Chinese dynasties of conquest (and intervention) (e.g., the Topa Wei, Liao, Jin, Xi Xia, Yuan, and Qing), whose rulers were not Chinese, who were more greatly influenced by the traditions of previous Inner Asian empires, and who could draw on stronger military/aristocratic elites from their own peoples to balance officials drawn from Confucian official-dom.[143] It was also less true for the predominantly Han Chinese Ming and Sui regimes, for reasons noted above.

Unfortunately, few reliable data exist to determine the extent to which the use of offensive force over static defense has been a major issue of debate among leadership groups during the 20th century. The modern Chinese state, both nationalist and communist, has often used offensive force in an attempt to establish stable buffer areas along the traditional periphery. Yet little if any evidence exists to suggest that this use of force was strongly contested by political officials. Obviously, since the collapse of the imperial order, Confucian values and interests have not played a role in internal leadership discussions or debates. However, broad-based political and bureaucratic interests and especially the imprint of dominant personalities have undoubtedly remained very strong as factors influencing overall decisionmaking. Until the 1990s, modern Chinese regimes have been led by assertive, charismatic founding figures with extensive military experience, such as Chiang Kai-shek, Mao Zedong, and Deng Xiaoping. Hence, as in the case of imperial China, these individuals almost certainly dominated, if not monopolized, leadership discussions over the adoption of coercive over noncoercive strategies, especially regarding such a critical national security issue as periphery defense. Moreover, as in the past, these leaders generally did not

---

[143]The authors are indebted to Edward Dreyer for this general observation, provided in a personal correspondence. Dreyer also observes that the dominance of essentially land-bound and continental-oriented Confucian officials within Han Chinese regimes greatly reinforced the existing tendency to denigrate the strategic significance of China's maritime periphery. Hence, the characteristic expression of Chinese naval abilities during most of the imperial era was not a blue water navy run by the state but, at most, a small coastal force for the defense of rivers and shores, and the occasional manipulation of non-state-run pirate fleets.

shirk from the application of force in efforts to pacify the heartland, consolidate (and in some instances expand) national borders, and influence the periphery.

Two significant partial exceptions during the Maoist era were the Korean War of 1950–1953 and the Vietnam War of 1965–1975. There is some evidence to indicate that both conflicts prompted significant debate among Chinese leaders, especially over whether and to what degree China should employ offensive force. During the Korean War, senior leaders responsible for economic affairs might have resisted extensive intervention in the Korean conflict because of its likely economic costs.[144] Nonetheless, it is almost certainly the case that, even in these instances, any debate occurred within narrow limits set by the paramount leader.

It is even more difficult to find instances in which broad-based bureaucratic interests played a major role in decisions to use force, as opposed to decisions regarding domestic development issues, where such factors have clearly played an important role. This is partly because the modern Chinese regime is only just emerging from an era of state formation and consolidation and beginning an era of more routinized maturation and development. Therefore, as (and if) this process proceeds, one might expect that the ascension to power during the post-Mao era of relatively uncharismatic political leaders possessing little military experience will result in greater internal debate over the use of force, perhaps duplicating, to some extent, the general lines of debate evident during the imperial era. This seems particularly likely given the increasing importance to China's national security of external economic ties and the growing role in policymaking of senior officials with extensive economic and bureaucratic experience.[145]

---

[144]Christensen (1996b), especially Chapter Five; personal correspondence with Christensen.

[145]There is some evidence to suggest that the limited application by China of military force for political ends (in the form of military exercises and missile firings) during the Taiwan mini-crisis of 1995–1996 provoked rather intense bureaucratic conflict. However, in this instance, the lines of debate were apparently between the Chinese military and the professional diplomats of the Ministry of Foreign Affairs, not civilian officials charged with domestic economic development. Swaine (1998a) (revised edition), p. 75.

In sum, domestic leadership competition or particular leadership views have at times exerted a decisive influence over the security behavior of the Chinese state. The highly personalized nature of China's leadership system has at times injected a strong element of instability and unpredictability into external security decisionmaking as leadership groups sought to manipulate foreign and defense policy in an effort to outmaneuver political opponents or build support among the Chinese populace. In these instances, the effect on policy content and direction has often been idiosyncratic, i.e., usually reflecting the personal whims or predilections of strong, charismatic leaders or the vagaries of the power struggle. This suggests that the influence of elite competition and individual leadership personalities on security policy has generally been greatest when the Chinese regime has been immersed in intense conflict or led by a strong, charismatic figure.

China's security policy has also been affected by domestic politics in a more regular and predictable manner as a result of the formation of leadership groups around enduring alternative policy approaches. Historically, the two most important policy debates affecting China's security behavior have been over autonomy and the use of force. During the imperial era, a relatively strong leadership consensus in support of self-reliant, coercive security strategies arguably occurred most often in the early or middle years of regimes, in response to repeated military provocations or insults to the authority or status of a strong Chinese state. Such actions permitted a convergence of interests between militant, charismatic, founding leaders and highly status-conscious Confucian officials. At the same time, during the height of most imperial Han Chinese regimes, the growing influence of civilian officials would often produce a preference for noncoercive security strategies, or at the very least a desire to avoid the excessive or prolonged use of force. During the modern era, China has been ruled, until the 1990s, by assertive, charismatic founding figures with extensive military experience. Hence, as in the case of imperial China, these individuals almost certainly dominated, if not monopolized, leadership discussions over the adoption of coercive over noncoercive strategies, especially regarding such a critical national security issue as periphery defense.

Also of note are those instances in which internal leadership conflict has led to a misguided rejection of noncoercive strategies in favor of a strategy of autonomy and offensive force. Such behavior has usually occurred during the latter stages of regime decline, at least during the modern period, and invariably produced disastrous results. Conversely, domestic leadership conflict has also at times resulted in the use of noncoercive measures of accommodation and appeasement when coercive policies might have been expected.

Chapter Four

CHINA'S CURRENT SECURITY STRATEGY: FEATURES AND IMPLICATIONS

The five basic features of Chinese security strategy and behavior presented in the previous chapter have persisted to the present day. However, contact with industrialized nation-states, the collapse of the traditional Confucian-Legalist order, and the emergence of Chinese nationalism have brought about several major changes in the specific definition of China's security objectives and concerns (i.e., what is understood by domestic order and well-being, threats to Chinese territory, and Chinese geopolitical preeminence) and hence the specific means by which such objectives or concerns could be addressed in the modern era. These changes generally brought about a hybrid "weak-strong" state security strategy that combined traditional "strong-state" efforts to control the strategic periphery with elements of a "weak-state" approach employing a relatively unsophisticated, territorial defense-oriented force structure and an extensive level of involvement in diplomatic balance and maneuver.

In recent decades, this strategy has undergone further changes, resulting in a modification and extension of the existing "weak-strong" state security approach of the modern era toward a highly "calculative" security strategy. The term "calculative," in this context, does not refer to the mere presence of *instrumental rationality*, understood as the ability to relate means to ends in a systematic and logical fashion and which is presumably common to all entities in international politics, whether weak or strong. Rather, the notion of "calculative" strategy is defined in *substantive* terms as a pragmatic approach that emphasizes the primacy of internal economic growth and stability, the nurturing of amicable international relations, the relative restraint in the use of force combined with increasing efforts to create a more modern military, and the continued search for asymmetric gains internationally. The reasons for this new strategy are ultimately rooted in the fact that China today requires high levels of undistracted growth in economic and technological terms, and hence significant geopolitical quiescence, to both ensure domestic order and well-being and to effectively protect its security interests along the periphery and beyond.

This chapter discerns the specific causes and features of China's present-day calculative security strategy and assesses the way this strategy could adversely affect U.S. interests and the stability of the Asia-Pacific region over the near to mid term. This period, defined as extending from the present to about the period 2015–2020, merits special scrutiny because it represents the *minimal* timeframe during which China, despite acquiring critical economic, technological, and military capabilities, will continue to depend on the success of the present U.S.-dominated international and regional order for its security. During this period, the actions of other states will most likely be the principal precipitants of any serious confrontations or conflicts with China, as the growth in relative Chinese power, being not yet complete, will limit Beijing's ability and willingness to pursue other, more assertive, geopolitical strategies. This chapter's discussion of the features and security implications of China's calculative strategy provides a basis for the analysis of the longevity of that strategy and the choices defining China's strategic directions over the truly long term—the period after 2015–2020. These two subjects are the focus of the next chapter.

FACTORS SHAPING CHINA'S CALCULATIVE SECURITY STRATEGY

The Benefits and Challenges of Economic and Technological Reform

After a period of nearly 30 years of communist rule, the Chinese economy began an unprecedented structural transformation in the late 1970s, thanks primarily to the market reforms of Deng Xiaoping. This transformation produced revolutionary improvements in Chinese growth rates, patterns and volumes of manufacturing and trade, personal income levels, state revenues, foreign exchange earnings, and levels of technology, all of which taken together portend a qualitative increase in national capabilities and, if continued over many decades, a shift in the regional and global balance of power.[1] Thanks to the fruits of the reform program initiated in 1978, China now perceives the acquisition of "comprehensive national strength"[2] as being within its grasp—strength, which if acquired, would enable it to both resolve its pressing internal developmental problems as well as reacquire the military capabilities and international political status it lost at the beginning of the modern era. The importance attached to concluding the ongoing reform program successfully cannot be underestimated because Chinese security managers clearly recognize that only sustained economic success can assure (a) the successful servicing of social objectives to produce the domestic order and well-being long associated with the memories of the best Chinese states historically; (b) the restoration of the geopolitical centrality and status China enjoyed for many centuries before the modern era; (c) the desired admittance to the core structures regulating global order and governance; and (d) the obtaining of critical civilian, dual-use, and military technologies necessary for sustaining Chinese security in the evolving regional order.[3]

At the same time, the continuation, over the long term, of China's recent economic successes will likely require far more extensive structural and procedural reforms than have taken place to date. These include more thoroughgoing price, tax, fiscal, banking, and legal reforms; the further liberalization of foreign investment practices, trade, and currency convertibility; the reform or abandonment of many state-owned enterprises; and the implementation of more effective environmental protection measures.[4] Such actions, at least in the near term, could significantly reduce growth rates, aggravate ex-

---

[1]The scope and significance of China's economic and technological achievements during the reform era are summarized in World Bank (1997a), pp. 1–16.

[2]Li (1990).

[3]A good exposition of the role of economic considerations in China's grand strategy, coupled with a defense of the claim that global stability will increasingly derive from Chinese strength, can be found in Song (1986).

[4]World Bank (1997a), pp. 17–96, for an excellent overview of the requirements for continued economic growth in China and the problems confronting future reforms.

isting social problems, and will almost certainly challenge deep-rooted bureaucratic and political interests. They could also significantly increase China's dependence on foreign supplies of critical materials, consumer demand, investment, technology, and know-how.[5] These possibilities could generate significant leadership debates over the pace and depth of future economic reforms and the structure and extent of Chinese involvement in the world economy. How China copes with these challenges holds potentially enormous implications for the future longevity and composition of China's calculative security strategy, and if not successfully addressed, they would prevent the growth of China as a world power.

Changing Capabilities and Orientations of Periphery Powers

Although China is thus changing dramatically and for the better, at least in economic terms, during the last 20 or so years, the fact remains that the capabilities and strategic orientations of the countries along China's strategic periphery have also changed.[6] In fact, the changes here have arguably been more radical, as far as relative national capabilities over time are concerned and, more significantly, the processes leading up to these changes have been in motion for much longer, in fact dating back to the end of the Second World War.[7] China's own economic ferment has thus begun at a point when the traditionally weaker states on its periphery have already increased their national power capabilities in a manner that would have been unrecognizable to previous generations of Chinese rulers, especially those managing the nation's fortunes at the high tide of the imperial era. Since the end of the Second World War, the sinitic states such as South Korea, Japan, Taiwan, and Vietnam, as well as

---

[5]For example, extensive fiscal reform and environmental protection efforts could temporarily divert resources from more productive pursuits, far-reaching state-enterprise reforms could exacerbate worker insecurity and lead to high levels of social unrest, and greater marketization and privatization efforts could provoke strong resistance at all levels of the Chinese system from profit-seeking capitalist government and party bureaucrats. See Swaine (1995b), pp. 57–80; Harding (1987), Chapter 10; and Lardy (1998).

[6]For a brief overview of the growth in capabilities along China's periphery, see Rohwer (1993).

[7]An overview of the processes leading to the rise of the peripheral states can be found in Tellis et al. (1998).

non-sinitic states such as India, have all emerged as independent, more-or-less strong, and stable political entities with significant and in some cases rapidly growing economic and military capabilities.[8] Moreover, several of these states have established strong political and security links with countries other than China, especially global powers such as the United States, and are becoming increasingly integrated into the international economy, although several countries (particularly Taiwan, Japan, and South Korea) have also recently established mutually beneficial economic and/or political connections with Beijing.[9] Areas along China's northern and western periphery, such as Outer Mongolia and the Central Asian Republics of the former Soviet Union, have also emerged as independent states, and even though they are not as strong and stable as the countries on the eastern and southern periphery and generally enjoy amicable and cooperative relations with Beijing, they have for the most part developed a primarily non-Chinese strategic orientation focused toward Russia and the Middle East.[10]

These developments suggest that, although the Chinese state has managed to incorporate formerly peripheral areas such as Tibet, Xinjiang, Manchuria, and parts of Mongolia into its orbit of control (sometimes by force and sometimes through deliberate sinicization), China now confronts a truly formidable challenge if it seeks to replicate its traditional goal of controlling or at the very least pacifying new periphery regions beyond the expanded heartland. Indeed, the past option of direct military force now presents enormous political, economic, and military dangers to the Chinese state not only from the actions of the major external powers such as the United States and Russia (which are often tied by security linkages to the peripheral states), but also directly from many of the peripheral states themselves. There is little doubt today that countries such as Japan, Vietnam, and India, to cite but three examples of states located along the eastern and southern periphery, are powerful and stable enough politically, economically, and militarily to ward off all but the most

---

[8]A useful survey of the power and preferences of the Asian states can be found in Malik (1993).

[9]The patterns of economic integration of the Asia-Pacific region are detailed in World Bank (1993).

[10]Snyder (1995).

violent—meaning nuclear—threats that can be mounted by Beijing. As a result, the principal peripheral area that Beijing can continue to threaten with overwhelming force remains Taiwan—an area long regarded by China as a province. Even in this case, however, the use of force is presented as a last resort to prevent the island from becoming permanently detached from the Chinese heartland.

The newly independent republics of Central Asia are also potentially susceptible to Chinese blandishments and coercion and could probably even become subject to Beijing's military power. But this remains a distant, merely hypothetical, possibility and one whose eventual success is by no means foreordained, especially if Russia is able to regain its traditional dominant position in this area. Beijing's primary interests in the region revolve around securing access to its vast, though as yet unexploited, energy supplies; moderating both pan-Turkic nationalism and militant Islam to sustain effective political control in the Xinjiang region; and encouraging regional economic development to develop trade and other economic linkages— all of which would be ill-served by the application of sustained military force directed at the Central Asian states.[11]

Exponential Growth in the Capabilities of Industrial Powers

Although most parts of the traditional Chinese periphery have thus experienced dramatic increases in national capability since the Second World War, the economic and military capabilities of major states in the wider international system have grown even more significantly. These developments, broadly understood, implied the further consolidation of Western power (and now include the integration of a formerly quasi-peripheral state—Japan—within the orbit of Western influence), which in turn was the result of two general processes. On the one hand, the economies of the major Western states in the international system benefited enormously from their participation in the U.S.-led process of privatized manufacturing and trade that has swept across much of Europe, North America,

---

[11]Useful surveys of Chinese interests in Central Asia can be found in Munro; and Burles (1999).

and Asia since the 1950s.[12] On the other hand, and partly as a result of this dynamic process of expanding privatization, the most developed industrial states, and particularly the United States, achieved major advances in technology that in turn served not only to greatly increase the lethality and effectiveness of their military capabilities but to actually increase the power differentials between the West and its many competitors.

These developments, taken together, implied that China today faces a significant disadvantage: unlike, for example, its Ming forebears in the 16th century, who could hold their own in the face of alternative centers of power such as Mughul India, Muscovy Russia, and Ottoman Turkey in the realms of technology and other national capabilities such as economic strength and military power, modern China (in both its Maoist and Dengist incarnations) has appeared on the international scene at a time when Western dominance is highly entrenched and almost self-perpetuating. Even more crucially, establishing and maintaining its capabilities as a major power in this environment require China to establish linkages with the highly successful economic system of the West, and consequently, both the preservation of security and the pursuit of power require a radically different level of global integration than was required of the Ming Dynasty four centuries earlier or of any other imperial regime. The price for the rejuvenation of Chinese power in the modern era is thus potentially high from the perspective of its traditional desire to maintain both autonomy and geopolitical centrality in Asia: Not only does the success of the U.S.-led postwar economic regime prevent Beijing from pursuing an isolated or a nonmarket approach to economic and military development (at least during the initial stages), but it also makes continued Chinese acquisition of economic and technological power hostage to the goodwill of Western regimes, markets, and suppliers. The ascent to power thus comes at the cost of limitations on Beijing's freedom of action and although it appears that this is a price China is by and large willing to pay, at least in the near term, it only makes the question of what Beijing's long-term directions would be—that is, the directions that can be pursued once

---

[12]This dynamic, together with the many changes occurring after 1971, is explored in some detail in Spero (1985), pp. 25–168.

the constraints relating to external dependency in the near term diminish—even more interesting.

Growing Domestic Social and Political Challenges

China certainly looks forward to the day when it can recover its rightful place in the sun—a yearning reinforced by past memories of both greatness and humiliation—but there is a clear recognition within the country's leadership that several obstacles must be overcome before China's claim to greatness rings palpably true within the region and world-wide. Although the external obstacles are clear and well-recognized, namely, China's dependence on external capital, technology, and markets, there has been a growing recognition, especially over the past 20 years, that the internal social, political, and organizational obstacles erected since the advent of communist rule in 1949 are just as, if not more, significant.[13]

The utopian and highly disruptive policies of the Great Leap Forward and the Cultural Revolution of the 1950s and 1960s created enormous chaos and uncertainty within China. By the 1960s and 1970s, a combination of continued population pressures, the institutionalized inefficiencies of a generally autarkic development strategy, and the highly rigid, repressive, and centralized political system associated with the Maoist regime had created great impoverishment and disillusionment. Taken together, such developments not only weakened the faith of ordinary citizens and officials alike in the leadership of the Communist Party and its official statist development strategy, they also resulted, more problematically, in a corrosion of political culture, which brought about the loss of leadership and popular virtue, made manifest by the appearance of pervasive corruption and the rise of a self-serving officialdom. These developments have significantly exacerbated the challenge to maintaining domestic order and well-being that resulted from earlier modern developments (including increases in China's population, discussed above), and place enormous pressure on the Chinese state to sustain high levels of economic growth over the long term.

---

[13]For a review of some of these challenges, see Harding (1994b).

Although the internal consequences of political and social corrosion are no doubt critical, insofar as they affect the prospects for national disunity, regional fissures, and social unrest, their external consequences are just as unsettling: They have given rise to a deliberate effort by the weakened and discredited organs of rule at wrapping themselves in the mantle of territorially defined notions of nationalism as they struggle to counter the corroding legitimacy of the communist state.[14] The effect of this dynamic has been to restore emphasis to the irredentist cause of "national reunification" while simultaneously setting the stage for the possible emergence of new, potentially dangerous, legal and ideological justifications that "could provide *lebensraum* for the Chinese people."[15] These justifications, taking the form of concepts such as *haiyang guotu guan* (the concept of sea as national territory) and *shengcun kongjian* (survival space),[16] feed off the newfound confidence that comes with two decades of high economic growth but could nonetheless bring China closer to a costly international conflict without in any way resolving the problem of infirm structures of rule at home. Even more important, they carry within themselves the potential for undoing China's larger calculative strategy and the geopolitical quiescence that Beijing is relying upon to complete its internal economic transformation.

The Emergence of a More Pragmatic Program of Military Modernization

The cost of weak government has been manifested in the material arena as well as in failures in the realm of legitimacy. This is seen most clearly when Chinese military capabilities are examined. There is little doubt today that, lack of resources apart—*a problem which in itself can be traced to leadership failure*—the inability of the Chinese armed forces to modernize adequately since at least the 1950s must ultimately be traced to the major shortcomings of China's economic system and its rigid and unimaginative bureaucracy and party

---

[14]Whiting (1995), pp. 732–734; Zhao (1997); and Pye (1995), p. 582.

[15]Kim (1997), p. 248.

[16]Kim (1997), p. 248.

structure. Most of the advances in China's military capabilities attained in the 1950s, 1960s, and 1970s came about primarily through incremental and marginal improvements of the largely obsolete Soviet weapons designs that became available to China during the heyday of the Sino-Soviet alliance of 1950–1962. During the 1960s and 1970s, an emphasis on Maoist self-reliance generally precluded any attempt to accelerate and deepen the modernization process by acquiring foreign military technologies and systems, and efforts to professionalize and modernize military practices and organizations were blocked by intrusive Maoist political and doctrinal controls.

By the mid 1980s, however, most Chinese civilian and military leaders clearly recognized that a strong and stable military force could not be built through a continued reliance on the failed autarkic and excessively ideological policies of the past. This recognition was facilitated, over time, by the gradual passing of those leaders, such as Mao Zedong, who were sympathetic to such policies for political or ideological reasons and was greatly spurred by the major military advances attained by Western powers—advances that were subsequently labeled the "military-technical revolution" (MTR) by Soviet theorists.[17] As a result of these factors, China's past impractical and insular approach to military modernization gave way to a new effort at examining and selectively incorporating advanced foreign military technologies while attempting to "indigenize" these qualities through licensed coproduction of complete systems, the incorporation of critical subcomponents, or the domestic absorption of knowhow, wherever possible.[18] This effort, in turn, required the creation of a more efficient, innovative, and productive defense industry establishment and the application of more purely professional criteria to military training and personnel selection. All of these requirements imply a much greater level of involvement with and dependence upon foreign, and especially Western, defense-related resources and know-how. They also demand the resolution of major,

---

[17]The key Soviet proponent of the MTR was Marshal N. V. Ogarkov. See Ogarkov (1982)—his seminal paper on the subject.

[18]Gill and Kim (1995) for a detailed review of China's arms acquisition strategy and constraints.

long-standing organizational and conceptual problems plaguing China's defense establishment.[19]

All in all, this shift in emphasis in military modernization from complete autarky to some more modest forms of dependence on external resources and know-how only reinforced the larger trend identified earlier: the growing reliance on outside powers for critical capabilities that can underwrite Beijing's rise to power and, by implication, the acceptance of certain constraints by China's security managers on its freedom of action as the price for the acquisition of those capabilities that are seen to advance its march to "comprehensive national strength" over the long term. At the same time, the ability of the Chinese state eventually to reduce its level of dependence on the outside and increase its freedom of action will depend to a great extent on its ability to carry out the more extensive economic reforms and overcome the kinds of structural and conceptual obstacles noted above.

The Rise of More Institutionalized, Pragmatic Forms of Authority and Governance

Although the problematic legacy of the past has greatly stimulated China's willingness to move in the new directions visible since 1978, other, more subtle, internal political changes have also coalesced to make the latest twist in Beijing's hybrid "weak-strong" state security strategy possible. These factors often go unrecognized because China's strong dependence on the external environment for continued economic success usually obscures the effect of internal transformations on Beijing's newest shift in strategy. Perhaps the most important internal change is the rise of more institutionalized forms of authority and governance. The gradual demise of charismatic authority in recent years, combined with the widespread repudiation of extremist ideological development strategies, has resulted in a more pragmatic, risk-averse brand of politics in comparison to the political and policy risks that could be taken by strong, militant, and charis-

---

[19]Such problems include (a) excessive adherence to self-reliance as a guiding principle; (b) lack of horizontal integration; (c) separation from the civilian commercial sector; (d) lack of skilled experts, managers, and labor; (e) poor infrastructure; and (f) technology absorption problems. Swaine (1996b).

matic leaders such as Mao in the heyday of the revolutionary era. In contrast to a previous generation of charismatic leaders who ruled by both force and popular acclamation, China's current leaders, lacking similar charisma and experience, have been forced to rule by creating a minimal policy consensus which involves, among other things, an "exchange of considerations"[20] both among leading party and government figures as well as the bureaucratic organs of state.[21] Survival in such an environment is contingent on success at the level of policy outcomes and, consequently, rash and imprudent external policies that could imperil the fortunes of the current leadership are likely to be avoided if for no other reason than because the individuals involved lack the awe-inspiring charisma that would insulate them against the worst political consequences of any serious failure.[22]

The gradually developing administrative institutions (including more institutionalized norms for leadership selection and removal), the increasing specialization among elites by expertise in various issue-areas, and the progressive replacement of violence by intra-elite bargaining as the primary means of capturing and sharing power have only reinforced the marked tendency toward policy pragmatism witnessed in the post-1978 era.[23] This development by no means implies the absence of strong contending views within the leadership or the elimination of traditional patterns of domestic leadership debate, discussed in the previous chapter. In particular, increasing, and unprecedented, levels of involvement with the outside could arguably heighten long-standing and deep-rooted Chinese sensitivities to cultural contamination and foreign manipulation and subversion. Arguments in favor of lessening Chinese dependence on the outside and increasing Chinese political and diplomatic autonomy could

---

[20]Following Chester Bernard, Waltz (1979), p. 113, uses this concept to describe relations between coordinate units. Although the relations among China's top leaders are not always coordinate relations, the mutual adjustment and accommodation that increasingly take place among various personalities and groups justifies the use of the phrase even in an environment that has room for nominal hierarchies.

[21]For a discussion of the evolution of the system of "collective leadership," see Wang (1995), pp. 103–119.

[22]Wang (1995), pp. 103–119.

[23]Pei (1998) and the discussion below of the prospects for long-term democratic change, for a detailed review of some of these developments.

gain greater currency if economic growth falters seriously or if Chinese involvement in international regimes or treaties are seen to obstruct the attainment of specific nationalist objectives, such as national reunification. Those who support China's greater involvement in world affairs, for whatever reason, would likely resist strenuously such arguments, thus creating the basis for significant leadership conflict. However, at present, and barring any major economic or social crises, such contention is not strong enough to abridge the evolving "rules of the game" pertaining to the peaceful, pragmatic pursuit and distribution of power, especially at the highest levels of the government and party. Also significant is the fact that there still exists a small though nontrivial threat of military intervention in the event of prolonged economic decline or elite strife.[24] This possibility, in turn, suggests that the majority coalitions currently behind China's pragmatic reform era policies have an even greater interest in ensuring, first, that a pacific external environment is created to the maximum extent possible (at least as far as China's own policies are concerned) and, second, that this environment actually yields visible dividends as far as Chinese economic growth and technological improvement are concerned.

Barring any catastrophic changes occurring outside of Chinese control, the net effect of these domestic transformations will be to reinforce the policy of pragmatism still further—a condition that can be expected to hold at least until China's power-political resurgence is complete, at which point there may arise new elites who seek to use the country's newfound power in more assertive ways to advance either their own particular interests or the national interest at large. Such elites could attain influence by combining nationalist pride in China's economic successes, Chinese great power aspirations, and elite and popular fears of foreign subversion to argue, for example, in favor of a more autonomous, strong state security strategy. Until that point is reached, however, the domestic leadership changes currently occurring in China appear to reinforce Beijing's appreciation of its dependence on the existing international system for continued growth and prosperity.[25]

---

[24]Swaine (1995b), pp. 38–39.

[25]For further details on these and other facets of China's leadership, see Chapter Five and Swaine (1995b), pp. 3–39, 95–104.

Lowered External Threats

China's willingness to recognize the price of dependence is certainly a significant facet of its present security strategy, but the larger and more consequential changes in its strategic environment that made this attitude possible must not go unnoticed. The gradual diminution in the levels of threat faced by the Chinese state since the 1970s created an environment where increased Chinese security-related interactions with other states became possible. This diminution occurred in part because the United States initiated a process of detente as a means of involving China in resolving its own problems with both Vietnam and the Soviet Union. When U.S. problems in Southeast Asia were resolved by the mid to late 1970s, the U.S. engagement of China as part of its larger strategy toward the Soviet Union only grew in intensity. Moreover, Beijing's freedom of maneuver compared to that of the Soviet Union actually increased (despite its own conspicuous inferiority) after the restoration of full Sino-U.S. diplomatic relations in 1979, thanks both to the positive externalities of U.S. nuclear deterrence and because the Soviets were more concerned with events in such far-off regions as Southwest Asia than with nearby competitors such as China. As a consequence of this gradual deepening of Sino-U.S. political relations, Washington drastically reduced its level of military assistance to Taiwan, dropped prohibitions on the sale of certain weapons and the transfer of many critical military and civilian technologies to China, and generally permitted a wide range of beneficial commercial dealings with the PRC.[26]

This turnaround in Sino-U.S. relations, along with initial signs of a decline in Soviet power, eventually spurred an improvement in China's relations with the Soviet Union, which ultimately produced a drastic reduction in military tensions between the two Eurasian powers, marked by high-level leadership visits and consultations, confidence-building measures along the Sino-Soviet border, and greatly increased economic and cultural contacts. Such an unprecedented reduction in the level of foreign threat posed to the Chinese

---

[26]For details, see Harding (1992), and Pollack (1999).

state in the modern era thus occurred at a time when the most important entity in the international system—the United States— appeared to be more supportive of China whereas its most consequential and proximate adversary—the Soviet Union—was progressively decaying in power-political capacity. This radical diminution in the range of traditional threats visible since the early years of the Cold War provided China with a substantial measure of political cover under which it could pursue the internal economic reforms—finally embarked upon in 1978 and accelerated in the mid to late 1980s—without excessive risk.

The general pacificity of its external environment allowed Beijing the luxury of downgrading military modernization to the last of the "four modernizations" (identified as agriculture, industry, science and technology, and national defense) in terms of relative priority and enabled China to undertake its market reform program for two decades continuously without any disproportionate diversion of its fruits into wasteful security competition.[27] The wisdom of this choice was only buttressed by the end of the Cold War, brought about by the final demise of the Soviet Union in 1992. This event provoked Jiang Zemin's authoritative assessment of China's strategic environment as "never having been more satisfactory since the founding of the Republic."[28] The relatively pacific external environment thus contributed to the emergence of a Chinese security policy that could focus on the long-overdue modernization of Chinese agriculture, industry, and science and technology. This focus enabled Beijing to lay the foundations for acquiring comprehensive national strength as opposed to embarking on a "quick and dirty" program of accelerated military modernization which, however much it increased China's coercive power in the short run, would eventually undercut its ability to become a true great power and reestablish the geopolitical centrality and respect it believes to be its due.

---

[27]Chen (1990).

[28]Cited in Kim (1996), p. 11.

THE MAJOR GUIDING TENETS AND POLICIES OF CHINA'S CALCULATIVE SECURITY STRATEGY

Given this backdrop, it is no surprise that Chinese grand strategy since the end of the Cold War has sought to maintain the orientation visible since 1978: the acquisition of comprehensive national power deriving from a continued reform of the economy without the impediments and distractions of security competition. The traditional objectives that the Chinese state has pursued over the centuries still remain and they *even now* constitute the ends to which all the efforts relating to economic growth and internal transformation are directed. These objectives include assuring domestic order and social well-being; maintaining an adequate defense against threats to the heartland; increasing the level of influence and control over the periphery with an eye to warding off threats that may eventually menace the political regime; and restoring China to regional preeminence while attaining the respect of its peers as a true great power marked by high levels of economic and technological development, political stability, military prowess, and manifest uprightness. Such objectives, however, cannot be pursued today through the assertive and sometimes militaristic solutions associated with the "strong-state" strategy of the past, in large measure because China presently finds itself "between the times": Although it may be a rising power, it is not yet sufficiently strong, at least relative to some of the key states on its periphery, if not beyond. Consequently, it is in many ways still a "consumer," rather than an entirely self-sufficient "producer," of security and its present grand strategy accordingly reflects the fact that its domestic and external environments constrain its preferred outcomes much more easily than its resources can produce them.

Not surprisingly, then, as has occurred at times in the past, China's grand strategy today is neither "assertive" nor "cooperative" in the most straightforward sense of those terms. Instead, in this instance, it displays a "calculative" streak which, though determined to prevent certain critical losses at all costs, is nonetheless characterized by an outward-oriented pragmatism designed to rapidly improve its domestic social conditions, increase the legitimacy of its governing regime, enhance its national economic and technological capabilities, and thereby ultimately strengthen its military prowess and improve its standing and influence in the international political order.

The logic underlying this "calculative" strategy is therefore simply one of *constrained maximization*, with China seeking to increase its power in a variety of issue-areas in as non-provocative a fashion as possible to avoid precipitating those regional or global responses that would seek to retard the growth of that power for all the time honored reasons associated with the "quest for equilibrium"[29] and "the creation of balances of power."[30] If successfully executed, the "calculative" strategy offers Beijing dual benefits, whether intended or not: On the one hand, it would desensitize China's political and economic partners to the debilitating problems of relative gains in Chinese capabilities and thus encourage continued foreign collaboration in the underwriting of China's rise to power.[31] On the other hand, it would, by accentuating China's desire for cooperation, provide Beijing with sufficient breathing space from external threats to uninterruptedly achieve its goal of increased national power.[32]

Given these considerations, the "calculative" strategy that achieved dominance in the 1980s can be summarized by its three guiding elements:

- First, overall, a highly pragmatic, non-ideological policy approach keyed to market-led economic growth and the maintenance of amicable international political relations with all states, and especially with the major powers.

- Second, a general restraint in the use of force, whether toward the periphery or against other more distant powers, combined with efforts to modernize and streamline the Chinese military, albeit at a relatively modest pace.

- Third, an expanded involvement in regional and global interstate politics and various international, multilateral fora, with an

---

[29]Liska (1977).

[30]Waltz (1979), p. 118.

[31]The problem of relative gains and its effect on cooperation is discussed in Grieco (1988).

[32]As Jiang Zemin candidly admitted, Beijing cannot afford to be aggressive because "China needs a long-lasting peaceful international environment for its development." Jiang Zemin (1995).

emphasis, through such interactions, on attaining asymmetric gains whenever possible.[33]

Together, these elements amount to a highly modified version of China's traditional "weak-state" strategy, designed to create the foundations for a stronger, more modern Chinese state.

How this strategy has concretely manifested itself will now be examined in the context of the policies China appears to be pursuing in four separate issue-areas (a) policies toward the United States and other powers, (b) policies toward military modernization, (c) policies toward territorial claims and the recourse to force, and (d) policies toward international regimes.

Policies Toward the United States and Other Major Powers

Given China's accurate appreciation of its status as a "still weak, but rising" power, the thrust of Beijing's security-related policies toward the United States as the preeminent power in the international system can be characterized as a two-sided effort focusing on "cooptation" on the one hand and "prevention" on the other. The effort at cooptation focuses essentially on developing and maintaining cordial relations with the United States to encourage it to consistently underwrite the continuing growth in Chinese power, whereas the effort at prevention seeks to hinder any U.S. efforts that may be directed toward frustrating the expansion in Chinese capability, status, and influence. This two-pronged strategy is grounded in the Chinese leadership's recognition that the United States subsists "in economic terms as an important trading partner and major investor" in China, while simultaneously remaining "in nationalistic terms as a major rival in a competition for 'comprehensive national strength.'"[34]

The efforts at both cooptation and prevention are manifested in direct and indirect forms. At the direct level, both are oriented first to

---

[33]This feature is also described as a "mini/maxi" code of conduct keyed to the maximization of security and other benefits through free rides or noncommital strategies and the minimization of costs to capabilities, status, or influence. Kim (1999).

[34]Yi Xiaoxiong (1994), p. 681.

convincing the United States to accept the rise of China as a stabilizing event both at the level of international politics and in the regional context of East Asia. Convincing the United States about the inevitability—in fact, the desirability—of the growth in Chinese power is essential to prevent any attempts at containment on the part of either the United States and its allies or other powers in Asia. It is also essential to forestall a heightened U.S. defensive counterresponse toward a rising China, especially one that—if it leads to greater military acquisitions, increased forward deployments, more robust operational tempos, and accelerated military R&D—would increase the gap in power capabilities between the United States and China still further. Such a reaction would thus force China to run a longer race to become a major power and also would provide Beijing's regional competitors with the political cover under which they could challenge Chinese interests more effectively. Both cooptation and prevention are therefore fundamentally oriented, as one scholar succinctly phrased it, toward legitimizing "a kind of 'hegemonic stability theory' with Chinese characteristics."[35]

To this end, China has attempted to maintain a variety of high-level interactions with the United States, at both the political and military levels. In all these exchanges, Chinese leaders have sought to secure U.S. support for the political, economic, and social transitions and transformations currently under way in China (including seeking a political imprimatur that can be used to fend off political opponents of cordial Sino-U.S. relations back home), while simultaneously attempting to weaken the level of support perceived to be offered by the United States to China's current or potential future adversaries, primarily the Republic of China, and in a different way to Japan as well. In the case of the former, Chinese efforts have been directed at encouraging a steady diminution of U.S. political and military support to the ROC, especially in the context of the latter's apparent efforts at achieving independence. Because U.S. support for the ROC is seen both as a direct challenge to China's sovereignty and as evidence of "an American mentality of 'not wanting to see the rise of a too powerful China,'"[36] Beijing has frequently exerted strenuous ef-

---

[35]Kim (1996), p. 5.

[36]Yi Xiaoxiong (1994), p. 685.

forts to weaken U.S.-ROC political ties.[37] Chinese objectives with respect to Japan are more complex in that Beijing recognizes that the U.S.-Japan Mutual Defense Treaty is a double-edged sword: Although it serves to restrain Japanese remilitarization in the near term, it could over time become the nucleus of a containment effort directed against China. Consequently, Beijing's effort at prevention here takes the form of a guarded disapproval of any deepening of the U.S.-Japan security relationship in the hope of encouraging the latter to atrophy naturally.[38]

Besides these political dimensions of cooptation and prevention, there is an economic dimension as well. Here, the principal objective of cooptation consists of being able to ensure continued access to U.S. markets which today constitute the wellspring of Chinese economic growth and prosperity. Consequently, assuring *permanent* "most favored nation" status has become the most important legal objective of direct cooptation at the economic level because it ensures that China's export-led growth strategy would find fulfillment in terms of ready access to the richest and most valuable market in the world for its consumer goods and light industrial products. Although China already has most favored nation status from the United States, this status requires annual renewal and is covered by a 1979 bilateral agreement between China and the United States rather than through membership in the General Agreement on Tariffs and Trade's (GATT) successor, the World Trade Organization (WTO). The recurrent renewal of this status, which is mandated by law, however, subjects the process of extension to a variety of political pressures, many of which have little to do with trade per se.[39] Consequently, China's abiding interest consists of convincing Washington to sup-

---

[37]Weakening the U.S.-ROC relationship has proved much more difficult than Beijing originally anticipated, in part because it is connected to U.S. domestic politics and the strong linkages between Taiwan and influential members of the U.S. Congress. China has repeatedly sought to increase its leverage over the United States concerning this issue, at times by offering to reduce or eliminate its exports of weapons of mass destruction and their associated delivery systems to some South Asian and Middle Eastern states in return for reductions in U.S. military assistance to Taiwan.

[38]For a representative example of the official Chinese position on U.S. strategic relations with Japan, see "Official Meets Japanese Envoy Over Defense Guidelines" (1998).

[39]A good discussion of China's interest in most favored nation status and in GATT more generally can be found in Power (1994); and Pearson (1999).

port its admittance into the WTO as a full member, *but on what amounts to preferential terms as a developing country.* Admittance to the WTO is important to the success of Beijing's export-led growth strategy in that it allows China access to *multiple* international markets on uniformly preferential terms; further, such access is ensured through a multilateral institution not fully under the control of the United States, thereby offering China opportunities to purse commercial and political interests (including those relating to Taiwan) outside of the restraints that may be episodically imposed within the framework of the Sino-U.S. bilateral relationship. Finally, it provides China with better cover against the protectionist policies of other developing countries while simultaneously accelerating Beijing's integration into the global economy.[40]

In addition to these direct *political and economic* efforts, there are other indirect efforts at cooptation as well. These include exploiting U.S. pluralist society to undercut any adverse political objectives that may be pursued by the U.S. government. In this context, corporate America, with its significant economic interests deriving from large investments in China, becomes a powerful instrument conditioning the shape of U.S. strategic policy toward China. And Beijing has not hesitated to use its sovereign powers of preferential access and large commercial orders to encourage U.S. business groups to lobby the U.S. government for consequential changes in its strategic policies as the price for continued, profitable, interactions with China.[41] These changes were usually sought in the issue-areas of human rights, the rules governing technology transfers, and nonproliferation. To be sure, the incentives for such lobbying exist even in the absence of any direct Chinese governmental intervention, but that implies only that the indirect mechanisms of prevention are even more profitable if China can secure a variety of advantageous political outcomes with little or no effort on its own part.

---

[40]Because Beijing seeks membership as a developing country, the United States has in the past blocked Chinese membership on the grounds that such status would allow China to continue a variety of restrictive trading practices even as it enjoys the fruits of preferential access to the markets of many developed countries. The rationale for China's wish to enter the WTO as a developing country is explicated in Wong (1996); and in Pearson (1999), pp. 176–177.

[41]Hsiung (1995), pp. 580–584.

Although the method of coopting U.S. policy through its domestic politics is perhaps the most visible element of China's indirect efforts, these efforts also occur in the realm of prevention as well, particularly at the international level. The best known attempts at influencing U.S. policy here consist of the various efforts made by Beijing over the years to orchestrate Asian sentiment against growing Japanese power, especially where manifestation of that power outside the home islands is concerned.[42] A similar logic underlies the occasional Chinese efforts to encourage an "Asia for Asians" sentiment: Here, the effort seems focused on convincing the United States, as well as other Asian states, that the "Asian way" remains a distinctive alternative to the Anglo-American modes of ordering social relations and that the Asia-Pacific region writ large can manage its affairs—whether in the arena of human rights or security—without outside assistance.[43] A more recent effort at indirect prevention consists of the increasingly energetic espousal by Beijing of a new multilateral mutual security structure for Asia—the so-called New Security Concept. Although some controversy exists over the meaning and intention of this concept, many observers believe that it is intended to replace the current U.S.-led bilateral security alliance structure of the Asia-Pacific region.[44] Irrespective of the details, the general orientation of such indirect efforts seems to focus on communicating to the United States that its present military and, to some extent, political, presence in East Asia, including its system of security alliances, is a waning vestige of the Cold War and hence should be muted considerably; nurturing a wedge between the United States and its formal and informal allies in Asia; and, finally, preparing the ground for an insular Asian theater where Chinese relative capabilities will not be eclipsed by the presence of larger extraregional political and military forces.

The United States is certainly the most important actor in Chinese strategic calculations, but it is by no means the only one. Conse-

---

[42]A typical example of Chinese thinking in this regard is Yu (1997).

[43]Such efforts do not appear to be part of a concerted, systematic strategy, however, but rather reflect the views of individual Chinese leaders, especially more conservative military figures.

[44]The standard presentation of the New Security Concept is contained in State Council Information Office (1998).

quently, it is not surprising that Beijing's efforts at cooptation and prevention are not restricted to the United States alone but rather extend to all other great powers in the international system. The objectives of these efforts are broadly comparable to those pursued against the United States and they revolve, for the most part, around lowering bilateral tensions and encouraging the major powers to assist China in its efforts at modernization. Thus, for example, relations with Russia are oriented primarily toward reducing the chances of political and military conflict between the two former antagonists and acquiring critical military technologies that cannot be obtained either from the United States or the West more generally. Although this essentially arms procurement relationship has now been baptized as a "strategic partnership," it is so only in name.[45] The economic meltdown in Russia after the demise of the Soviet Union has resulted in Russian defense industries scrambling for customers simply to survive. China's high growth rates and its increasing concern with maritime, rather than continental, issues (including the threat of Taiwanese independence) make Beijing the perfect customer and, not surprisingly, the Russian military-industrial complex—with the hesitant acquiescence of the Russian leadership—has responded by providing a variety of weapon systems or technologies, some of which will be license-produced in China itself.[46]

Where military products from Great Britain, France, and Israel are concerned, Chinese interests revolve more around specific subsystems rather than finished platforms or weapons systems, but China's primary strategic interest in developing relations with these states, and with the Europeans more generally, consists of being able to ensure access to diversified sources of civilian and dual-use technologies and, more broadly, to preserve positive political and economic relations that contribute to China's overall development.[47] Where relations with China's immediate East Asian neighbors such as Korea, Japan, and even Taiwan are concerned, the main objective of

---

[45]"Can a Bear Love a Dragon?" (1997); and Anderson (1997). The notion that the Sino-Russian relationship constitutes "the beginning of a new quadrilateral alignment in East Asia in which a continental Russo-Chinese bloc balances a 'maritime' American-Japanese bloc" (Garver, 1998, Chapter Five) is at the very least extremely premature.

[46]Blank (1996). At the same time, Russia's leadership apparently disagrees over the appropriate level and composition of Russian arms sales to China.

[47]Gill and Kim (1995).

cooptation seems to be an effort to encourage greater direct and portfolio investments in and trade with the Mainland. In the specific case of Taiwan, this interest is in large part motivated by China's strong desire to increase Taiwan's overall level of involvement in and dependence upon the Mainland, as a way to increase Chinese political leverage over Taiwan. The benefits in terms of capital transfers, increased employment, and domestic wealth generation are deemed to be critical enough to encourage deeper economic participation on the part of these countries, even if their longer-term political interests may diverge substantially from China's. In any event, the general principle underlying these relationships seems to be the same: to use China's growing market and economic wealth to secure those resources that cannot be procured from the United States while simultaneously using these transactions to provide its non-U.S. partners with an economic stake in China's continued growth.

Deepened relations with China's non-U.S. partners also has other advantages. Where significant arms-producing states such as Great Britain, France, and Israel (and other European states as well) are concerned, China seeks to manipulate access to its commercial market to prevent these states from providing arms and military technologies to Taiwan.[48] Such transfers, it is feared, could reinforce the Taiwanese desire for independence while simultaneously vitiating the deterrence China seeks to impose through the application of its older and relatively more obsolescent weaponry. Apart from the specific benefits in relation to Taiwan, deepened relations with other powers also provide benefits in relation to the United States. At the very least, deepened relations constitute a "diversification strategy,"[49] which gives Beijing some political and economic instruments that can be used to prevent the creation of a strong U.S.-led anti-Chinese coalition in those issue areas where U.S. and non-U.S. interests may not fully coincide. Thus, these relationships give Beijing improved leverage in dealings with the United States and they could become *in extremis* the routes by which China circumvents any future U.S. efforts at restraining either its policies or its growth in capabilities more generally. As one scholar summarized it, "to Chinese leaders, [political] diversification offers obvious bargaining ad-

---

[48]Shambaugh (1996b), pp. 1301–1302.

[49]Yi Xiaoxiong (1994), p. 678.

vantages as it signals other powers that they are not indispensable and that China can avoid and resist foreign pressures without seriously hindering its national security."[50]

Policies Toward Military Modernization

As part of its current "calculative" strategy, China has sought to develop a range of military capabilities to sustain an expanded level of political and operational objectives. These objectives include (a) securing the defense of Chinese sovereignty and national territory against threats or attacks from all manner of opponents, including highly sophisticated military forces; (b) acquiring the ability to counter or neutralize a range of potential short-, medium-, and long-term security threats along China's entire periphery, but especially in maritime areas; (c) acquiring the ability to use military power as a more potent and versatile instrument of armed diplomacy and statecraft in support of a complex set of regional and global policies; and (d) eventually developing the power-projection and extended territorial defense capabilities commensurate with the true great power status expected in the 21st century. These complex objectives may be summarized, at least over the near term, as an effort to reduce China's existing vulnerabilities while increasing the utility of its military forces to secure diplomatic and political leverage.[51]

The efforts at reducing vulnerability have materialized at two different, though related, levels. The first level consists of a slow but determined effort at nuclear modernization. As indicated previously, the range of Chinese nuclear capabilities today are modest, at least relative to the capabilities of the superpowers during the Cold War. Despite the presence of much larger arsenals in the Soviet Union and the United States, the Chinese historically seemed disinclined to increase the size of their nuclear inventory presumably because, first, they were satisfied that the mutual deterrence relations between the United States and the Soviet Union generated sufficient positive externalities that precluded the need for a significant expansion of capabilities—specifically, such relations meant that only a small

---

[50]Yi Xiaoxiong (1994), p. 678.

[51]A good summary of the multidimensional facets of China's military modernization can be found in Shambaugh and Yang (1997).

strategic force capable of conducting a credible retaliatory strike against either Soviet or U.S. cities and major U.S. military bases in Asia was deemed sufficient to deter both states from attacking China; and, second, their modest but not insignificant capabilities already allowed them to support some primitive kinds of selective nuclear operations, well before they either developed the accompanying doctrine that justified such operations or were given credit for such capabilities in the West.[52]   The ability to execute such selective operations derived more from the diversity of their nuclear holdings, which included small numbers of land- and sea-based ballistic missiles, manned bombers and, more important, tactical nuclear weapons,[53] and the locational uncertainty of many of these force elements than from a deterrence architecture that emphasized the possession of a large "hyper-protected force for intra-war deterrence, with long endurance and excellent communications and control."[54] Given these calculations, the Chinese are believed to have developed a diversified arsenal of about 450 warheads—an inventory similar in size to that maintained by Great Britain and France; for such medium powers, a strategy of limited deterrence was deemed to be sufficient in the face of the complex nuclear deterrence regime maintained by the United States and the Soviet Union during the Cold War.[55]   Despite the many limitations of this arsenal, it is obvious that the Chinese value their nuclear weapons both for the status they bestow on them in the international system and because they remain the only effective deterrent in all situations where Chinese conventional military power may be found wanting.

---

[52]For an analysis of the evolving doctrinal justifications of China's nuclear modernization effort, see Johnston (1995/96).

[53]China's development of tactical nuclear weapons, principally in the form of artillery warheads, atomic demolition munitions, and shells for multiple rocket systems, apparently began in the 1970s in response to increasing military tensions with the former Soviet Union. It has continued since, however, despite the collapse of the USSR and the improvement of political relations with all significant military powers along China's borders. These capabilities have never been acknowledged by China but observations of People's Liberation Army (PLA) training exercises and underground nuclear tests have led many observers to conclude that such capabilities exist. See Caldwell and Lennon (1995), pp. 29–30.

[54]Schlesinger (1967), pp. 12–13.

[55]Goldstein (1992).

Given these considerations, China's efforts at nuclear modernization have not focused on increasing the size of the nuclear inventory per se but rather on reducing its vulnerability to preemptive strikes by the more sophisticated forces of the industrialized powers. The efforts here have been directed primarily toward improving "the survivability of [its] strategic forces, develop[ing] less vulnerable basing modes, and mak[ing] general improvements in the accuracy, range, guidance, and control"[56] of its missile forces. Consistent with these goals, China appears to have focused primarily on developing new land-based, solid-fueled, road-mobile missiles such as the DF-21, DF-31, and DF-41 to replace older liquid-fueled missiles such as the DF-5A as well as producing a new class of warheads thought to be either miniaturized or of smaller yield and weight to increase targeting flexibility and launcher mobility.[57] Other developments include developing a new second-generation replacement sea-launched ballistic missile, the solid-fueled JL-2, and possibly a small fleet of four to six more advanced ballistic missile submarines, as well as a new bomber, the FB-7, as a replacement for its antiquated H-5 and H-6 fleet. There is also some speculation that China's nuclear modernization includes improving its tactical nuclear capabilities as well as developing new nuclear warheads for its short-range ballistic missiles such as the DF-11 (M-11). Almost all available evidence relating to these programs suggests that the pace of development and acquisition is generally slow. This is usually taken to imply that China does not view these systems as very much more than an evolutionary progression of its already existing capabilities—a progression required both for prudential reasons relating to the new demands of operating in a unipolar environment (in which the United States could conceivably target more nuclear weapons on China) and for technical reasons relating to combating obsolescence.[58]

---

[56]Caldwell and Lennon (1995), p. 30.

[57]On Chinese warhead R&D objectives, see Garrett and Glazer (1995/96).

[58]One caveat to this general statement could exist, however. Some observers of China's nuclear weapons modernization program believe that Beijing has recently decided to enhance significantly its theater nuclear weapons capability as its only effective means of deterring the threat or use by the United States of highly effective long-range precision-guided, and stealthy conventional weaponry. Such weapons were used by the United States with virtual impunity during the Kosovo conflict of 1998.

The second level of efforts aimed at reducing vulnerability occurs in the conventional realm. China's labors in this area are much more concerted and its achievement much more significant. The priority attached to conventional modernization derives from a variety of factors. First, it reflects an appreciation that Chinese conventional forces and weaponry are more useable instruments of power than its nuclear capabilities.[59] Second, given China's evolving threat environment, Beijing believes it may be faced with "limited theater" contingencies that require the use of its conventional forces in the near to mid term and, consequently, must prepare diligently for their use in a variety of situations where even modest differences in relative capability could radically affect the kinds of outcomes obtained.[60] Third, the economic reforms conducted since 1978 have produced dramatic changes in China's strategic geography, in that its most valuable economic and social resources now lie along its weakly defended eastern and southeastern territorial periphery as opposed to the secure interior of the heartland as was the case during the Cold War. This development, in turn, has put a premium on the development of new kinds of conventional forces—primarily air and naval— and new concepts of operations that are quite alien to the traditional continental orientation of the Chinese military.[61] Fourth, the nature of China's potential adversaries is seen to have changed: The solution of a "peoples' war," which might have sufficed against land powers such as the Soviet Union, is now viewed to be irrelevant in the context of future maritime adversaries such as Taiwan, Japan, and the United States, where "limited wars under high-tech conditions" would increasingly require material and ideational resources of the sort that China does not currently possess.[62] Fifth, and finally, China appears to have been greatly impressed by the experience of the Gulf War where the technologically superior coalition forces provided a sharp and pointed preview of the devastating punishment

[59]Chu (1994), pp. 186–190.

[60]Munro (1994); and Godwin (1997).

[61]Chu (1994), pp. 187–188. Also see Swaine (1998b).

[62]Chu (1994); Swaine (1998b); and Godwin (1997).

that could be inflicted on any adversary possessing an obsolete force structure, doctrine, and capabilities.[63]

These five considerations, taken together, have forced a reevaluation of China's ability to execute effective border defense aimed specifically—*at least in the near term*—at preventing the loss of possessed and claimed territories, both contiguous and offshore. Because China's contiguous land borders, however, are relatively secure at this time, thanks both to Chinese diplomacy and China's potential neighboring adversaries' current unwillingness to press their claims (each for their own reasons), the most visible dimensions of the conventional modernization have involved air and naval forces. This is not to imply that land force modernization has been overlooked. China is engaged in ongoing efforts to reduce the overall size and streamline the structure of the PLA to improve its qualitative capabilities.[64] The mobility, firepower, logistics, and communications assets of PLA ground forces are being improved as a prudential measure should they be required for combat operations in some land border areas as well as for internal pacification. Yet despite these initiatives, air and naval modernization has overshadowed all else because improvements in air power are now viewed as critical for the success of *all* military operations, and modernized naval capabilities are seen as indispensable for the defense of offshore claims, especially those relating to Taiwan and the South China Sea, and for the defense of China's increasingly important strategic assets along the coast.

Contingencies involving Taiwan in particular have provided a sharp focus for China's conventional modernization efforts in recent years. This includes developing both interdiction (including morale-breaking) capabilities against Taiwan as well as denial capabilities against Taiwan's potential defenders, primarily the United States. The requirements pertaining to the interdiction of Taiwan have resulted in a substantial effort to strengthen China's missile order of battle, primarily short-range ballistic missiles such as the M-9 and M-11. These missiles are viewed by the Chinese as uniquely capable

---

[63]See Frolov (1998) for a review of China's modernization initiatives precipitated by the lessons of the Gulf War.

[64]Godwin (1992).

of sowing mass panic on Taiwan or destroying Taiwanese military installations with little advance warning. Contingencies involving Taiwan have also resulted in consequential efforts to improve Chinese air battle management capabilities over the Taiwan Strait and allow China to use its recent or imminent arms acquisitions from Russia—advanced air superiority aircraft such as the Su-27, advanced air defense systems such as the SA-10 and SA-15, and new surface and subsurface capabilities in the form of Soveremenny destroyers and Kilo submarines—with consequential effect. Although each of these Russian-built weapons systems addresses critical deficiencies in China's basic force structure and was almost certainly acquired as part of Beijing's overall modernization effort, each system also has a particular operational relevance in the Taiwan theater.

Because combat operations directed at Taiwan may require that China contend with the forward-deployed naval capabilities of the United States, Beijing has also embarked on a serious effort to acquire capabilities that could increase the risks accruing to any U.S. attempts at armed diplomacy or outright intervention. These efforts have focused principally on improving China's ability to detect, track, and target U.S. carrier battle groups by multiple means as far away as possible from the Mainland. This includes developing air- and ground-launched cruise missile systems for standoff attack, sea denial capabilities centered on subsurface platforms as well as anti-surface attack and mine warfare systems, and information attack capabilities centered on antisatellite warfare, electronic warfare, and deception and denial operations. Although many Chinese capabilities in this area are modest at present, improving these capabilities will remain a critical priority over the long term.[65]

This is true a fortiori because the objectives of China's conventional modernization effort are not near-term goals alone. Rather, Beijing's search for increased diplomatic and political leverage—consistent with its growing status and in response to the changing security environment of the modern era—will presumably require that it eventually be able to operate independently throughout most of the Asian

---

[65]A good summary of Chinese efforts in this regard can be found in Khalilzad et al. (1999) and Stokes (1999).

littoral. Serving this objective by itself will likely require that the Chinese military be able to at least hold extraregional forces at risk, if not master them entirely. The quest for increased diplomatic and political leverage, therefore, has already begun in terms of efforts to operationalize extended sea and information-denial capabilities. These include developing new maritime and space-based surveillance capabilities, new modernized diesel and nuclear attack submarines incorporating several Russian technologies and subsystems, new surface combatants equipped with better surface-to-surface and surface-to-air capabilities, new air-, surface-, and subsurface-launched tactical cruise missiles, possibly new directed-energy weapon programs, and new information-warfare initiatives in addition to exploring the offensive use of space.[66] Although many of these programs remain in the very early stages of development, when combined with new kinds of naval aviation capabilities in the coming decades, they could eventually coalesce into capabilities that will allow for an extended Chinese naval presence and power projection capability throughout much of East Asia.[67]

China's current conventional military modernization programs are thus designed to serve pressing near- and medium-term needs, while still allowing for the possibility of an evolutionary expansion over the long term as Chinese economic capabilities increase in size and importance. It is important to recognize, however, that the long-range strategic objectives associated with China's potential long-term economic capabilities and great power aspirations such as the acquisition of *extended sea control* over maritime areas extending far into the Pacific Ocean—especially those regions described by Chinese naval strategists and leaders as the "first and second island chains"[68]—do not determine *current* Chinese weapons acquisitions and modernization programs in any direct, immediate, and straightforward fashion. Rather, the role of broad strategic concepts, such as the control over the first and second island chains, is more regulative than constraining: That is, these concepts provide general benchmarks for the future, they identify certain desired capabilities that Chinese force planners likely aspire to incorporate into their

---

[66]Stokes (1999).

[67]Godwin (1997).

[68]For an excellent analysis of this concept, see Huang (1994).

force structure over the long term, and they no doubt justify the PLA Navy's modernization agenda in competition with the other armed services. But they do not provide programmatic guidance for near-term military acquisitions. These acquisitions are still determined primarily by the PLA's focus on deterring or defeating attacks on Chinese territory, both actual and claimed, both continental and maritime, through the acquisition of limited air, sea, and information-denial capabilities. The larger strategic concepts then simply serve to ensure that these near-term military acquisitions are not *fundamentally inconsistent* with China's likely long-range aspirations of attaining some level of extended control over or at the very least presence within distant operational areas that will become relevant to its security interests as its overall national power increases.

In their effort to achieve these objectives—developing a force capability that resolves near-term challenges while simultaneously being capable of supporting longer-term aspirations—Chinese security managers have recognized that the military modernization efforts of the state must be built on a prior foundation of indigenous scientific, technological, and economic capabilities. Hence, the level of resources devoted to military modernization has increased at a pace that is intended neither to undermine the attainment of essential civilian development priorities nor to unduly alarm both the peripheral states and the major powers and thus erode the generally benign threat environment facing China today. This is, in essence, the clearest manifestation of the "calculative" strategy. And, although the advantages of the current approach, which focuses on slowly developing indigenous capabilities (as opposed to embarking on a rapid, highly costly, and difficult acceleration of foreign acquisitions), are clear to Beijing, it is important to recognize that the success of this strategy, other things being equal, could nonetheless erode the relative power capabilities of China's major regional competitors, including the United States, so long as the pace of economic growth in China continues to exceed that of its competitors. *Superior economic growth rates are therefore critical* because they represent, in principle, fungible resources that can be garnered by the state and applied to the acquisition of some specific capabilities—military or technological—that one's competitors may have. To that degree, even an inward-focused modernization that greatly increases

China's economic capabilities relative to other major powers will, more than any other, likely contribute to a change in the *overall* relative balance of power in Asia and beyond over the long term.

Policies Toward Territorial Claims and the Recourse to Force

China's approach to territorial claims remains a subset of its general strategic approach toward the peripheral states under the calculative strategy. This strategy in effect has resulted in China pursuing a generalized good-neighbor policy that has focused on strengthening its existing ties in Northeast and Southeast Asia, mending ties wherever possible in south and west Asia, and exploring new relationships in Central Asia.[69] This omnidirectional effort at developing good regional relations is centered on a sharp recognition of many critical geopolitical realities. First, the peripheral areas will continue to remain highly important for Chinese security, just as they did historically, even as they continue to host new sources from which many consequential challenges to Chinese power may emerge over time. Second, China today remains incapable of altering the structure of relations with many of its peripheral states through force or the threat of force, and although Beijing may even prefer to reinstate some of the traditional patterns of control and deference it has enjoyed in the past, it is impossible to do so without further increases in relative Chinese power. Third, renewed contentions with key peripheral states could obliterate the prospects for a peaceful regional environment and, by implication, frustrate China's desire for "comprehensive national strength." It is in this context that recent Chinese initiatives at defusing old territorial disputes ought to be considered.

China certainly has territorial disputes with many important states on its periphery, including Russia, Japan, Vietnam, and India. Most of these disputes derive from the colonial era when national boundaries were often adjusted idiosyncratically in accordance with the local balances of power present at the time. As a result, China often "lost" marginal portions of border or peripheral territory, as for example when the British annexed the northern tip of Burma in 1886.

---

[69]Hsiung (1995), pp. 576–577.

The actual nature of these losses is difficult to discern because the character of Chinese control in these relatively small areas was often weak, occasionally nonexistent, and sometimes merely a function of the suzerain relationships enjoyed by Chinese rulers with the local rulers of these territories. Many of these disputes remained unresolved because China and its Asian competitors were relatively weak for most of the postwar period, and because the Cold War, which dominated the bulk of this era, enforced a "pacification" of these disputes, even when the power-political capabilities to resolve these contentions may have existed in some cases.

Aside from these marginal losses, however, Chinese security managers often refer to the much larger deprivation and humiliation ·suffered by China over the centuries. If all the territories claimed, occupied, or directly controlled by China since its unification in the third century B.C. were matched against its current physical holdings, the presently disputed marginal territories would fade into insignificance. For example, during the early Han Dynasty, Chinese control extended beyond its current boundaries to portions of present day Central Asia and northern Vietnam. During the early Tang, even larger portions of Central Asia came under Chinese rule. Similarly, during the Ming Dynasty, China controlled or occupied parts of Vietnam, and under the early Qing, China controlled Mongolia and large portions of the Russian Far East (see the maps in Chapter Three). In fact, even if only the more recent territorial losses suffered during the "century of national humiliation" (lasting from roughly 1840–1940) were iterated, the previous conclusion would still hold. Despite occasional references to these losses suffered historically, the Chinese state appears to have by and large accepted the borders it inherited in 1949, preferring instead to pursue mostly marginal claims as opposed to seeking renewed control over the larger expanses of territory it may have controlled or occupied at one point or another in its history. The absence of these larger claims serves to underscore China's present conservatism where territorial revisionism is concerned.[70] The extent of its greater losses is

---

[70]For a clear statement of current Chinese conservatism regarding territorial issues, see Mao (1996). This work makes no reference to the possibility that China might in future lay claim to former Chinese lands now under the undisputed control of other states.

nonetheless worth noting if for no other reason than it serves as a marker identifying territorial interests that in some cases *might* be pursued in more concerted form if favorable changes take place in the future regional balance of power.

For the moment, however, Chinese territorial interests are focused mainly on disputes involving Russia, along the Ussuri River and along the Sino-Russian border west of Mongolia; India, principally in Aksai Chin and in the Indian northeast with respect to the McMahon line and the status of the Indian state of Arunachal Pradesh; the South China Sea, where China and several Southeast Asian states have claims on the Spratly Islands; Japan, over the Senkakus; and, finally, Taiwan, which remains a complex dispute over both the political status of the island and the right to rule.

Beijing's "calculative" strategy has resulted in a two-pronged approach aimed at securing Chinese interests with respect to these territorial disputes. First, if the dispute in question is both intrinsically trivial and marginal to China's larger interests, Beijing has sought to resolve it amicably to pursue its larger goals. The border disputes with Russia, for example, are evidence of this approach where China's overarching interest in improving its political relationship with Moscow and securing access to Russian military technology has resulted in quick, it is hoped permanent, solutions to the Ussuri River dispute.[71] Another similar example pertains to the speedy resolution of the border disputes with Kazakhstan and Kyrgystan: Given Chinese interests both in preventing external support to the separatist movements in Chinese Central Asia and in ensuring access to the energy reserves of the trans-Caucasus, Beijing moved quickly to amicably delimit its border with both these newly independent states.[72]

---

[71]See "Agreement Between the Government of the Union of Soviet Socialist Republics and the Government of the People's Republic of China on the Guidelines of Mutual Reduction of Forces and Confidence Building in the Military Field in the Area of the Soviet-Chinese Border" (1990); and the later treaty, "Agreement Between the Russian Federation, the Republic of Kazakhstan, the Kyrgyz Republic, the Republic of Tajikistan and the People's Republic of China on Confidence Building in the Military Field in the Border Area" (1996).

[72]"Agreement Between the Russian Federation, the Republic of Kazakhstan, the Kyrgyz Republic, the Republic of Tajikistan and the People's Republic of China on Confidence Building in the Military Field in the Border Area" (1996).

Second, if the dispute in question is significant but cannot be resolved rapidly to China's advantage by peaceful means, Beijing has advocated an indefinite postponement of the basic issue. This tactic has been adopted, for example, in the case of the territorial disputes with India, Japan, and several of the Association of Southeast Asian Nations (ASEAN) states. The basic logic underlying this approach has been to steadfastly avoid conceding any Chinese claims with respect to the dispute, while simultaneously seeking to prevent the dispute from vitiating the pacific environment that China needs to complete its internal transformation successfully. Such an approach has at least several advantages: It positions China as a conciliatory state seeking to resolve all outstanding disputes peacefully. It does not increase the demands on China's military forces at a time when the PLA is relatively weak and when the Chinese economy needs all the breathing room it can get. It prevents balancing coalitions from arising against China in the event Beijing pursued more coercive strategies. And, it delays the resolution of these disputes at least until the balance of power changes substantially in favor of China. At that time, both simple usurpation and coercive bargaining *might* become more attractive, although it is unclear today whether the Chinese leadership would actually conclude that the benefits of such actions easily exceed the costs.

Under the "calculative" strategy, therefore, China has sought to avoid further losses of territory at all costs (except when the losses are deemed to be truly insignificant relative to the benefits of some other competing goals). Whenever intrinsically valuable territory is at issue, however, China has sought to preserve the status quo—not giving up its sovereign claims, but preferring to avoid any application of force, so long as the other parties to the dispute do not attempt to change the status quo ante either. This logic has applied even to the dispute over Taiwan, where China would prefer to freeze the island's presently ambiguous status. It would prefer not to employ force to resolve the issue but may nonetheless be compelled to do so because the principle of avoiding significant territorial loss—particularly of an area possessing enormous nationalistic significance as a Chinese province—would demand a military reaction, no matter how costly, if the Taiwanese sought to change the status quo unilaterally. In general, therefore, the reluctance to employ force to resolve the outstanding territorial disputes remains a good example of the "calculative" strategy at work. Although it represents a sensitivity to the logic of relative material capabilities that has been evident in Chinese strategic behavior since the imperial era, including a straightforward recognition that the PLA may simply not have the capacity to prevail in some force-on-force encounters that may occur, a more important aspect is Beijing's likely perception that most of these disputes can be resolved down the line to China's advantage by any means of its own choosing if its national capabilities are allowed to grow rapidly and undisturbed in the interim.

Although China's reluctance to seek recourse to force or the threat of force at present is intimately bound up with the demands of the calculative strategy, especially as it applies to the issue of territorial disputes, it is important to recognize that there is no reason why this should be true either in principle or over the long term. That is, China could use force for reasons that have little to do with its territorial disputes, e.g., as a consequence of deteriorating political relations with other powers or simply because of dramatic increases in China's military strength. This is unlikely today, especially given the imperatives of the calculative strategy, but it may become relevant as Chinese power grows over time. It may also become relevant in the context of a larger irredentist agenda, especially one emerging from a chauvinistic nationalist desire to reopen the territorial questions arising out of a century of national humiliation. Although this will remain a concern for all of China's neighbors confronted by its steadily growing capability, at least in the policy-relevant future most Chinese applications of force will probably be intimately bound up with attempts to stave off threatened territorial losses, as opposed to the pursuit of some other autonomous power-political goals.

Policies Toward International Regimes

The calculative strategy currently pursued by Beijing has resulted in China adopting an "instrumental" attitude toward international regimes. This implies that China possesses neither an intrinsic commitment nor an intrinsic antipathy to the existing international norms and organizations but approaches these simply in terms of a pragmatic calculation centered on the benefits and losses of participation and nonparticipation. Consequently, it has pursued a wide range of strategies with respect to both existing and evolving international regimes which, depending on the issue-areas in question, can range from full participation in search of asymmetric gains, through contingent cooperation in pursuit of reciprocal benefits, to outright–overt or covert–defection. The manifestation of such a wide range of behaviors is by no means unique to China: It is in fact typical of most states, since consistently simple and straightforward behaviors—either in the direction of cooperation or of defection—are usually manifested only by those few states that either disproportionately benefit from the regime or are disproportionately penalized by it. The established great powers usually fall into the first category, and the manifestly revisionist states usually fall into the second. All other states that occupy the middle ground, that is, those that are both favored and disadvantaged by prevailing regimes in varying degrees, would adopt behaviors similar to China's. Since Beijing encounters a variety of international regimes in the areas of economic development, trade, technology transfer, arms control, and the environment, this fundamental calculus is often reflected in different ways.

First, China either participates or has sought to actively participate in all regimes that promise asymmetric gains where accretion of new power or maintenance of existing power is concerned. In this category lie all the regimes connected with the international economy, global trade, the diffusion of technology, and international governance. Participating in these regimes enables China to connect more effectively to the global market system that today, more than any other, has been responsible for the meteoric growth witnessed since 1978. Not surprisingly, China has expressed great interest and has engaged in arduous negotiations in an effort to join organizations such as the WTO, which could assure it uniform access to the markets of both advanced industrialized countries and developing economies alike. Toward that end, it has made various efforts to reform its domestic legal and patent system to ensure the protection of intellectual and material property rights to secure continued access to the technology and know-how brought by multinational corporations to China. It has striven valiantly, however, to enter the WTO on preferential terms as a developing country, since entry on such terms provides it access to multiple international markets but would not require that it eliminate, either immediately upon entrance or soon thereafter, many of the domestic regulations that impose barriers to free trade within China.[73]   Because of this quest for asymmetric gains, the United States had for several years prevented China from securing membership in the organization, and although the Chinese leadership has often declared that membership as a developed country is "absolutely unacceptable," given the growing domestic concerns about the adverse social consequences (e.g., unemployment and labor unrest) that might result from China's deeper integration with the global economy following WTO entrance,[74] it seems that, on balance, the search for "WTO membership is still high on China's trade diplomacy agenda."[75]   The issue of WTO membership represents the clearest example of the search for asymmetric gains, but China's continued linkages with other international organizations—economic and political—provide examples of its efforts to sustain existing power and privileges.   China has profitably interacted with the International Monetary Fund (IMF), the IBRD, and other financial institutions that promise preferential access to capital, technical know-how, and resources.   Where international governance is concerned, China has continued to participate fully in the United Nations (UN) for reasons connected with both status and interests: Its acknowledged standing as a permanent member of the Security Council distinguishes it from powers of lesser standing and enables it to shape global and regional policies—especially in a unipolar environment—that may affect Chinese interests or those of its allies.[76]   As Samuel Kim has shown, China has sought to use a wide variety of UN institutions and fora to maximize political, economic, financial, and image benefits while minimizing any losses or risks.[77]

Second, China has sought to participate in all international organizations and regimes where consequential policies adverse to China's interests might be engineered as a result of Beijing's absence. In this category lie all those regional regimes that China initially resented

---

[73]For an excellent summary of the issues involved in China's quest to join the WTO, see Rosen (1997).

[74]For a discussion of such concerns, which derive from China's primary security objective of maintaining domestic order and well-being, see Pearson (1999), pp. 182–183.

[75]Wong (1996), p. 296.

[76]For instance, see speech by then PRC Foreign Minister Qian Qichen (1994).

[77]Kim (1999), especially pp. 60–71.

but was eventually constrained to participate in, mainly to ward off future losses that may have accrued in its absence. The best examples here remain China's participation in the ASEAN Regional Forum and the ASEAN Post-Ministerial Conference.[78] China's early disinterest in these bodies was rooted in an effort to avoid being "cornered" by enmeshing multilateral arrangements where China's greater bargaining power—visible in the purely bilateral relationships it enjoys with its smaller neighbors—would be neutralized by participation in a large forum that brought together all its many potential competitors simultaneously. Once these fora acquired a life of their own, however, Beijing realized that its lack of participation could result in these institutions adopting policies that might not be in China's best interests. To forestall this possibility, China became a late entrant to these bodies. Its initial participation was the result of a constrained choice, but China has realized that these institutions may offer future benefits and consequently its desire to continue participating may be motivated as much by the hope of future gains as it is conditioned by the current desire to avoid immediate losses.[79]

Third, China has sought to undercut—through participation—those regimes that threaten the political interests of its communist government. The best examples of these are in the issue-areas of human rights, personal liberties, and political freedoms. All international regimes in these arenas that seek to fundamentally change the balance of power between individuals and the state are perceived to threaten China's governing regime which, though in evolution, still affirms the primacy of the party and the state. Not surprisingly, China's political leadership, and occasionally sections of its elite as well, have viewed universalist declarations pertaining to human rights and political freedoms either as an interference in China's domestic affairs or, more significantly, as an insidious effort to undermine the stability of the Chinese state with a view to preventing its rise in power or replacing it entirely with a democratic regime.[80] The Chinese discomfort with such regimes, however, has usually elicited cooptational responses when the necessity of assuaging interna-

---

[78]Foot (1998).

[79]Klintworth (1997); Vatikiotis (1997); Wanandi (1996); and Bert (1993).

[80]Nathan (1999); and Nathan (1994).

tional public opinion is deemed to be critical. Thus, for example, China supported the Universal Declaration of Human Rights in part because support for such resolutions bestows benefits in the realm of international public opinion, because the declaration itself is unenforceable, and because the language in the statement is loose enough to lend itself comfortably to a variety of political systems and practices.[81] Consistent with the objective of shaping international opinion, China has in fact attempted to offer alternative visions of what good politics entails, one of which emphasizes the communitarian requirements of order over individual preferences of freedom and is supposed to represent an "Asian way" that allegedly comports more appropriately with regional traditions and values. In attempting to offer such an alternative vision, which implicitly legitimizes the existing power relations within China, Beijing has managed to secure a considerable degree of support from other authoritarian countries in Asia, all of which view the contemporary concern about human rights, personal liberties, and political freedoms as merely another particularist, Western view of political arrangements rather than as universal norms—a view that allegedly either intentionally or unintentionally is used by Western powers to beat up on the Asian states to perpetuate their own dominant influence.[82]

Fourth, China has sought to overtly or covertly undercut or defect from those regimes that threaten its political and strategic interests and generally to adhere to those regimes that advance such interests. A well-known example of such Chinese behavior can be found in the issue-area of proliferation of weapons of mass destruction. Chinese policy has evolved greatly in this area. From an early posture that condemned Western and Soviet-U.S. arms control efforts as a form of "sham disarmament" designed to perpetuate superpower dominance (thus leading to calls for widespread proliferation as a means of defeating such "superpower hegemony"), China has now reached the conclusion that "high entropy" proliferation—meaning a highly proliferated world with few "rules of the nuclear road"[83]— would be

---

[81]"Envoy Comments on Declaration on Human Rights Defenders" (1998).

[82]For one example of a defense of the "Asian way," see Zakaria (1994).

[83]Molander and Wilson (1993), p. xiii.

prejudicial to its interests in principle.[84]   Thus, over the years, it has progressively joined international regimes such as the Biological Weapons Convention (BWC) (1985), the Non-Proliferation Treaty (NPT) (1992), the Chemical Weapons Convention (CWC) (1993), and the Comprehensive Test Ban Treaty (CTBT) (1996) (and has agreed to abide by the guidelines of the Missile Technology Control Regime— MTCR (1991)), though often with great reluctance and not without several attempts to water down the level of commitments imposed by such regimes. Although Beijing has now accepted its legal obligations under these regimes, its record at compliance, however, has in some instances been less than reassuring.[85]   In practice, it has assisted the WMD programs of some countries along or near its periphery such as Iran and Pakistan. In effect, those countries deemed vital for the success of Chinese regional security policies have at times been partly "exempted" from the universal obligations Beijing has undertaken with respect to proliferation. Some Chinese assistance in this regard has been simply a product of poor domestic control over its military-industrial complex, but it has in other more egregious instances been a deliberate consequence of state sanctioned policy.[86]   This behavior led one analyst to conclude that Chinese proliferation behavior exemplifies a perfect case of "different rules for different exports,"[87] suggesting that in general Chinese behavior in the arena of export controls "does not demonstrate a clear pattern of either compliance or violation."[88]

Fifth, China has gone along with those international regimes that notionally provide joint gains, if the initial private costs of participation can either be extorted, shifted, or written off. The best example of such behavior is found in the issue-area of the environment, where the efforts to control greenhouse gases, restrict carbon dioxide

---

[84]For a review of early Chinese attitudes, see Pillsbury (1975). A good discussion on current Chinese attitudes to high-entropy proliferation can be found in Garrett and Glaser (1995/96), pp. 50–53.

[85]A good survey of the Chinese record with respect to participation and compliance can be found in Swaine and Johnston (1999); and Frieman (1996). See also Garrett and Glaser (1995/96); and Johnston (1996a).

[86]For details, see U.S. Senate (1998), pp. 3–16.

[87]Davis (1995), p. 595.

[88]Frieman (1996), p. 28.

emissions, and reduce the level of pollutants more generally have been supported by China only after several attempts to shift the costs of such compliance asymmetrically on to other states. More specifically, China's reluctant accommodation of regime interests in instances such as the Montreal Protocol has been clearly a function of its ability to extort resources from the developed states as the price for its participation in such regimes. As Samuel Kim succinctly concluded, "China's 'principled stand' on the global campaign to protect the ozone layer was issued in the form of thinly disguised blackmail: China refused to sign the 1987 Montreal Protocol without the promise of big cash and greater 'flexibility' on the use and production of chlorofluorocarbons (CFCs)."[89] On this matter, as in many others, China's eventual participation in this and other international regimes was conditioned by multiple considerations.[90] To begin with, Beijing has perceived that Chinese interests *eventually* would be advanced, even if only marginally, by the regime in question; hence, it has complied only after attempts at resistance, defection, or free riding were perceived to fail.[91] Further, its participation in many instances becomes contingent on the success of institutionalized cost shifting, that is, on China's ability to exploit its relative importance to get other participants to bear a portion of Beijing's costs as the price of Chinese participation in the regime. In the issue-area of environmental protection, for example, Elizabeth Economy notes that "fully 80 percent of China's environmental protection budget is derived from abroad. Overall, China is the largest recipient of total environmental aid from the World Bank and has received extensive support from the Global Environmental Facility, the Asian Development Bank, the United Nations Development Program, and bilateral sources."[92] Finally, the decision to participate usually represents a shrewd appreciation of the relative power of stronger states involved in the issue-area in question, especially the United States and its other OECD partners, as well as an attempt to play "quid pro quo," in that the benefits of Chinese participation and support are offered in

---

[89]Kim (1991), pp. 40–41.

[90]Sims (1996).

[91]Such behavior is also evident in the arms-control arena, as suggested by Swaine and Johnston (1999).

[92]Economy (1998), p. 278.

the expectation that the goodwill gained could be cashed in in other issue-areas where the gains sought by China would presumably be higher.[93] For all such reasons, China has participated in international regimes such as the Montreal Protocol where the costs of participation though initially high could be borne through external assistance and possible future exploitation.

Sixth, China has also participated in regimes where the costs of unilateral defection were very high. The best example here remains China's willingness to participate in the CTBT. Given the relatively modest capabilities of China's nuclear arsenal, all early indications suggested that China would either abstain from participation or exploit the opposition to the CTBT emerging from other states, such as India, to avoid signing the treaty.[94] Over time, however, it became clear that the United States had staked an inordinate amount of diplomatic and political resources to have the treaty signed by all the major nuclear-capable powers in the international system. The sheer pressure applied by the United States and the implications of a Chinese refusal to participate—perhaps affecting technology transfers, membership in the WTO, and MFN status—finally resulted in a Chinese accession to the treaty, but only after Beijing concluded a final series of underground nuclear tests. To be sure, other considerations also intervened: the declining utility of nuclear weapons, the absence of any need to expand China's present nuclear capabilities in radically new directions, the recognition that China's growing power capabilities would always allow for a future breakout from the treaty at relatively low cost in *force majeure* situations, and the not inconsequential image concerns associated with China's desire to be seen as a responsible great power and as a just and principled state. All these factors combined with a sensitivity to the high political costs of being a nonsignatory finally ensured China's successful participation in the CTBT, even though, other things being equal, it might have preferred to unilaterally "defect" on this, more than any other, issue.[95]

---

[93]This calculus is of course also evident in other policy areas, including bilateral diplomatic, economic, and security relations with the United States.

[94]Garrett and Glaser (1995/96), pp. 53 ff.

[95]For a good discussion, see Johnston (1996b).

BENEFITS AND RISKS

Pursuit of the calculative strategy, as manifested in the four issue-areas analyzed above, has resulted in significant security gains for the Chinese state during the past decade. First, it has greatly strengthened domestic order and well-being by producing sustained, high rates of economic growth and major increases in the living standards of many Chinese. Second, it has greatly increased China's international leverage, especially along its periphery, and raised its overall regional and global status and prestige. Third, it has resulted in an expansion in its foreign economic presence and an increase in its political involvement and influence in Asia and beyond. Fourth, it has also generated a huge foreign currency reserve as well as provided the Chinese state with the financial wherewithal to purchase advanced weaponry and critical technologies from foreign states, thus compensating, in part, for the significant continued shortcomings in its military capabilities.[96] Fifth, in perhaps the greatest achievement of all, it has contributed—despite the numerous unresolved disputes between China and its neighbors—to the maintenance of a relatively benign external environment that enables Beijing to make the processes of internal economic growth more self-replicating than ever before.

All told, therefore, the calculative strategy has paid off handsomely for China: It has put it along a path that, if sustained, could make China the largest economy in the world sometime in the first half of the 21st century. Even more significantly, it has allowed such growth to occur as a result of an export-led strategy that increasingly employs significant proportions of imported technology and inputs—an amazing fact signifying that China has been able to rely upon both the markets and, increasingly, the resources of its partners to create the kind of growth that might eventually pose major concerns to its economic partners, *all without greatly unnerving those partners in the interim.* This does not imply that China's partners in Asia and elsewhere are unconcerned about the implications of China's growth in power. It implies only that such concerns have not resulted, thus

---

[96]For example, Chinese purchases of advanced weapons from Russia are to a significant extent a testimony to the failure of China's defense industry to indigenously produce many such critical systems.

far, in efforts to constrain China's growth because the desire for absolute gains on the part of all (including China) has outweighed the corrosive concerns brought about by the problem of relative gains. This represents the true success of the calculative strategy. By being explicitly premised on a refusal to provoke fear and uncertainty as a result of provocative Chinese actions, Beijing has succeeded, whether intentionally or not, not only in desensitizing its trading partners to the problems of relative gains but it has also, by rhetoric *and* actions aimed at exploiting all sides' desire for absolute gains, created the bases for the kind of continued collaboration that inevitably results in further increases in Chinese power and capabilities. Carried to its natural conclusion, the Chinese transition to true great-power status could occur in large part because of its partners' desire for trade and commercial intercourse so long as Beijing is careful enough not to let any security competition short-circuit the process in the interim.

The desire to avoid such competition is certainly China's intention, especially given its continued weakness in certain critical measures of economic and military power relative to the United States and key peripheral states such as Japan, Russia, and India. This being so, it is most likely that Chinese state-initiated revisionism of the international arena will be minimal in the years ahead and especially before, say, the period 2015–2020, which by most indicators is the *earliest* date when relative power capabilities would begin to be transformed to Beijing's advantage. That fact notwithstanding, the very successes of the calculative strategy, insofar as they precipitate unintended external and internal developments, could produce new security problems, for both China and the Asia-Pacific region at large, that might worsen before 2015.

First, the significant, albeit incremental, advances in China's military capabilities, combined with the emergence in the late 1980s and early 1990s of tensions over territorial issues such as Taiwan and the Spratly Islands, have raised anxieties among both the peripheral states and the Western powers over whether, and to what extent, China will seek to use its steadily growing military capabilities to resolve local security competition and more generally to establish a dominant strategic position in East Asia over the long term. The lack of clear-cut answers to these questions, as a result of both Beijing's ambiguity and its own ignorance about its future security environment in the long term, as well as simple systemic uncertainty (meaning, the fear of an unknown future), have given rise to a variety of regional counterresponses. A few of the more capable regional states have initiated a variety of military modernization programs that are at least partly motivated by long-range concerns over China's increasing capabilities and the uncertainty about the future U.S. regional presence, and several of the weaker states have begun exploring new diplomatic and political forms of reassurance.[97] If these counterresponses continue to gather steam, Beijing might be faced with a gradually deteriorating regional environment wherein more and more energetic military acquisitions and counter-acquisitions as well as competitive efforts at alliance formation begin to displace all the positive benefits of the calculative strategy over time.[98] The net result of such a dynamic would be the return to a more adversarial regional environment. Such an outcome may not by itself arrest China's relative growth, but it would nonetheless degrade the enthusiasm with which the regional states participate in China's economic renewal—with all the implications that has for technology transfers, direct and portfolio investments, market access, and global economic growth more generally—while simultaneously increasing the premium placed on military as opposed to other less-lethal instruments of interstate relations.[99]

Second, China's rapidly expanding involvement in foreign trade, technology transfer, and investment activities, combined with its growing participation in various international fora, has generated tensions with many of the advanced industrial states over issues of reciprocity, fair access, and responsibility. In part, this has been a direct result of the calculative strategy which, by positioning China in a

---

[97]A good survey of these regional developments, together with the role played by the interaction of external fears (including local rivalries) with internal growth, domestic business interests, and the search for regional prestige, can be found in Ball (1993/94). Beijing has attempted to reassure the international community about its intentions through the issuance of a defense White Paper in July 1998, but the lack of authentic information about budget expenditures and numbers and the likely disposition and purpose of forces makes it a less-than-complete document.

[98]The current Asian financial crisis could significantly reduce the pace of such a development because it has constrained the ability and willingness of many Asian countries to expand their military arsenals in response to increasing Chinese capabilities. For a broad survey of these developments, see Simon (1998).

[99]Friedberg (1993/94) concludes that such an outcome is in fact likely.

generally "exploitative" mode, has made it less sensitive to the external costs of maintaining high growth rates. Not surprisingly, China today is viewed by some Western observers, in some instances, as an unfair economic partner and multilateral regime participant that often chooses to free ride or defect from international and bilateral agreements or understandings and generally resists opening up many of its markets unless forced to do so. If such a sentiment gathers steam, there would be an increase in economic and political retaliation directed against China.[100] Although such actions may be intended merely to secure reciprocal "good behavior" in the economic realm, it could have unintended consequences in other areas. Given the strong suspicion in Beijing about emerging Western, and in particular, U.S., efforts at containing China, even purely economic retaliation may be read as part of a larger more concerted effort to bring China to heel. This perception, in turn, could lead to Chinese recalcitrance and obstructionism in other issue-areas such as proliferation, attitudes toward the U.S. presence in Asia, and the like, and before long could result in a tit-for-tat game that clouds more aspects of Chinese relations with the West than were initially at issue.[101]

Third, China's increasing dependence on foreign markets, maritime trade routes, and energy supplies has contributed to a growing sense of strategic vulnerability in Beijing to external economic factors, and this could result in increased pressures for expanding China's ability to control events beyond its borders. These pressures are reinforced by the fact that the concentration of China's major economic centers along the eastern and southern coastline, combined with the dramatic advances occurring in military technology, has increased Chinese vulnerability to a crippling military attack executed from standoff distances well outside the traditional defensive perimeter sought to be maintained by the Chinese state. Chinese responses to issues of resource and market dependence thus far have been both restrained and marginal, at least in military terms. For example, for energy dependence, China has sought to rely increasingly on the international market (and hence, from a security perspective, continues to depend on the U.S. interest in defending the oil-rich Arab states); develop stable, long-term energy supplies from key Central

---

[100]Sanger (1997).

[101]Shambaugh (1996a).

Asian energy producers; increase internal efficiency in the extraction of domestic resources and in manufacturing processes in general; and maintain good relations with the Gulf states, in part through the supply of lethal military and in some instances WMD technologies. Thus far, China has not responded to this problem by seeking unilateral solutions built around the development of power-projection forces able to operate at great distances from the Chinese Mainland. The problems of increased vulnerability to threats against existing or claimed Chinese territories, however, have apparently resulted in programmatic decisions *initially* aimed at acquiring military instruments capable of maritime barrier operations (such as the creation and maintenance of naval exclusion zones) and *eventually* securing and maintaining nearby offshore zones of influence through at least defensive sea control operations (such as the establishment of a sustained naval presence able to repel armed incursions into its area of operation).[102] These solutions, although conservative today, have the potential to develop into more powerful capabilities, including those required for offensive sea control in the form of forward operations throughout much of Asia-Pacific and the Indian Ocean areas.[103] Most emerging great powers in the past naturally developed such capabilities as their own perceptions of vulnerability increased. If China proves an exception to this past pattern (either by choice or because of a failure to develop the requisite economic and military capabilities), it could face a combined regional and extraregional response that makes the need for such capabilities even more imperative over time.

Fourth, the end of the U.S.-Soviet strategic rivalry as a result of the collapse of the Soviet Union, and the emergence of the United States

---

[102]The judgment that China's modernization of its naval and air assets includes elements of an explicit battlespace control (as opposed to mere denial) capability is based on both the diverse types of weapons platforms and support systems the Chinese are acquiring or attempting to acquire (e.g., long-range surface and subsurface combatants, more capable early warning and precision-strike assets, space-based surveillance capabilities, and possibly one or more aircraft carriers), and the inherent logic of geopolitics, technology, and operational considerations. Such factors suggest that the maintenance of a robust sea-denial capability over time will eventually require increasingly more effective sea-control capabilities, especially if China wants to maintain the security of maritime regions for hundreds of miles beyond its coastline, as is implied by the "islands chain" concept.

[103]The technologies required to sustain such operations are assessed in Tellis (1995).

as the sole global superpower have served to reduce Washington's strategic rationale for maintaining amicable security relations with the Chinese state. This factor, combined with the images of brutality and totalitarian repression resulting from the forcible suppression of large numbers of peaceful Chinese demonstrators in June 1989, the often-acrimonious Sino-U.S. disputes over economic and human rights issues, and a growing confrontation between Washington and Beijing over Taiwan, has significantly raised the Chinese sense of threat from the United States in the 1990s. Indeed, in recent years, U.S. policies toward China have been increasingly viewed as directly threatening core Chinese national security interests. The notion of "peaceful evolution,"[104] for example, threatens the Chinese state's conceptions of domestic order and well-being, continuing American support for Taiwan (including the political and military assistance that makes its supposed drive toward formal independence possible) threatens the Chinese vision of territorial integrity and unity, and the widespread discussions within the United States of the possible utility of containing or "constraining" China threatens the Chinese desire to recover its status and reestablish a position of geopolitical centrality in Asia. All in all, then, the demise of the Soviet Union created a situation in which Chinese grand strategic interests and those of the United States do not automatically cohere. This creates an opportunity for the growth of new irritants in the bilateral relationship. If such irritants are not managed successfully, they could eventually increase to a point where they radically undermine the success of any calculative strategy pursued by Beijing.

Fifth, the emergence of autonomous factors in the regional environment that affect Chinese core interests but which Beijing may be unable to control could bring about an escalation of tensions with other powers even before the calculative strategy runs its natural course. Among the most critical such issues are the future of Taiwan and the

---

[104]This term is used by many Chinese elites to describe a U.S. strategy to weaken and eventually destroy the existing Chinese political system from within, through the promotion of Western political and social values and structures in China. As Betts notes, "the liberal solution for pacifying international relations—liberal ideology—is precisely what present Chinese leaders perceive as a direct security threat to their regime." Betts (1993/94), p. 55.

Spratly islands.[105] The democratization of the political process on Taiwan that has taken place since the 1980s has led to a steady shift in political power, away from pro-reunification forces associated with the Mainlander-dominated Nationalist Party to independence-minded forces associated with the native Taiwanese-dominated Democratic Progressive Party.[106] Moreover, continued high growth rates, expanding levels of foreign trade and investment across the region, and the accumulation of enormous foreign exchange reserves have given Taiwan new avenues for asserting its influence in the regional and global arenas. These political and economic trends lay behind Taiwan's determined effort, begun in the early 1990s, to increase its international stature and influence as a sovereign state through an avowed strategy of "pragmatic diplomacy."[107] Such behavior, combined with Beijing's increasing reliance on territorially defined notions of nationalism, noted above, and its growing fear that Washington is directly or indirectly supportive of Taiwan's efforts, have served to strengthen China's sense of concern over Taiwan and increase its willingness to use coercive diplomacy, if not outright force, to prevent the island from achieving permanent independence. Hence, future attempts by Taiwan to strengthen its status as a sovereign entity through, for example, the attainment of a seat in the United Nations, as well as Chinese perceptions of growing Western (and especially U.S.) support for such behavior, could provoke Beijing to undertake aggressive political and military actions (including, perhaps, a direct attack on Taiwan) that would likely precipitate a confrontation with the United States, greatly alarm China's Asian neighbors, and generally destroy the incentives for continued restraint and caution basic to the calculative strategy.[108]

A similar outcome could conceivably occur as a result of developments in the South China Sea. Despite episodic altercations with Vietnam and the Philippines, China has thus far generally exercised considerable restraint in the pursuit of its claims to the Spratly

---

[105]The future of the Korean peninsula would also be an issue directly affecting China even though no sovereignty claims are at stake here.

[106]Friedman (1994), especially Chapter 8; and Tien and Chu (1996).

[107]Yue (1997).

[108]For a good summary of these issues see Cheung (1996).

Islands, agreeing to shelve the sovereignty dispute with other claimants and pursue joint exploitation of any possible resources located in the area. However, such restraint could diminish significantly in the future if other states were to become more aggressive in advancing their claims to the area, or if large viable oil or natural gas deposits were discovered beneath the islands or seabed of the region. The attraction of plentiful nearby energy resources to an increasingly energy-import-dependent China could prompt Beijing to undertake efforts to seize control of all or some of the Spratlys or restrict naval transit of the area and thereby precipitate dangerous military confrontations with other claimants and possibly the United States. Such a development, in turn, would almost certainly erode China's ability or willingness to pursue its current calculative strategy.[109]

Sixth, the increasing wealth and the general liberalization of society that have resulted from the reforms have generated a variety of social ills and economic dislocations which together have contributed to growing fears of domestic disorder within China. These ills, which include endemic corruption, rising crime rates, significant pockets of unemployment, growing regional income disparities, overcrowding in cities, and increased strikes and demonstrations, have given rise to a perception both within China and abroad of a growing "public order crisis."[110] These developments, combined with China's increasing dependence on external resources, markets, and investment capital and growing fears over the increasing acceptance by many Chinese of "decadent and corrupting" Western cultural products, have led some Chinese elites and ordinary citizens to espouse a modern version of the traditional argument favoring greater developmental autonomy, limited foreign contacts, a more centralized, coercive state apparatus, and accelerated efforts to develop the capabilities necessary to control the periphery.[111] Such arguments might over time provide renewed power to those more isolationist-oriented conservatives in the Communist Party and the military who, though currently out of favor, nonetheless could gain greater popular and elite support for their views if China's domestic and

---

[109]An excellent discussion of China's strategic calculus with respect to the use of force in the South China Sea can be found in Austin (1998), pp. 297–326.

[110]Austin (1995).

[111]Zhao (1997), pp. 733–734; and Chen (1997).

international environment were to deteriorate rapidly, even before 2015–2020. The core of this potential internal crisis, such as it is, derives in part from the increasing hollowing-out of the Communist Party from below. As a result, the struggle for domestic order becomes simultaneously a struggle for national discipline and political survival. In such circumstances, the increasing importance of the PLA as the guarantor of domestic security coupled with the rising attractiveness of an authoritarian ideology of "order-first" could combine to create domestic transformations that would make China more fearsome in appearance and, thereby, undercut the trustworthiness required for the success of its calculative strategy.

Any of these six developments occurring either independently or in combination could result in enormous pressures to expand and rapidly accelerate improvements in China's military and economic capabilities as well as increase its external influence to simultaneously establish political and economic dominance over the periphery, ensure continued high rates of domestic economic growth, and provide leverage against future great power pressure. Although these objectives remain in some sense the distant goals to which the present calculative strategy is arguably directed, the pursuit of these aims will become much more fervid and may be undertaken by more coercive means in the near to mid term if a breakdown in the calculative strategy occurs. In fact, many observers have noted that, by the early 1990s, the Chinese state had already apparently moved some distance in developing a military "fallback" solution in the event of a conspicuous failure of the calculative strategy. This solution has entailed an increased level of defense spending and the progressive implementation of a new defense doctrine keyed to the acquisition of capabilities to undertake offensive, preemptive, conventional attacks beyond its borders, coupled with enhanced efforts to create a more survivable and flexible nuclear deterrent capability.[112]

Whether these developments materialize in "strong" form still remains to be seen, but at any rate they raise two critical questions that demand scrutiny and, if possible, an explanation. First, assuming

---

[112]Regarding PLA doctrine, see Godwin (1997). For Chinese nuclear force modernization, see Johnston (1996b).

that no mishaps occur in the interim, how long can the calculative strategy be expected to last? Second, what, if any, posture can be expected to replace the calculative strategy after the latter has successfully run its course? The next chapter attempts to provide tentative answers to both these questions.

Chapter Five

CHINA FACES THE FUTURE: THE FAR TERM

The challenges facing China's calculative strategy, even in the near term, should not be underestimated. As indicated in the previous chapter, a variety of external and internal factors could coalesce to undermine both China's efforts at pragmatism and its desire to economize on the use of force. This could result in serious crises in a variety of issue-areas—such as Taiwan, the Spratlys, Tibet, Korea, WMD proliferation, and trade—which could compel Beijing to adopt more muscular policies toward both the United States and its regional neighbors. Assuming for the moment, however, that no catastrophic revisions of the calculative strategy are forced in the near to mid term, the "natural" longevity of this strategy then becomes an interesting question. That is, the issue of how long China's calculative posture would survive *assuming rapid and continuing economic growth* becomes a question of great relevance for policy because the answer to this question enables both China's regional neighbors and the United States to anticipate future changes in Beijing's attitudes and prudently prepare accordingly. Unfortunately, this question cannot be answered with any certitude, but it is possible to identify the conditions under which the calculative strategy would naturally evolve over the long term, thereby providing a basis for understanding those circumstances that portend a consequential change in China's future strategic direction.

ASSESSING THE "NATURAL" LONGEVITY OF THE CALCULATIVE STRATEGY

The key to assessing the natural longevity of the calculative strategy lies in examining more closely why the strategy was devised to begin with. The reasons essentially boil down to the fact that China is a rising but not yet strong power, whose further growth in capabilities depends fundamentally on the quality of its external environment. This *strong* dependence on the external environment is manifested not simply by Beijing's desire for peace to prevent the distractions of security competition but, more fundamentally, by its continuing need for external markets, capital, and know-how to maintain its current export-led strategy of growth. The continuing growth necessary to maintain domestic order and well-being and complete China's ascent to power thus depends on the actions of others: access to their markets, capital, and technology, which is contingent on Beijing not posing a threat both to the regional states and to the international system in general. This recognition, more than any other, has guided the development of the calculative strategy and it is, therefore, reasonable to suggest that, *ceteris paribus*, China's adherence to this approach will endure at least as long as its acquisition of comprehensive national strength is incomplete.

This argument, in effect, implies that the quality of China's external environment, *at least in the first instance*, remains the key variable that determines the degree to which China can attain its principal power-political goals, namely, the ensuring of domestic order and well-being, the attainment of strategic influence and, if possible, control, over the periphery, and the restoration of geopolitical preeminence. The realization of these goals—whenever that occurs—will represent an important culminating point in China's modern political history in that it will have completed an evolutionary sequence from weakness to strength. Beginning with being a weak state in the late Qing, China has progressively evolved into a weak-strong state under communist rule, only to possibly end up as a strong state once again at some point in the distant future, perhaps still under communist rule, but more likely enjoying some other more liberalized form of political governance.

If and when this process is completed, the wheel will have turned full circle and—other things being equal—China could, once again, be faced with the opportunity to employ some of the traditional strong-state strategies not witnessed since the highpoint of the imperial era. Whether such strong-state strategies are in fact employed will also depend on the quality of China's internal environment. The issue of the institutionalization and democratization of China's political order (discussed below) certainly becomes relevant here, but other considerations relating to the spatial distribution of wealth and power internally, the social forms that arise as a result of new economic inequalities, and the character of the convergence that develops between holders of economic and political power will all play a critical role in how future strong-state strategies evolve and are manifested. These variables, in interaction with external imperatives, will shape how China's leadership determines and executes its preferred strong-state strategies in the future and while these strategies cannot be discerned in their detail right now, it is possible to at least identify broad alternatives. Before this exercise is conducted, however, it is important first to assess how certain key variables will affect China's continued commitment to its present calculative strategy and how changes in these variables might demarcate the timeframe within which any future shifts in strategy might take place.

The discussion in this chapter, which pertains to the possibility of a shift in China's present calculative strategy to something resembling the strong-state strategy of the imperial era, must not be interpreted to mean that China currently seeks to *consciously and deliberately* shift out of its present strategy at some point in the future. Nor must it be understood as a simplistic stratagem of "lying in wait," wherein the Chinese state patiently bides its time until the balance of power shifts to its advantage before it can revert to a supposedly "normal" pattern of muscular behavior. The premises underlying the discussion here, in fact, do not impute any sinister motives to China's calculative strategy. They are sensitive, however, to *structural* transformations in the international order, especially to changes in relative capability among countries and to the implications of those changes for international politics. In particular, they incorporate the supposition that as Beijing's relative capability changes for the better, its interests will expand proportionately, as will the spatial and institutional realms within which those interests are sought to be defended. It is therefore possible, for purely structural reasons, that China's currently limited objectives—domestic order, peripheral stability, and geopolitical recognition—may gradually evolve in the direction of more expanded interests requiring that it "exert more control over its surroundings."[1]

The possibility that such an expansion of interests may occur over time is precisely what makes the Chinese transformation so interesting and so pressing from the perspective of U.S. *grand strategy* because it directly intersects with U.S. efforts to preserve its own preeminence even as it struggles to maintain a stable regional order in Asia. In fact, it would be surprising if such an expansion of interests did *not* occur as Chinese capabilities increase because, as historians often point out, expanding interests as a function of expanding power have invariably been the norm throughout recorded history for three reasons.[2] First, rising power leads to increased international interests and commitments. Second, as rising powers gain in relative power, they are more likely to attempt to advance their standing in the international system. Third, rising power inexorably leads to increasing ambition. Taken together, these considerations imply that China's "dependence on the favor of its neighbors, [which] has been comparatively high" when it subsisted as a weaker power, may not survive its ascent to greatness when, as a true superpower, it will have all the capabilities to "behave boldly," and perhaps be "more inclined to force its will upon others than to consult with them."[3] Such changed behaviors are possible because, as Robert Gilpin succinctly concluded, "the critical significance of the differential growth of power among states is that it alters the cost of changing the international system and therefore the incentives for changing the . . . [existing] . . . system.[4]

Because of such considerations, the possibilities for change in China's current calculative strategy, the conditions governing such a change, and the timeframe within which such change could take place all become questions of pressing analytical interest. It is in this context that the proposition, "China's adherence to a calculative strategy will endure *at least* as long as its acquisition of comprehen-

---

[1]Roy (1996), p. 762.

[2]See Gilpin (1981); Kennedy (1987).

[3]Roy (1996), pp. 761–762.

[4]Gilpin (1981), p. 95.

sive national strength is incomplete," can be broken down into three specific dimensions.

First, China's commitment to a calculative strategy will be a critical function of the extent and structure of its economic capabilities. To begin with, this implies that Beijing's freedom of action will be conditioned substantially by the size of its GNP both in absolute and in relative terms. The size of absolute GNP (both in an aggregate and in a per capita sense) will determine the degree to which China is able to service its vast internal developmental needs. Fulfilling this objective is critical to ensuring domestic order and well-being to both attenuate the volatility of intrasocietal relations and increase the legitimacy of the Chinese state. Given the importance of these two objectives, it is unlikely that China would shift from its currently profitable calculative strategy before it can attain those relatively high levels of absolute GNP that are "convertible into virtually all types of power and influence."[5] Such an achievement would allow it to further reduce the numbers of near-to-absolute poor, estimated to consist of about 170 million people in 1995; preempt urban poverty which, despite being as low as 0.3 percent of the urban population in 1981, could become a matter of concern as urbanization increases and China's state-owned enterprises are reformed; and arrest the growing inequality across the urban-rural divide (an income gap that explains at least one-third of total inequality in 1995 and about one-half of the increase in inequality since 1985) and also interprovincial disparities (which account for almost one-quarter of the total inequality in 1995 and explain one-third of the increase since 1985).[6]

Although attaining a high level of absolute GNP contributes to improving the quality of life of China's population and, by implication, gives China an opportunity to pursue other political objectives, Beijing will also have to be sensitive to its GNP levels in relative terms. This measure defines China's standing in comparison to its peers and, to that degree, it suggests the freedom of action that China is likely to enjoy relative to other states in the international system.

---

[5]Knorr (1973), p. 75. For a dissenting view on the easy fungibility of power, see Baldwin (1979). For an analysis of the relevant constituents of national power in the postindustrial age, see Tellis et al. (forthcoming).

[6]The World Bank (1997b), pp. 1–13.

Economists debate how to calculate relative GNP among states, but the critical issue here is that a China with higher GNP relative to its competitors will acquire commensurate political weight and, consequently, will have a greater capacity to embark on efforts to remake or shape the international political order to better suit its own needs and preferences.[7] Because such an effort cannot be undertaken so long as China is outside the league of "hegemonic"[8] states—that is, states powerful enough to determine or decisively influence the nature of the rules and institutions governing global politics—it is unlikely that Beijing would shift out of its calculative approach before attaining global economic preponderance, especially when it is locked in a situation where the calculative strategy remains the cheapest route through which it can acquire hegemonic capabilities in the sense described above. Most assessments suggest that China would not become the world's preeminent economic power before 2015–2020 (when measured in purchasing power parity (PPP) terms) *at the very earliest* and, while it might exceed the size of the U.S. economy at that point, it would still trail far behind the United States and many other Western countries when measured in terms of per capita GDP.[9]

Although the size of GDP, both in absolute and relative terms, is important, the issue of China's economic structure also bears on the question of when Beijing might shift from its calculative strategy. The economic structure of a country defines its degree of structural preparedness for an autonomous pursuit of great-power goals. In considering this fact, it is important to recognize that, despite its rapid economic growth, China today still remains predominantly an

---

[7]Knorr (1973), p. 75, summarized this notion by defining "two sides to nation power": one, which "is concerned with what a country can do to other countries," and the other, which "concerns a country's ability to limit what other countries do to it."

[8]The terms "hegemonic state" or "hegemonic behavior" are employed in this study in the technical manner suggested by U.S. international relations theory, where they refer to the structure-defined, global rule-making capacity of certain great powers, rather than in the Chinese sense where such terms convey a pejorative meaning, and are most often used to describe oppressive and predatory behavior by strong states.

[9]The World Bank (1997a), p. 21. It is quite clear that China will be unable to sustain its target of 8 percent growth in the near term, but even rates of 5–6 percent would still be impressive relative to growth rates in the rest of the global economy. For an analysis of the prognosis for future Chinese growth and why its growth rates are likely to slow down during the next decade, see Wolf (1999).

agricultural country, when measured by employment (50 percent) though not by sectoral contributions to GDP (20 percent).[10] Any shift out of its current calculative strategy would therefore be prudent only when its structural transformation is complete—that is, when it has developed a large, skilled, industrial workforce able to autonomously produce the range of civil and military instruments required to sustain an independent political trajectory as well as an effective service sector that produces the complex enabling capabilities required by both an industrial society and a modernized military.

This shift from agriculture to industry and services, when measured by employment, may come about faster than is usually imagined. In contrast to the United States and Japan, which took over 50 years to reduce the share of agriculture in the labor force from 70 percent to 50 percent, China has succeeded in doing the same in less than 20 years. Assuming that this process continues at such a pace, China would be able to reduce the proportion of agricultural labor to about 20 percent of the total labor pool by 2020 and perhaps even further in the years beyond. At somewhere around this point, it is expected that both the contribution of the industrial and services sector to GNP, and the size of the industrial and services workforce as a fraction of total employment, will roughly approximate those proportions currently holding in typical upper-middle-income countries today.[11] Even more significantly, however, it is expected that the level of technology "domesticated" by the Chinese economy will reach significant enough levels to make indigenous "niche" capabilities fairly commonplace.

Finally, the level of dependence on the international economy will be the final, albeit *arguably least important*, factor (in the economic realm) that determines when a shift from the calculative strategy is possible.[12] In the late 1970s, China's foreign economic relations

---

[10]The World Bank (1997a), p. 22.

[11]The World Bank (1997a), p. 22.

[12]This factor is arguably least important as a structural indicator of China's possible shift from the calculative strategy because, although levels of external economic dependence might restrain a state from acting more assertively, they will not in any sense guarantee such restraint. As argued below, the historical record does not show that economic dependency significantly lowers the likelihood of conflict between

contributed about 13 percent of its GDP. In 1995, that figure jumped to almost 30 percent—a proportion comparable to that of other large developing countries.[13] This significant, though not exceptional level of dependence, at least in comparison to the other East Asian economies that rely on foreign trade for almost 60 percent of their GDP, clearly indicates why the calculative strategy remains essential for continued Chinese economic growth. Only when China reaches the point where it becomes like a large *developed* country—that is, one pursuing an internally driven growth strategy that exploits the diversity of resources and markets within its own borders—would it experience significant economic incentives to shift toward the more normal, risk-acceptant, international political behaviors associated with true great powers. Even if the levels of foreign direct investment (FDI) it receives continue to remain high at that point—China already receives 40 percent of the FDI going to developing countries and is the largest recipient of FDI after the United States today—its ability to shift from a calculative strategy would not necessarily be impaired so long as its internal economic environment is strong and stable and the Chinese market is seen to offer opportunities that are profitable enough for foreign investors despite any of the uncertainties that may be induced by Beijing's perhaps more assertive international political behavior.[14]

Equally significant here is the nature of China's dependence on its external environment for natural resources. Today, Chinese exports are dominated by a variety of labor-intensive manufacturers, with primary products accounting for only a very small share of total trade. As its economic growth continues, however, it is likely that China will become a large net importer of many primary products including food grains and energy. Any increased dependence here could in principle lead to two opposed kinds of policy outcomes: It could lead to a continuation of the calculative strategy as political conservatism and military restraint are oriented toward maintaining good relations with key suppliers. This approach would emphasize

---

states. The most important structural factor influencing strategic behavior is the aggregate level of national power, as measured by economic and military capabilities.

[13]The World Bank (1997a), pp. 84–85.

[14]Foreign portfolio investment is minimal and 75 percent of the cumulative investment here comes from ethnic overseas Chinese.

continued market solutions to the problem of scarcity. It could also lead to a more assertive political strategy as China, fearing the unpalatable consequences of dependency, begins to contemplate unilateral, exclusivist, solutions to the problem of resource constraints—solutions that require, among other things, the development of privileged political relations with certain key suppliers and the acquisition of potent military forces designed to preserve the lines of supply, protect the supplies themselves, and finally provide for the security of the suppliers.

Which solution will be applied over time cannot be forecast a priori, but what remains certain is that any successful effort to reduce dependency, especially in the arena of energy supplies, would give China significant opportunities to change its calculative strategy assuming, of course, that its overall growth patterns remain unchanged. Almost all analyses today suggest that China's dependency on foreign energy sources will steadily increase, at least until the year 2010 and possibly even to 2020 and beyond.[15] However, one study suggests that after 2025, Chinese dependence on foreign energy may actually begin to drop as alternative domestic sources of energy are exploited, increased efficiencies accrue in industrial production, and conservation and energy management measures, combined with the economies forced by steadily rising energy prices, finally begin to bear fruit.[16] If this assessment is correct, it is likely that China would be faced with some additional opportunities to shift from its calculative strategy at some point during or after the circa-2020 timeframe.

Second, China's commitment to a calculative strategy will be a critical function of the nature of its military capabilities, its operational effectiveness, and the character of regional power relations. Besides the issues related to economic capability and dependence on foreign trade, an important consideration underlying the need for a calculative strategy is the generally poor state of the Chinese military. This force, which was designed primarily to provide a deterrent capability in the realm of land warfare during the Cold War, would be outclassed today in many circumstances involving both the seizure and control of contested land territories and the advanta-

---

[15]For a good survey and analysis of these sources, see Downs (unpublished).
[16]Freris (1995).

geous resolution of maritime disputes involving China's offshore claims. China presently does not have the military capabilities to pursue any political strategy that requires more than an economy of force in the conventional realm, particularly where its regional peers are concerned. This reflects its significant military weaknesses caused, in part, by the new operational demands that have arisen in the course of the last 20 odd years, the concomitant civilian demands placed on available Chinese resources by the imperative of maintaining relatively high growth rates, the steady expansion of the areas of interest deemed essential to Chinese security, and the serious qualitative degradation that the PLA has had to endure over several decades as a result of China's internal political and economic cataclysms at a time when many of its regional peers were steadily acquiring new and sophisticated military technologies. Any changes in the presently dominant calculative strategy in a direction other than universal cooperation and restraint in the use of force would thus require at the very least a significant improvement in Chinese military power, especially at the conventional level, and relative to China's larger Asian neighbors and the United States.

Such improvement could increase China's warfighting potential along three generic levels of capability. At the first and simplest level, China would need to develop a range of military capabilities that would allow it to *deny* its adversaries the free use of a given battlespace. This capability is essentially negative in that it seeks primarily to prevent China's competitors from completing their desired missions successfully. At the second, intermediate, level, China would move beyond merely denial capabilities to something resembling positive *control*, thereby allowing it to operate within a given battlespace without inordinate risks to its own forces. This level of capability bequeaths China the ability to use certain battlespaces in the pursuit of some tactically limited goals. At the third and most demanding level, China would actually have the capability to *exploit* its positive control over a given battlespace to bring coercive power to bear against the strategic centers of gravity valued by its adversaries. This level of capability would represent the most assertive use of its military prowess in that it would permit China to conduct a variety of forcible entry operations involving land, air, and sea power, that hold either the homeland or the strategic assets of its adversaries at grave risk.

Since the principal external military challenges to China today are perceived to be maritime and concern unresolved disputes over either the ownership or the sovereignty of several offshore areas, it is likely that China would make no fundamental change in its calculative strategy until it reaches the second level of capability, that is, until it acquires the military wherewithal (measured in terms of weapons systems, organic support, and operational capabilities) to dominate and control the local battlespaces along its periphery. To be sure, China already has significant denial, and in some cases even exploitative, capabilities that can be brought to bear against those adversaries who seek to disturb the status quo to its disadvantage in areas close to China's borders, especially its interior, continental borders. But, it still lacks many of the military instruments and operational skills needed to control the peripheral battlespaces on a continuing basis (both near and far) and it is still far from acquiring the capabilities that would allow it to exploit control in support of some more assertive forms of forcible entry involving land, naval, and air forces.[17]

The PLA today does possess a large and growing force of conventionally armed short- and intermediate-range ballistic and cruise missiles, which it could use for interdicting targets either in the homelands of its regional neighbors or at sea. It also has a large force of short-range attack aircraft and numerous surface and subsurface naval combatants, which could likely overwhelm, though probably at some cost, the capabilities of many smaller nearby regional states. These instruments, however, are more useful for denying others the objectives they may seek or for deterring them or, failing that, punishing them should they embark on any military operations against Chinese territory. They are much less useful for acquiring and sustaining effective control over the foreign battlespaces of interest to Beijing, at least when major regional competitors are concerned, and they would be quite inadequate for prosecuting the kind of forcible entry operations that would be most threatening to China's most important neighbors.

---

[17]A good assessment of the PLA's current ability to project power can be found in Godwin (1997).

This incapability, both at the intermediate and at the higher ends of the scale, derives from the fact that the People's Liberation Army Navy (PLAN), for example, does not have carrier battle groups or even surface action groups built around platforms with tactically matched capabilities; it has a small marine force capable of amphibious landings, but it is incapable of anything resembling amphibious assault under conditions of forcible entry.[18] Similarly, the PLAAF does not have any worthwhile expeditionary air capabilities (despite the inherent speed and flexibility of all air power), and even the mostly obsolete long-range airframes it does have are not rapidly deployable for campaigns outside their permanent bases. The PLAAF cannot even transport its relatively large number of airborne units en masse, much less insert and support them in the face of significant air and ground opposition emanating from the major regional powers.[19]

None of this should be taken to imply, however, that China would be absolutely unable to undertake any successful military actions within the maritime areas adjacent to its coastlines. To be sure, Beijing certainly has the ability to seize lightly defended or undefended areas claimed by smaller regional neighbors such as the Philippines or Vietnam, or to prevent such neighboring powers from occupying such contested areas. China has in fact clearly displayed this capability in the case of disputed islands in the South China Sea. It has also demonstrated the capability to strike with ballistic missiles at fixed offshore targets within about 100 nautical miles of the Chinese Mainland and it could probably conduct small-scale blockades which, despite their operational limitations, could still have serious *political* effects against weaker powers such as Taiwan or some of the smaller ASEAN states. All these abilities, which are most effective against the marginal Asian states, do not in any way undercut the general conclusion that China currently confronts major limitations in the arenas of extended battlespace denial, control, and exploitation against most major Asian powers such as Japan, Russia, and India.

----

[18]Jencks (1997).

[19]Jencks (1997).

Not surprisingly, China has begun several efforts to acquire a range of capabilities intended, first, to *deny* its most capable adversaries the use of the appropriate battlespaces through which they could challenge Chinese interests (especially interests associated with the defense of territory directly under the control of or claimed by the Chinese Government), and, second, to ultimately give its own forces some measure of *control* over those battlespaces even in the face of concerted opposition. In the near term, this has resulted in significant efforts at acquiring modern, long-range, land-based tactical aviation platforms such as the Su-27 and its derivatives, together with air-to-air refueling platforms; indigenously developing a variety of more modern and versatile combat aircraft such as the J-10, the FC-1, and the FB-7; seeking new command and control and surveillance capabilities in the form of both Airborne Warning and Control System (AWACS) and improvements in the existing electronic warfare/ground control intercept (EW/GCI) net; making limited acquisitions of modern wide-area surface-to-air missile defenses in the form of the SA-10 and SA-11; and substantially modernizing its naval warfare capabilities, acquiring various new weapons, sensors, communications, and propulsion systems for both its surface ships and its submarines. Although China has not paid comparable attention to its land forces modernization, it has nonetheless sought to streamline and improve the capabilities of its ground forces including its airborne quick-reaction forces. Most of the improvements here have focused on increasing unit mobility, improving combined-arms training, and modernizing logistics and combat support.

These capabilities taken together will undoubtedly improve China's warfighting capability over time. The essential questions, however, are where will the most significant improvements likely occur and over what time period. No definitive answers can be offered to these questions, since the acquisition and effective integration of the kinds of capabilities needed to underwrite a muscular foreign policy over the long term will require continued success in a variety of complex political, economic, and organizational realms. These include the sustained, high-priority, endorsement of the senior leadership; higher levels of financial resources; a well-run, innovative, and robust research and development system; a technologically advanced and quality-driven manufacturing base; a systematic education and training program at all levels within the military, including more realistic combat simulation and training; an institutionalized system of developing, testing, and improving operational and tactical doctrine; and an efficient organizational, managerial, and command structure to coordinate all the above dimensions. Many of these elements are not yet in place and even those that are confront significant obstacles. These include limited funds for equipment and training; antiquated logistics; an excessive emphasis on self-reliance at all levels of the defense industry system; a lack of horizontal integration among key military structures; severe technology absorption and utilization problems; a lack of skilled experts, managers, and workers; and low education levels among soldiers and officers.[20]

Consequently, straightline extrapolations of future military capabilities derived from existing baselines and past rates of development are fraught with pitfalls. Nonetheless, if it is assumed for the sake of argument that it is largely a matter of time before most of the existing financial, technical, organizational, and conceptual obstacles confronting China's military modernization program are either greatly reduced or eliminated altogether, and that the general rate of improvement seen in the past decade will at least persist, if not accelerate, over the next two decades, then it is likely that China will attain the following generic military capabilities by about the year 2020:

- At the conventional level: significant battlespace denial and improved battlespace control capabilities within about 250 n mi of China's coastline, marked by (a) major improvements in land- and sea-based antisurface and long-range precision-strike capabilities, (b) significant improvements in electronic warfare (including information denial) and space-based monitoring and surveillance capabilities, and (c) moderate, evolutionary gains in the ability of air, ground, and maritime forces to conduct joint, offensive operations abutting China's maritime and land borders.

---

[20]Swaine (1996b). Regarding PLA training, also see Blasko, Klapakis, and Corbett (1996). For analysis of the professionalization of the PLA officer corps, see Mulvenon (1997a).

- At the nuclear level (strategic and tactical): a more accurate, versatile, and survivable nuclear force characterized by (a) an improved, secure second-strike capability against the United States and Russia, able to penetrate even the thin ballistic missile defense (BMD) systems that may be deployed by both countries by 2020; (b) an enhanced nuclear and conventional counterforce strike capability against a significant number of targets in Japan, Korea, India, and Russia; and (c) some ability to integrate discrete nuclear and chemical weapons use with conventional operations on the battlefield.

Overall, it is likely that China will succeed by and large in fielding many elements of a 1990s-era military inventory, if not an actual warfighting force, by the year 2020. However, the Chinese military will likely have limited niche capabilities in certain warfighting areas such as space exploitation, information warfare, and directed-energy weaponry and may even be successful at integrating some technologies and concepts deriving from the revolution in military affairs. Although such limited achievements may appear reassuring at first sight from the perspective of preserving regional stability, this may be deceptive. This is because the potential for basic shifts in the calculative strategy will be determined not simply by the adequacy of China's force structure and the absolute effectiveness of its military as measured by state-of-the-art capabilities but also by the regional balances of power.[21] It is in this context that possessing elements of a 1990s-style force even in 2020 may not be entirely disadvantageous (especially if it is an *effective* 1990s-style force), in large measure because such capabilities may be sufficient for the political objectives China may seek in that timeframe and because China's regional competitors may not be much further along either. As far as the maritime periphery is concerned, China faces four distinct sets of actors—the Southeast Asian states, Taiwan, the United States, Japan, and more remotely, India—and as the analysis below suggests, even a 1990s-style force could yield significant, even if still limited, dividends for China's security policy by 2020, especially if the Chinese military can develop the technical and operational capabilities by then to effectively control some battlespaces out to about 250 n mi from its frontiers.

---

[21]For an excellent survey and analysis of these balances see Betts (1993/94).

As far as the Southeast Asian states are concerned, China already has the capability to overwhelm any combination of these actors in naval force-on-force encounters, assuming that no extraregional assistance is forthcoming. This capability will be further reinforced by the year 2020. This assessment derives first from a simple correlation of the competing orders of battle. Chinese numerical superiority generally suffices to negate even the superior technology that could be mustered by the Southeast Asian states. The latter dimension, in any event, must not be exaggerated: Although the ASEAN countries have in recent years acquired some impressive combat aviation and anti-surface warfare technologies—Malaysia has 8 F-18s and 18 Mig-29s, Thailand has 36 F-16s, Singapore has 17 F-16s, Indonesia has 11 F-16s, and Vietnam has about 6 Su-27s—these capabilities exist in relatively small numbers. Their integration into the existing force structure will not be effortless in all cases save Singapore, the combat proficiency of all Southeast Asian operators, barring the Singaporean Air Force, is an open question, and it is unlikely, in any case, that all these relatively sophisticated aircraft would ever face the PLAAF or the PLAN in any unified or coordinated fashion. In most contingencies that can be envisaged (e.g., in the South China Sea), Chinese naval and air forces would have a considerable advantage over the military forces of one or even several ASEAN states. This judgment would be altered only if ASEAN in its entirety attained the unprecedented ability to deploy military forces in concert or if extraregional intervention is presupposed in the form of either sea- or land-based U.S. power, land-based Australian air power, or land-based British or French air power.

Chinese advantages over Taiwan will continue to increase over time. For the moment, and probably for several years to come, the relatively superior ROC Air Force, which is in the process of integrating into its force structure aircraft such as the F-16, the Mirage 2000, and the Indigenous Defense Fighter in tandem with airborne warning and control platforms such as the E-2T, can effectively blunt the worst threats that could be mounted by the PLAAF. However, Taiwan's ability to protect itself from Chinese military pressure over the long term confronts significant obstacles. The ROC military, for example, has serious problems with integrating its existing equipment, its training regimes are not entirely adequate, and its air and naval bases, air defense system, and command and control infrastructure remain vulnerable to barrage fires of Chinese missiles. Moreover, the Taiwanese armed forces are still organizationally "stovepiped" in many undesirable ways; they continue to possess a force structure that is not entirely congruent, in terms of both equipment and training, to the needs of island defense; and they will remain disadvantaged by their relative lack of numbers and the continuing constraints imposed on access to sophisticated military technology. China's continuing modernization of its air, naval, and missile forces as well as its command and control capabilities over the Taiwan Strait will only increase the levels of effective punishment it can inflict on Taiwan in a crisis. Although China will still be unable to successfully invade Taiwan through an amphibious assault or seal off the island through a total naval blockade, these weaknesses may not be very consequential if it believes it can successfully coerce Taiwan through increasingly accurate conventional missile fires and air attacks coupled with a damaging, albeit partial, air and subsurface blockade (or even a simple *guerre de course*) directed at Taiwanese commerce and shipping.[22]

Achieving this objective successfully presumes, of course, that the United States and its military forces would be entirely absent from the equation. Precisely because this presumption cannot be assured, China's military modernization has focused a great deal of attention on increasing the risks that can be imposed on any intervening U.S. force. In practice, this has meant attempting to cope with the threats posed by U.S. carrier battle groups operating off the Chinese coast or adjacent to Taiwan. Several of the military systems currently under development by the Chinese are oriented to acquiring the capability to detect, track, target, and attack a carrier battle group operating within about 250 n mi off China's eastern coast. These include airborne, naval, and space-based surveillance platforms; advanced diesel-electric submarines with wake-homing torpedoes; long-range tactical cruise missiles with terminal homing; and, long-range interceptors and attack aircraft.

It is likely that despite all China's efforts in this regard, it will proba-bly be unable to defeat a U.S. naval force that was fully alerted, pos-

---

[22]For a reading of Chinese assessments of the military balance in relation to Taiwan, see Cheung (1996), pp. 13–17; for other readings, see Jencks (1997).

sessed adequate capabilities, and was committed under very clear rules of engagement. Unfortunately, there is no guarantee that U.S. military forces would be always employed only under such conditions: In fact, it is very possible that in the early days of a crisis, particularly in the context of a sudden attack, the United States would be able to muster a battle group composed of only a single aircraft carrier and its escorts. Under such conditions, even a force as powerful as a carrier battle group may not be able to survive dense and coordinated multi-azimuth attacks unscathed. This ability to threaten U.S. carrier battle groups operating at close distances to the Chinese Mainland will only increase over time. By the year 2020, China will almost certainly be able to mount significant denial efforts involving, inter alia, air- and space-based detection and cueing and long-range attacks by high-speed surface-to-surface missiles (SSMs) and air-to-surface missiles (ASMs), smart mines, and torpedoes. Even then, however, none of these capabilities may suffice to conclusively defeat a U.S. CVBG in battle. But that may not be required if Chinese military modernization succeeds in providing Beijing with an important benefit it lacks today—the ability to significantly raise the cost of U.S. military operations along the Chinese periphery and, to that degree, eliminate the advantage that the United States currently enjoys of being able to operate with impunity throughout the East Asian region.[23]

Chinese advantages over Japan will probably remain minimal in most warfighting areas for a long time to come. In part, this is because Japan has and will continue to have access to the best U.S. technology, intelligence, and weapons. Having planned for operations against the Soviet Navy during the Cold War, Japan also has the advantage of a long lead as far as training and orienting its military forces to deal with open-ocean attack is concerned. Both the Japanese Navy and Air Force remain highly proficient operators and it is most likely that, in the event of a conflict, the Japanese Self Defense Force (JSDF) would be able to eliminate all Chinese open-ocean surface capabilities within a matter of days, if not hours. Japan would nonetheless continue to remain vulnerable in some warfighting arenas. The newer Chinese subsurface capabilities, assuming that they are deployed in significant numbers, will tax even

---

[23]This critical point is made most perceptively in Goldstein (1997/98), pp. 53–54.

Japanese antisubmarine warfare (ASW) capabilities thanks both to the nature of ASW operations and the peculiar geophysical environment in the East and South China Seas. Japan will also continue to be vulnerable to ballistic missile attack and the extent to which this problem would be attenuated by the year 2020 is uncertain for both political and operational reasons.[24] Finally, Japan would be constrained by any surprise Chinese occupation of its disputed island territories because, lacking any amphibious capabilities for forcible entry, it would be forced to rely entirely on the United States or on its own air power to eject the intruders.

All things considered, therefore, if present trends continue, China's military modernization will likely precipitate some significant changes in the regional balance of power by the year 2020. China will be able to execute denial and control, if not exploitative, operations against all the Southeast Asian states, if the latter are unable to coordinate their response and are unaided by an outside power. A similar conclusion holds for Taiwan, assuming that present trends in the realm of politics and military access continue. China will also likely acquire significant, albeit limited, denial capabilities against the United States in Asia—capabilities it does not possess today. And, through its growing subsurface capabilities, it will be able to deny Japan the free use of its water spaces in a way that it cannot do today. Whether these changes will suffice to induce a shift in China's calculative strategy at that point is unclear, but they certainly contribute toward altering the structural conditions that make for the possibility of such a change.

Third, China's commitment to a calculative strategy will be a critical function of developments in its domestic politics, including the nature of its regime and institutions. Domestic politics remains the last, and in many ways the least understood, factor contributing to a possible shift in the calculative strategy over time. The long-term influence on security strategy exerted by domestic political issues is most closely related to the question of systemic change associated

---

[24]By 2020, China will likely possess several hundred short- and medium-range ballistic missiles able to deliver either nuclear or conventional warheads to targets anywhere in Japan with a high degree of accuracy. It is unclear whether Japan either directly, or via the U.S. military, will be able to field an effective missile defense system by that time.

with the possible collapse of communism and the emergence of a democratic form of government on China.

There is a substantial body of opinion which believes that China is still a classic communist state, at least where its political regime and institutions are concerned.[25] As such, the problems of political repression, religious persecution, exploitative trade practices, and proliferation of weapons of mass destruction are viewed to be the natural consequences of a regime implacably hostile to the West in general and to the United States in particular. Such a perspective inevitably leads to the suggestion that the problem of regional stability demands a radical transformation of the Communist Chinese regime. It is supposed that such a transformation, which replaces the currently authoritarian political order with new demo-cratic structures and institutions, would inevitably produce geopolit-ical tranquility because of all the arguments associated with the con-cept of "democratic peace." These arguments essentially boil down to the claim that, since democratic states do not fight wars with one another for structural and normative reasons, the advent of Chinese democracy would inevitably lead to peace between China and its major competitors such as Japan, the United States, and India—which are also democracies—as well as with the nascently democra-tizing states in Northeast and Southeast Asia. The intellectual logic of the claims associated with democratic peace, thus, makes the question of the natural longevity of the calculative strategy quite ir-relevant: If China democratizes, the competitive character of its cur-rent antagonisms toward Taiwan, Japan, Southeast Asia, the United States, and India largely disappears and, consequently, the calcula-tive strategy is inevitably and completely transformed into a coop-erative strategy similar to that followed by all other states in the so-called "zone of peace."

Even if the logic of democratic peace is unquestionable on both theoretical and empirical grounds, the problem of a possible shift in China's currently calculative strategy still remains relevant because of all the difficulties associated with the transition to democracy. If China becomes completely democratic, the question of adversarial

---

[25]See, for example, Krauthammer (1995).

relations between itself and its neighbors may well disappear,[26] but until that point is reached, however, the issue of how changes in the current regime affect the propensity for conflict and cooperation remains both real and relevant. As Mansfield and Snyder have argued,

> countries do not become democracies overnight. More typically, they go through a rocky transitional period, where democratic control over foreign policy is partial, where mass politics mixes in a volatile way with authoritarian elite politics, and where democratization suffers reversals. In this transitional phase of democratization, countries become more aggressive and war-prone, not less, and they do fight wars with democratic states.[27]

The question of transitioning to democracy acquires special currency in the case of China only because, despite the arguments offered by many critics of the present regime in Beijing, the Chinese have experienced a nontrivial movement toward democracy since 1978. To be sure, this "democratization" has not resulted in the one measure of reform so central to democrats in the West—periodic free and open elections—but it has nonetheless precipitated significant structural changes that have both altered previous patterns of elite politics and increased the forms and extent of mass participation in political life.

This process of regime transformation is significant from the viewpoint of Chinese grand strategy because its introduction of a new class of winners and losers in domestic politics and of a new set of pressures and incentives on political elites as a whole could portend a transformation in the way Beijing views its role in the world and in the means by which it fulfills that aspiration. This process will almost certainly be neither benign nor trouble-free and Mansfield

---

[26]The persuasiveness of the "democratic peace" argument will be discussed in greater detail below.

[27]Mansfield and Snyder (1995), p. 5. This finding has been challenged by Wolf (1996); Weede (1996); and Thompson and Tucker (1997). See also the rejoinder by Mansfield and Snyder (1996b). These arguments, centered considerably on methodological issues, cannot be adjudicated here and, consequently, Mansfield and Snyder's arguments are employed not necessarily as an endorsement of their theoretical fitness but because they provide plausible descriptions of how a democratizing China could behave in destabilizing ways in the future.

and Snyder have in fact argued with solid supporting evidence that "states that make the biggest leap in democratization *from total autocracy to extensive mass democracy* are about twice as likely to fight wars in the decade after democratization as are states that remain autocracies."[28] If this assertion is true, it is not difficult to see why the question of domestic, especially regime, change becomes so relevant to the future of the calculative strategy and why it is essential to examine the contours of that change in China and assess whether it could produce the instability and war that scholarship often warns about when speaking about the process of democratic transition.

In general, there are four basic mechanisms through which the democratization process can lead to conflict. First, the transition to democracy, being essentially tentative and evolutionary, tends to generate relatively infirm institutions that create opportunities for authoritarian groups (or entrenched authoritarian elites) to pursue policies that would not be ratified by the populace in more mature democracies. Second, the process of democratization creates new winners and losers in the political realm, thereby generating complementary incentives for losers to arrest their loss of internal power through external adventures and for winners to protect their gains by any means necessary, including war. Third, the competitive jostling for advantage between survivors from the ancient regime and the new elites often precipitates external attention, aid, and occasionally direct intervention, as the foreign allies of both groups seek to resolve the ongoing struggle on terms favorable to their own interests. Fourth, and finally, the chaotic processes of democratization create new "ideational spaces" where radical ideologies, which might not have survived under more normal political conditions, can feed off existing discontent and grow into political movements that survive mainly by belligerence and the threat of war.[29]

Whether any of these mechanisms, or a combination thereof, could actually manifest themselves in China and affect either the duration or the evolution of the calculative strategy depends fundamentally on the *character* of the democratization process currently taking place. Assessing this issue requires a brief analysis of (a) the restruc-

---

[28]Mansfield and Snyder (1995), p. 6.

[29]These processes are explored in Mansfield and Snyder (1995), pp. 26–34.

turing of governing institutions, including the patterns of intra-elite competition and civil-military relations; (b) the role of the new winners and losers in the current economic and political reform process; (c) the external linkages and constituencies supporting various contentious groups within China; and (d) the prospects for the reemergence of an "ideology of order" and its effect on both domestic politics and external relations.

The process of economic reform and opening up to the outside under way since the late 1970s, the simultaneous passing of China's founding revolutionary generation of charismatic leaders, and the Chinese state's increasing reliance on economic growth for political legitimacy and domestic order have together precipitated major changes in institutional structures and relationships and in past patterns of intra-elite competition and contention, leadership selection, and policy formulation and implementation. The demands for greater predictability and efficiency of a market-led, outward-oriented pattern of economic development and the emergence of a new leadership generation of relatively noncharismatic "bureaucratic technocrats" with specialized party or government experience have created a generally risk-averse style of leadership politics that places a premium on consultation, pragmatism, and policy performance. These imperatives have gradually led to reductions in the overall power of centralized party structures; extended the influence of state administrative institutions at all levels; increased functional distinctions among military, government, and party institutions; and generally strengthened the authority of formal administrative institutions and processes over informal, personal and ideological bases of power. They have also produced a more regularized, codified structure of leadership selection and removal and increased proscriptions on the use of force or unilateral leadership decisions to resolve both power and policy conflicts.[30]

The reforms, generational change, and an increasing emphasis on economic growth have also brought about major changes in civil-military relations. In particular, the process of professionalization and institutionalization evident across the party-state structure,

---

[30]For a general discussion of the reform process and its effect on the Chinese polity, see Harding (1987); Lieberthal and Lampton (1992); and Lieberthal (1995), especially Part Three, pp. 155–240, and pp. 314–330.

combined with the passing of many revolutionary military elders, is creating a more professional military, separate and distinct in function and outlook from civilian institutions and less-willing and less-able to intervene in senior leadership politics. China's military leadership is becoming more concerned, as a group, with protecting and advancing its professional, institutional interests, particularly force modernization for national defense and the maintenance of domestic order. In other words, top military leaders are less concerned with influencing the balance of power at the top of the party-state system than with ensuring that the policies passed by that system preserve their professional interests.[31]

Despite such major developments, strong resistance remains within many sectors of Chinese society and especially among China's political and military leadership to (a) the emergence of genuinely autonomous political, social, and economic power centers outside the control of the central party-state apparatus; (b) the establishment of a genuinely independent legal system that protects the interests of individual citizens against arbitrary acts of repression and coercion by the state; and, in general, (c) an acceptance of the importance of overt and institutionalized forms of political competition to China's future growth and stability.[32] In effect, most Chinese leaders believe that the continued high levels of economic growth deemed necessary for regime legitimacy, social stability, and the creation of a strong and prosperous state can be sustained primarily by expanding and deepening the existing process of marketization and administrative reform, without encouraging or permitting significantly greater levels of political openness.[33] The military in particular serves both as a

---

[31]For a comprehensive assessment of the changing structures and roles of the Chinese military during the reform era, see Shambaugh and Yang (1997), especially the chapters by Shambaugh, Joffe, Swaine, and Dreyer.

[32]This is not to deny that a kind of "shadow pluralism" exists in the Chinese political process in which the success of official policies increasingly depends upon the consent of institutions and groups that have their own resources and are less dependent on the party-state apparatus. However, the Communist Party leadership has thus far granted these new social forces little formal recognition or institutionalized access to the political system. See White (1994), pp. 75–76.

[33]As one Chinese observer states, the main goals of political reform in China today include (1) the enhancement of the (administrative) legal system, (2) the elimination of government interference in economic enterprises, (3) the reduction and simplification of bureaucratic structures, (4) the improvement of democratic monitoring sys-

stimulus for continued market-led economic growth[34] and as a brake on pressures for greater political liberalization.

Because of such elite resistance and the continued successes of China's economic reform program, the political reform process over the near to mid term will probably not, in and of itself, generate a fundamental change in the regime's basic adherence to the calculative strategy. It is possible that a severe and prolonged economic decline could lead to the collapse of the communist regime and the emergence of forces supportive of democratic change over such a time period. However, it is very unlikely that even these developments would result in a genuinely democratic polity. An intense fear of chaos, the absence of coherent civilian institutional alternatives to the Communist Party, the weakness of socioeconomic organizations capable of formulating and channeling nonstate interests, suspicions of foreign manipulation and subversion, and the presence of a generally conservative and increasingly professional military all suggest that it is far more likely that economically induced social chaos would lead to either a more repressive, insecure Chinese state or a complete collapse of central authority and a prolonged period of political disorder.[35]

At the same time, the very processes of economic development and reform and the concomitant emergence of a new leadership generation with greater ties to the outside are undoubtedly generating more complex and internally cohesive social, bureaucratic, and economic groups with interests separate from those of the ruling Communist Party leadership. Over the long term, continued administrative rationalization, marketization, and privatization, along with a deepening of involvement with outside economic entities, will undoubtedly sharpen the contradiction between the forces of social, economic, and political pluralism and the restrictions pre-

---

tems, (5) the maintenance of stability and unity, and (6) the development of so-called "democracy with Chinese characteristics." See Liu (1997), p. 9.

[34]Military support for continued marketization stems not only from its commitment to force modernization but also from its direct involvement in business activities, undertaken to augment the insufficient revenues it receives from the government. See Mulvenon (1998). This arguably holds true today despite recent efforts to remove the military from business.

[35]For a more detailed discussion of such scenarios and their implications for Chinese foreign policy, see Swaine (1995b), pp. 104–109.

sented by a largely rigid, monolithic power structure. As a result, the Chinese state will likely confront increasing social pressures to redefine the rules of the game and reshape China's key political institutions to maintain economic efficiency and productivity and more effectively handle a variety of social problems arising from extensive economic development and reform.[36]

The intensity of such pressures and hence the degree of urgency in responding to them will likely depend, first, on economic factors. If the regime is experiencing a serious economic decline, but not a wholesale collapse, formerly satisfied social and economic groups will likely demand greater influence over the policy process, and the leadership will likely be more inclined to undertake some type of significant political reforms as a means of averting further economic decline and social unrest. Even in the absence of economic decline, however, it is likely that the ongoing development and reform processes in themselves will eventually require efforts at more extensive political restructuring.[37] However, rather than introduce far-reaching democratic reforms, which would almost certainly be viewed as an invitation to chaos (especially if the economy were in decline), China's leaders will more likely be compelled, over the long term, to establish a version of an authoritarian, corporatist state, in which (a) organically formed social and economic groups (e.g., industrial labor, business, and agricultural associations) are formally recognized and granted significant, albeit limited, roles in the political and policy process, (b) existing political institutions such as the People's Representative Congresses are given greater authority, (c) government and party involvement in economic activities is severely curtailed, and (d) a more formalized relationship is established between central and local governments that reflects the realities of growing local power. In this system, some significant level of institutional

---

[36]White (1994), p. 76.

[37]Specifically, requirements for attaining more advanced levels of economic development, including greater access to information and technologies, more freedom to innovate, and a greater ability to respond quickly and efficiently to changes in market demands, combined with a growing need to channel and coopt various social pressures arising from such development (e.g., worker unemployment and displacements), will likely increase pressures to cede more genuine decisionmaking power and authority to an increasingly larger number and variety of socioeconomic actors. Such increasingly influential nonstate groupings will, in turn, likely demand greater influence over those political, social, and economic policies that determine their fate.

pluralization would likely exist, but ultimate power would almost certainly remain in the hands of the Communist Party, whose national leadership would not be determined by open and competitive elections nor fundamentally constrained by an independent judicial authority.[38] Moreover, such a relatively "autonomous," growth-oriented regime would likely place a great emphasis on beliefs associated with "developmental nationalism" (rather than legal or democratic concepts) to legitimize its efforts.[39] In short, the Chinese state would most likely attempt to reduce the tensions between the newly emergent forces of pluralization and the existing political-economic structure by implementing a set of middle-range political reforms loosely associated with the Chinese notion of "new authoritarianism" (*xinquanweizhuyi*).[40]

This process of incremental political adaptation to emergent socioeconomic forces could extend over many decades, if properly handled and assuming reasonably high rates of economic growth. However, the enormous challenges posed by the need to simultaneously adapt to a diversity of new socioeconomic interests with growing power and influence, assuage the concerns of older party, government, and military elites, and maintain relatively high growth rates suggest that an authoritarian developmental regime would likely confront a variety of increasingly severe political and social problems over the long term that could hold significant implications for the longevity of the calculative strategy. For example, rifts over

---

[38]Efforts to divert and deflate political opposition by granting a limited role to opposition parties could occur under this political system, but true power-sharing would likely be excluded, for reasons already cited.

[39]The full contours of such a significant, yet limited, political reform agenda are discussed by White (1994), pp. 75–77, 89–90. In sum, they include "the separation of the Party from the state administration, the removal or weakening of Party organizations within enterprises, the radical reduction of direct official controls over economic activity, measures to bring about the internal restructuring of the Party itself, reform of existing 'mass organizations,' and greater space for autonomous organizations in 'civil society'" (p. 90).

[40]This viewpoint, espoused by a variety of Chinese intellectuals, advocates a *gradual* transition toward full-fledged democracy through a staged, centrally directed process involving the introduction of a market economy that changes the balance of power between state and society, the gradual expansion of the space available for the organized expression of socioeconomic interests, and the incremental introduction of forms of democratic participation, representation, and competition. See White (1994), p. 87, and footnote 14, which presents various Chinese sources for "new authoritarianism."

power distribution and policy issues would likely emerge (and grow in intensity) between party reformers and representatives of other influential political forces, including democratic activists, state and military institutional interests, and representatives of key social groups. These contending elites would likely use quasi-autonomous institutional power bases, links to various influential social strata, and even foreign entities (such as Western business or democratic groups) to advance their positions. Moreover, in the absence of the legitimizing and constraining functions provided by a full-blown democratic system and legal infrastructure, some elites would probably attempt to employ chauvinistic brands of nationalism to strengthen their position, including appeals to antiforeign sentiments. Some elites might even be tempted to provoke external conflicts. This would be especially likely under conditions of low economic growth, given the tremendous reliance of the regime on "developmental nationalism" for its legitimacy. Even in the absence of poor economic performance, efforts by an authoritarian developmental state to impose tough economic and social decisions regarding issues of poverty, insecurity, distribution, and sovereignty could pit reformers against populists. In such a climate, citizens might increasingly view the state's limited political reform efforts as a form of self-serving, elitist corruption and thus might support politicians who reject greater political and economic reform and openness in the name of populist nationalism.[41]   In this context, the age-old Chinese domestic leadership debate between autonomy and foreign involvement could come into play with a vengeance. Moreover, the role of the military in these developments would likely prove decisive. It could alternatively serve to ensure the continuity of political and economic reform, to bolster the forces of popular nationalism, or, if internally divided, to permit (or accelerate) a descent into chaos.

Such growing political fissures and conflicts could thus result in erratic shifts in the external policies of the Chinese state, between periods of calculative and assertive behavior, or, alternatively, in a wholesale and prolonged period of more aggressive behavior or even chaos, especially under conditions of economic disarray. However, all of the above suggests that such potentially disruptive politically

---

[41]McCormick (1994), especially pp. 109–110. Also see McCormick (1990).

induced behaviors are far more likely to occur over the very long term, and not during the near or mid term, i.e., before 2015–2020.

When the above three variables affecting the longevity of the calculative strategy are considered synoptically, it is possible to argue that *barring external perturbations* Beijing's present calculative orientation will endure for some time to come. This pragmatic course, which emphasizes increased, multidimensional, interaction with the West coupled with an economy of force toward its regional neighbors, is by no means a product either of high-mindedness or of an ideological conversion to a worldview centered on the primacy of reason over force and the desire for cooperative security. Rather, it is emphatically a *realist* strategy deriving from a shrewd recognition of China's still substantial political, economic, and military weakness. So long as these weaknesses persist, it is unlikely that the calculative strategy would be perceived as having entered the zone of diminishing returns and the analysis undertaken in this section clearly suggests that China's many weaknesses will not be redressed in any fundamental way before the 2015–2020 timeframe. Assuming that present trends hold, it is only during this timeframe *at the very earliest* that the Chinese economy would *begin* to rival the U.S. economy in size, diversity, and orientation and that the Chinese military will acquire the wherewithal to mount credible denial threats aimed at its strongest regional adversaries such as the United States, Japan, and India, while simultaneously maintaining a modicum of control or exploitative power over smaller competitors such as Taiwan, Vietnam, and the Southeast Asian states. Although disturbances in domestic politics (especially major upheavals brought on by severe economic problems) could no doubt occur at any point between now and the year 2020, the analysis above suggests that it is unlikely that the process of democratization *despite being mainly illiberal* could lead to any radical shift in the calculative strategy in the interim, largely because the evolving institutions of rule, the dominant leadership and social groups in the Chinese polity together with their foreign supporters, and the new intellectual and ideological forces unleashed by the reform process all profit from the success of the calculative approach—at least until such time as China acquires comprehensive great power capabilities.

The structural factors, all taken together, then suggest that the calculative phase of China's grand strategy will be relatively long and drawn out and, by 2020, will already have been in play for about 40 years. This fact ought to be borne in mind whenever any discussions about "the coming conflict with China"[42] take center stage in political discourse: China today is a weak country and although it may still challenge the United States and its regional neighbors on various issue-areas in the near term, these challenges for the most part would be driven mainly by a desire to stave off potential losses and in many cases may be precipitated by the actions of other states. The other kinds of challenges that China could mount—challenges driven either by a desire for extended acquisitive gains or by a quest for control over the global system—are arguably still a long time away and would not occur except as part of a systemic "power transition" taking place at the core of the global system.

This transition, which results from episodic structural "shifts in the international distribution of power,"[43] probably would not begin to arise in the case of China and the United States before the next two decades, if at all. This is also corroborated by Modelski and Thompson's pioneering work on long cycles in international politics, which suggests that the next "macrodecision" relating to leadership in the global system would not emerge before 2030 when measured by current estimates of long-term economic growth interpreted in terms of Kondratieff waves interacting with cycles of hegemonic change.[44] *If* one believes that global stability and economic growth currently derive from the presence of the United States as the world's *sole* superpower, then the United States no doubt has to prepare for this possibility right away—including doing all in its power to prevent such a transition from successfully coming to pass—but a passing of hegemonic leadership to China is by no means either inevitable or imminent. Although the uninterrupted success of Beijing's calculative strategy (and the high growth rates that accompany it) will no doubt ensure its inevitability over time, a great deal depends on what the United States does or does not do in the interim.[45] *At the very least, if secular trends hold, this transition is not*

---

[42]Bernstein and Munro (1997) make this point in their recent book with this title.

[43]Organski and Kugler (1980), p. 4.

[44]Modelski and Thompson (1996), pp. 4–10.

[45]This point is made correctly—and most emphatically—in Nye (1991).

imminent and though the analysis in this chapter dates it out to about 2015–2020 or thereabouts—at the very earliest—it may in fact be postponed even further (or may never take place at all) depending on developments both within the United States and in the Asian region at large.

In fact, even the circa 2015–2020 time point represents the earliest moment *of a longer time interval* when the achievement of economic primacy by China would begin to slowly interact with the continued accretion of more effective military capability. Thus, it is best understood, if all goes well for Beijing in the interim, as the *beginning* of an extended phase during which rising Chinese power will slowly be consolidated, and not as a magic threshold through which a hegemonic China dramatically appears *deus ex machina* the following year. Needless to say, the period leading up to this point, and the current calculative strategy that goes with it, may extend considerably longer if Beijing faces a slowdown in its historically high rates of growth, or experiences difficulty in shifting from its export-led strategy to a domestically driven pattern of growth, or confronts an environment of continued U.S. global and regional strength, or experiences national convulsions relating to the management of domestic political, economic or social change; or undergoes a significant internal regime transformation that institutionalizes liberal democracy over time. This last development will not obviate the problems of a global power transition, but it may attenuate its most destabilizing characteristics, including the propensity for war.[46]

Again, none of this implies that China's interim calculative strategy will be problem-free and that all conflicts, should they arise, would occur only in the wider context of a global power transition. A variety of altercations over Taiwan, Tibet, the Spratlys, proliferation, trade, and market access could still occur in the near term, but these would be mainly "normal" disputes as opposed to "systemic" conflicts, that is, disputes pertaining to the contested issue at hand, rather than explicit or implicit struggles over control of the international system. To be sure, even such "normal" disputes, if they occur with great intensity and result in significant Chinese losses, could result in a shift from the presently dominant calculative strategy and, over time,

---

[46]This point is discussed in greater detail below.

precipitate a frantic Chinese effort to increase its military capabilities to acquire those permanent power-political advantages that would immunize it against the worst depredations imaginable. If the normal disputes identified above lead to such an outcome, they will have succeeded in transforming what are otherwise routine competitive transactions between states into a more significant and consequential rivalry over leadership of the international system. Under such conditions, Beijing may alter its current calculative strategy much faster than was earlier anticipated with the intent of preventing further losses, if not securing outright gains. Such relatively sudden, aggressive shifts in Chinese security behavior have, in fact, occurred in the past, in response to intensified confrontations with the outside. Should these aberrations not occur, however, it is most likely that the calculative strategy will persist for at least another two decades and that the really interesting and critical issues of great power competition, including possible conflict to determine the dominant power in the system, will not begin to manifest themselves before that time.

BEYOND THE CALCULATIVE STRATEGY

If it is assumed that China's calculative strategy continues uninterrupted and without mishap for the next two—perhaps several—decades, the question of what replaces it over the long term becomes an issue of great relevance. This question becomes particularly interesting because the initial premises that underlay the strategy—China's relative weakness and its general dependence on the external environment for continued economic growth—may not continue to remain salient during this time period. Thus, if it is assumed (a) that China's economic growth continues more or less uninterrupted, (b) that this growth becomes largely self-sustaining because it has successfully shifted to an internal strategy of exploiting its domestic markets, and (c) that China's rate of growth generally remains higher than the rates of growth experienced by its competitors, the need for continued reliance on a calculative strategy would becomes less pressing because the constraints imposed by external dependence would gradually diminish at about the time when Beijing was continuing to experience a substantial accretion of relative national power. The assumption that China's economic growth both continues uninterrupted and is higher than that enjoyed by its competitors is crucial because the issue of what replaces the calculative strategy becomes interesting only if China acquires those comprehensive national capabilities that signal a *systemic disequilibrium* arising from a differential growth of power among the key entities in the international system.[47]

If China acquires this level of national capabilities—such that a power transition at the core of the global system becomes possible— what would Beijing's grand strategy turn out to be? Clearly, it is unlikely to persist with the calculative strategy because this strategy, being born primarily of weakness and dependence, will have transformed the circumstances that generated it and, thus, will have outlived its necessity and usefulness. At this point, the calculative strategy will slowly atrophy and be transmuted into another strategy that better comports with China's new power and capabilities. What would this successor strategy be? At least three alternative strategies are possible: a chaotic China, a cooperative China, or an assertive China.

The Irony of Success: A Chaotic China?

At least one distinguished observer has, in effect, argued that the international system will never be confronted with the challenges of such a power transition because China's emerging success will only lead to "a terminal crisis within the next 10 to 15 years."[48] The making of this crisis, which has been described as nothing less than the "coming Chinese collapse,"[49] is seen by such observers as having multidimensional causes that span the economic, social, and political realms. At the economic level, for example, the high Chinese growth rates that could lead to a global power transition are seen to be absolutely unsustainable over time because they rely on an "extensive" strategy involving increasingly larger injections of factor inputs rather than an "intensive" strategy that exploits rapid improvements in factor productivity. Moreover, China's pace of growth is seen to incur diminishing returns over time primarily because of

---

[47]The assumption, for instance, underlying Dibb (1995).

[48]Goldstone (1995).

[49]Goldstone (1995), p. 35.

capital rather than labor shortages. These capital shortages would only be exacerbated because the current approach of relying on export-led growth for capital accumulation would require that the United States incur a trade deficit of about $6,000 billion by the year 2020—almost 48 percent of its GDP—simply to sustain the present trend in China. Not only would such mechanisms of accumulation be unsustainable in a political sense, they would also be increasingly unsustainable in an economic sense since—under these assumptions—diminished U.S. prosperity would slowly choke off the market for Chinese goods and products over time.[50] Once other considerations such as the burdens of China's state-owned enterprises, the fragility of its banking system, and the limitations of its technology base are factored in, the Chinese inability to fuel a power transition on economic grounds alone seems to be a conviction held by most pessimistic analysts.

The dilemmas at the social level are seen to exacerbate the economic difficulties alluded to above. Here, the rising regional disparities between the coastal and inland provinces, coupled with the increasingly pervasive corruption seen at all levels in Chinese society, is viewed as preparing the way for consequential challenges to regime legitimacy and in the limiting case, even civil war.[51] Even if such outcomes can be avoided, the pessimists argue that China's successes cannot be sustained: The continuing growth in the absolute size of the population, the peculiarity of its demographic composition, including the large youthful population combined with a dramatic shortage of females (due to high female infanticide and abortion of female children), and the problems of shifting a high proportion of the rural population into the urban sector are seen as making for substantial social chaos, not to mention consequential economic interruptions.[52] The interaction of these two realms is seen to be increasingly problematic as Chinese agriculture is viewed as having entered the stage of unsustainable development: looming food shortages are anticipated, with China's grain deficit in the year 2030 estimated to be nearly double the global reserves of grain avail-

---

[50]Gunter (1998).

[51]See Kaye (1995b) for a good overview of some of these problems.

[52]Mulvenon (1997b).

able in 1994;[53] a significant shortage of potable water is also forecast as the water table appears to be falling at the rate of almost one meter per year in the northern parts of China; and massive environmental degradation is assessed as affecting agricultural output and public health, even leading to international disputes. In fact, one analysis, assessing all these factors insofar as they affect the carrying capacity of the land, concluded that "the long-term strategic goal of China's population policy should be to limit the population below one billion, or ideally, below 700 million,"[54] clearly an estimate some distance away from the 1.6 to 1.7 billion people China is expected to have in the 2020+ timeframe.

The political challenges are also perceived to be both daunting and unmanageable. Despite the clear success of the Chinese economy in the past 20 years, the pessimists note that the central government has been increasingly unable to siphon off the growing wealth proportionately through taxation, thereby resulting in the new elites being able to progressively undercut the regime's own power and preferences.[55] This problem, caused by the rise of new power centers in China with all the threats they embody for cohesion and unity, is exacerbated by fundamental disputes within the ruling regime itself. These disputes center on the degree of control sought to be maintained over the economy, polity, and society; the pace of change; and the appropriate methods of change.[56] The future of the PLA, its relationship to the party, and the dilemmas afflicting its principal missions—defense of the country against external threats, or defense of the party against internal opposition, or defense of the populace against arbitrary government—all make the looming crisis of governability even more treacherous and burdensome.[57] Finally, the decline in the party's direct control over society; the increasing discontent within its traditional bastions of support, the peasants and workers; and the rise of a new generation of successful social elites who care little for the party or the traditional communist regime are

---

[53]Brown (1995).

[54]Cohen (1995), p. 224.

[55]Shirk (1993).

[56]Kaye (1995a).

[57]For an excellent analysis of China's current civil-military dynamic, see Joffe (1996). See also Paltiel (1995).

all together seen as producing a situation where "fiscal decay at the center, conflicts among elites, and the rise of banditry and war-lordism along the periphery" reproduce conditions analogous to the periods of decay in imperial China, conditions that, it is concluded, "the latest 'dynasty' [in Beijing] appears unlikely to break."[58]

With these assessments, the pessimists among China analysts would argue that the calculative strategy, whatever its virtues, will inevitably terminate, at best, in a chaotic and, at worst, in a collapsing China, understood either as the systemic atrophy of the state or the fissi-parous fracturing of the polity, with non-Han regions such as Tibet, Xinjiang, and Mongolia eventually breaking away. Far from prepar-ing for an inevitable power transition where China would challenge the United States for regional and global leadership as a result of its continuing economic growth and distension in military power, the real challenge for Washington, according to this school, consists of "how best to anticipate [China's] collapse and prevent it from triggering international crises."[59] The possibility of a meltdown in China after four or more decades of high economic growth would certainly turn out to be anticlimactic, representing a rare oddity in international history. The only example of such an outcome in modern times would probably be the Shah's Iran, where a rapid surge in wealth and power occurred only to be consummated in a traumatic revolutionary collapse. A similar outcome in China would be simply catastrophic, in part because of the gigantic scale of the problem (compared to Iran), in part because of the much deeper levels of Western involvement (in all areas of activity), and in part because a candidate great power armed with nuclear weaponry (as opposed to merely a regional power) is involved. A collapsing, or even a chaotic, China thus makes for frightening international challenges that simply bedevil the imagination.[60]

---

[58]Goldstone (1995), p. 51. As discussed in Chapter Three, downward spirals of eco-nomic decline, elite corruption and contention, and social decay and unrest almost invariably preceded the collapse of Chinese states in the past.

[59]Goldstone (1995), p. 52.

[60]Waldron (1995b). Some Western (and perhaps some Chinese) observers believe that a Chinese collapse would likely result in the rise of a democratic China and should thus be viewed as a positive development to be encouraged or even promoted by for-eign governments. However, a Chinese collapse would far more likely result in chaos and perhaps even civil war, as suggested above. Hence, efforts to encourage govern-

Fortunately, this outcome today is judged by most sinologists to be a remote possibility and, in any event, the reasons for such judgments and the debates between the pessimists and the optimists over the future of China cannot be either evaluated or settled here.[61] The possibility of a chaotic or collapsing China must simply be acknowledged and the fact that it might not occur must also be confronted. In fact, if the latter outcome obtains *as most sinologists today believe,* the question set out earlier only demands further examination: What replaces the calculative strategy eventually if China's relatively rapid rate of growth in national power continues for several decades and does not result in any collapse in the interim? If this question is taken as the focus of the heuristic exercise that follows, it is possible to argue that China's long-term choices lie between *cooperation* and *assertion,* if chaos and collapse are outcomes ruled out of bounds for analytic purposes. These choices are identified mainly on the basis of certain theoretical conceptions of how the international system is constituted and operates and they also draw from historical evidence of how other rising powers have behaved in the past and from observations about the historical behavior of strong Chinese states presented in Chapter Three. Although this may not be the ideal methodology for discerning China's future grand strategic trajectories, it is nonetheless the best procedure available to scholars and policy analysts today. It allows for adducing fairly coherent and systematic expectations of how China might behave—expectations that can be progressively refuted over time based on how Beijing's actions actually turn out.

The Triumph of Reason: A Cooperative China?

The competing notions of a "cooperative" and "assertive" China are meant to convey certain "ideal types," since it is not possible to describe any political entity so far out into the future in detail. Both ideal types are intended to depict some stark, central characteristics of a possible China and its derivative behaviors. Both assume that

---

ments to promote a Chinese collapse are reckless and irresponsible. Moreover, the costs of a collapsing China are inestimable, thus making it worthless as a policy option. For a further discussion of the precipitants of collapse in China and its consequences for Chinese external policy, see Swaine (1995b), pp. 104–109.

[61]Nye (1997).

China has completed its economic reform program successfully and that it has acquired the kind of power capabilities associated with true great powers, but each provides a radically different vision of both the direction in which China may proceed and the ends to which its newly acquired power is directed.

A cooperative China is essentially one that became, and behaved like, a Kantian entity in world politics, i.e., a liberal, democratic, polity. As any other such state, it would consider itself bound by, and obligated to pursue, standards of behavior that are conceived and defended in terms of a transcendentally grounded conception of universal human rights and mutual obligations.[62] The core of the liberal regime is centered fundamentally on a "respect for persons," that is, a belief in the proposition that individuals are to be always treated as the subjects rather than as the objects of action. In international relations, the principle of "respect for persons" translates itself into the right of states to be "free from foreign intervention."[63] As Michael Doyle succinctly summed up this logic, "since morally autonomous citizens hold rights to liberty, the states that democratically represent them have the right to exercise political independence."[64] In other words, liberal states, respecting the autonomy of their own citizens, would by extension not interfere with the rights of other similarly constituted states. They might interfere with, and in fact even prosecute, wars with other nonliberal states, but among liberal states, a "zone of peace, a pacific union"[65] would ostensibly obtain "despite numerous particular conflicts of economic and strategic interest."[66] It is important to recognize that the existence of a pacific union does not imply the absence of interstate rivalry or disagreement; it implies only that whatever these conflicts, they shall not be resolved by any "self-regarding" solutions such as war— solutions that inherently embody a large-scale abridgment of respect for others.

---

[62]The transcendental foundation of Kant's liberalism is discussed systematically in Reiss (1995).

[63]Doyle (1983), p. 213.

[64]Doyle (1983).

[65]Doyle (1983).

[66]Doyle (1983), p. 214.

Although such respect is no doubt accorded only to fraternal democratic peers (and not to nondemocratic competitors), a cooperative, democratic China would nonetheless be good news as far as the United States is concerned because its entry into the liberal union would result in a sharp diminution of the war-proneness that could otherwise accompany China's rise as a great power.[67] A cooperative China—even though notionally still a potential challenger in power transition terms—would thus not only engender pacific relations with the dominant power, the United States, but would also produce cordial intercourse with the other great powers in the international system, all of whom happen to be—luckily—liberal democratic states as well. A cooperative China, in this context, would display several distinguishing characteristics as far as international politics is concerned. To begin with, it would be generally acceptant of the prevailing international order into which it entered. This acceptance would be centered principally on the recognition that an international order that respected the rights of persons—even if initially U.S. dominated—would be in China's interests so long as it allowed for the cultivation of profitable personal and social relations that contributed to enhancing the utility and welfare of both Chinese citizens and the Chinese state. In these circumstances, even those facets of the prevailing system that were incongruent with Beijing's interests would cease to be bothersome to China as they would be altered eventually in one of two ways: either through evolutionary, market-centered mechanisms that allowed China's relatively greater economic power to produce outcomes that reflected its own preferences over time, or through more deliberate mechanisms such as international institutional rules and organizations that would alter the existing structures of advantage in a direct and considered way as a natural consequence of China's growing geopolitical weight.

Further, a cooperative China would strongly emphasize interdependence and collective security. These twin emphases would naturally grow—in terms of liberal logic—from both ideological and pragmatic considerations. Interdependence would be deemed essential for the continued vitality of the pacific union as more complete specialization and the growing density of interactions, economic and political,

---

[67]As Betts phrased this argument, "what is good for China turns out to be good for everyone." Betts (1993/94), p. 55.

would serve to strengthen the union both in absolute terms and against its potential adversaries and to increase the costs of defection. This strengthening, in turn, would enlarge the union as more states seeing the fruits of interdependence seek to join the liberal zone of peace—by engineering internal transformations if necessary—thus contributing to an increased level of pacificity throughout the international system. The emphasis on collective security, though distinct from interdependence, becomes a natural corollary to interdependence in the economic realm.   The elimination of self-regarding solutions such as war, at least within the pacific union, creates the opportunity for broader conceptions of security where an attack on one state can be treated as an attack on all. Such responses, which aim at producing "automatic obligations of a collective character,"[68] would generally result in a low *individual* propensity by each state to use force as a means of settling international disputes, perhaps even those involving nondemocratic states. This reticence to use force in an autonomous fashion not only bestows great economic benefits to every liberal state, but it also results in the creation of a formidable collective defense capability despite the reduction in military burdens borne by any *individual* state. The ideological commitment to *posse comitatus* thus neatly dovetails with practical advantages of reduced national defense burdens stemming from collective security arrangements.

Finally, a cooperative China would display a conspicuous willingness to seek joint gains rather than unilateral advantage. This disavowal of the traditional strategy of seeking unilateral advantage derives simply from the recognition that no benefits accrue to such a strategy in the zone of peace. In an environment of turmoil, unilateral gains are valuable and ought to be pursued because they give their possessors advantageous capabilities that can be transformed into military instruments. These military instruments provide great benefits in a world of security competition where threats to life and property are endemic. If security competition ceases to exist, however, as it ostensibly does within the pacific union of states, the pursuit of unilateral advantage is irrational and possibly counterproductive. It is irrational because, in a realm where interstate competition is mostly economic, the notion of relative gains quickly becomes

---

[68]Morgenthau (1968), p. 296.

irrelevant. The search for relative gains cannot be sustained in strong form even in an environment where a zone of turmoil coexists with the zone of peace so long as the latter is stronger than the former, especially in military capabilities. Since the zone of peace presently and for the foreseeable future consists of the most powerful states in the international system, it is unlikely that China would need to pursue unilateral advantages on the grounds that it might be threatened by entities located in the zone of turmoil. Further, the pursuit of such a policy would undermine the collective security arrangements that liberal states have traditionally sought to create. To that degree, it would also be counterproductive because, by giving rise to suspicions about Beijing's intentions, it could destroy the trust and cohesion already existing within the zone of peace and thereby end up further threatening both Chinese security and the security of all other liberal states.

This depiction of a cooperative China represents a Weberian ideal type—that is, a pure, unadulterated, conceptual abstraction of a certain phenomenon—but it is nonetheless useful because it depicts a particular political orientation which, though unalloyed at the analytical level, could materialize through some approximation in reality. A cooperative China in practice would be generally a status quo as opposed to a revisionist power; it would value highly continued economic interdependence and would place greater faith in institutional as opposed to unilateral solutions for security; it would abjure the use of force whenever possible, relying on it only when its physical security is clearly and presently threatened; and, it would, in all its international affairs, place a premium on the attainment of joint gains to cement the underlying interests of all the major states as opposed to merely enhancing its own. If such a cooperative China, or some version of it, is at all possible, the critical question consists of explaining how and why such an outcome would be sustained in the face of the fact that Beijing has—by now—grown in power capabilities and could well choose to behave in a far more unilateral manner, as have past great powers in world politics.

In principle, four possible arguments could be adduced in support of the expectation that China would behave as a cooperative state even after it joins the ranks of the great powers. Each argument, either directly or by implication, suggests that, even after it acquires great power capabilities as a result of its present calculative strategy, China would have good reason to abjure "self-regarding" behaviors in world politics in favor of alternative "other-regarding" postures that increase peace and collective security.[69]

The first such argument in favor of a cooperative China is drawn from liberal theories that emphasize the value and pacifying effects of *economic interdependence.*[70] This argument asserts that since China's growth in capabilities was essentially a product of its participation in a liberal economic order—where commercial interdependence between states allowed its trade-driven growth to produce stupendous increases in economic wealth—there is little reason for Beijing to abandon such a fruitful strategy even after it acquires real great power status. This belief is grounded, in the first instance, on ``the expectation that China will need to pursue absolute gains simply to resolve its vast developmental problems *for a long time to come.* Since China's population will lack the living standards enjoyed by its contemporaries, even when Beijing becomes a consequential actor by most aggregative measures such as GNP, the size of military forces, and the like, the interdependence argument asserts that the pursuit of absolute gains would still continue so that trade-driven growth can enable the lowest deciles of China's population to be slowly absorbed into the ranks of its successful and wealthy citizenry.

Even after this point is reached, however, a strong form of the interdependence argument asserts that Beijing would continue to pursue absolute gains because there is no reason why a prosperous China should not want to be even more prosperous—that is, when measured by the benefits it obtains *when compared to itself under some alternative international regime.* This desire to be even more prosperous and even more successful than it was at that point in time—a presumption consistent with the liberal belief that human beings are incessantly concerned with improving material well-being—would compel China to become sensitive not only to the costs of alienating its trading partners but also to the minuscule benefits afforded by assertive postures involving military force in comparison to the more productive forms of international intercourse associated with trade,

---

[69]For a good reading of how differing versions of liberalism affect the prospects for peace, see Betts (1993/94).

[70]The classic statement of this position remains Russett (1967).

interdependence, and collective security. Both the high expected costs and the low expected benefits of noncooperation, therefore, conspire to keep Beijing's sociable posture on a fairly even keel because the alternative strategy of assertion would only result in diminished absolute gains, lowered economic growth, and increased suspicion and hostility throughout the international system, all of which taken together reduce the collective benefits enjoyed by all states and by implication also reduce the gains obtained by China itself.

The second argument for continued cooperation by China, even after it acquires true great power capabilities, is related to the economic interdependence argument but is quite distinct from it. This argument, centered on claims about *the changing nature of power in the international system*, asserts that the traditional assertiveness associated with great powers in the past is obsolete because power today derives less from the tools of violence and coercion than it does from the legitimacy, the effectiveness, and the strength of both domestic regimes and national governments within a country.[71] The reasons for such a transformation in international politics are numerous and vary from theorist to theorist. One scholar argues that the changing nature of power is produced by the obsolescence of war, an outcome which, even in its conventional variety, is brought about simply by the utter destructiveness of modern combat, thus making it completely useless as a tool of great power assertiveness.[72] Other commentators have divined the changing nature of power to be a function of the "postmodern states"[73] now inhabiting the international system. These states, infected with the viruses of individualism, cosmopolitanism, and prosperity, are seen to be part of what Machiavelli once called a "world grown effeminate"[74]—a world of lost *virtu* which heralds the rise of new powers that cannot nourish the internal restiveness required to fuel the machines necessary for war and expansion. Still other theorists argue that the changing nature of power derives from the diminishing returns now accruing to conquest and territorial acquisition. The growing disutility of *lebens-*

---

[71]Luard (1988).

[72]Mueller (1989).

[73]Buzan and Segal (1996).

[74]Machiavelli, II, 2.

raum in the modern period is supposed to set sharp limits on the utility of assertive strategies, since the international diffusion of science and technology, the possibility of knowledge-based increases in production at home, and the relative ease of trade and commerce over subjugation all combine to reduce the benefits produced by military might at least as far as the possibility of military conquest and occupation is concerned.[75]

Numerous other justifications for the belief in the changing nature of power may be adduced, but at bottom all such justifications are rooted in the central claim that "the costs, risks and difficulties in applying force are rising, while the benefits derived therefrom are declining."[76] This conviction more than any other underwrites the belief that all rising powers in the future will sustain greatness more as "trading states" than as the traditional imperialist entities of the past. China, too, will not be an exception to this rule. The examples of Germany and Japan today are already seen as evidence of how growing national power can manifest itself in cooperative international postures: both states have generally declined to engage in military expansion or pursue coercive uses of force; both states have used commerce, trade, and economic intercourse, as opposed to security competition, as a way to expand their national power; both states have sought to strengthen international regimes and institutions as a way to order global governance and increase their national security; and, finally, both states have declined to use "self-regarding" strategies for producing political safety in favor of collective security arrangements that emphasize joint gains in the form of "regulated, institutionalized balancing predicated on the notion of all against one."[77] Such behaviors, it may be argued, represent an alternative future for *all* rising powers and, consequently, China— which arguably has other good reasons for being a cooperative state[78]—may also come to define its greatness over time in terms

---

[75]Rosecrance (1986), pp. 13–14, 24–25.

[76]Orme (1997/98), p. 138.

[77]Kupchan and Kupchan (1995), p. 52.

[78]For many Chinese, these reasons include the apparent "fact" that China has historically abjured interfering in the internal affairs of foreign political entities, employed force against such entities only when its physical security was clearly and presently threatened, and generally rejected efforts at foreign expansion.

that accord with the changing notion of power manifested today by Germany and Japan.

The third reason for the belief that China would assume a cooperative posture even after it attains great power capabilities is rooted in the claims associated with the *nuclear revolution*.[79] Theorists who argue that nuclear weapons have radically transformed the fundamental ordering principles of international politics suggest that a resurgent China would be more cooperative than other great powers in the past simply because the presence of nuclear weapons sets sharp limits on the assertiveness that can be displayed by new rising powers. Because nuclear weapons have increased the costs of conflict to a point where mutual destruction awaits all entities involved in any systemic war, the most extreme forms of political assertiveness—unrestrained warfare that threatens the homeland of an adversary—have been sharply curtailed, at least as far as great and rising powers armed with nuclear weapons are concerned. Equally important, the possession of such weapons in the hands of all the key global powers implies that most rising states would be immunized against the worst depredations—such as preventive war—which may be contemplated by a declining dominant power. This immunity to ultimate destruction, then, prevents rising powers from having to actively thwart any military efforts that may be made by a declining dominant power to arrest the shifting balance of power: All such efforts will not only rapidly incur diminishing returns but may in fact accelerate the adverse power trends if they ultimately threaten the larger objective of economic and societal renewal facing the declining dominant power.

The presence of nuclear weapons, therefore, should make for remarkably peaceful power transitions, at least when viewed in historical terms. Implicitly, they should also make for significantly cooperative rising powers, since their presence implies that the latter, despite their growing capabilities, will be unable to decisively threaten other nuclear-armed states in the international system. By the same token, the extant great powers would be unable to decisively threaten the new rising powers either. This pacificity, brought about by fears of mutual assured destruction, is also seen to

---

[79]Jervis (1989).

engender other beneficial effects in that the horrendous dread of systemic conflict simultaneously serves to dampen both limited wars and crisis behavior for reasons that are linked to the unacceptable consequences of nuclear escalation. All these reasons, therefore, might be used to suggest that a Chinese ascent to great power capabilities might be less problematic than other power transitions in history: Being unable to make truly significant alterations in the global balance at the expense of other competing states, China would sooner or later discover the virtues of a cooperative posture, given that assertive policies would be unable to make any but the most peripheral gains.

The fourth and final argument for believing in a cooperative China, even after it acquires true great power status, is rooted in the expectations of the *democratic peace*. Although China is by no means democratic today, there is little doubt that a slow process of democratization has been under way since 1978. The sphere of personal freedoms has increased; the capricious exercise of state power has been reduced, especially as far as threats to the lives of Chinese citizens are concerned; and the development of institutions pertaining to the rule of law, the respect for property, the adjudication of disputes, and the exercise of power is gradually under way. If this process continues without interruption, it is possible that China would slowly acquire the accouterments of all democratic states even as it slowly grows in national power capabilities, thus producing at some point after about 2020 the happy conjunction of great power married to a substantially, if not fully, democratic regime.

This rise of China as a democratic great power could be held to presage a cooperative international posture for all the structural, if not normative, reasons usually associated with democratic peace. Among these would be the consolidation of internal institutional constraints on the power of the most important national leaders, the rise of formal or informal checks and balances within the Chinese government (especially between the Chinese Communist Party and the National Peoples' Congress and between the Communist Party and other emergent autonomous political parties), and the integration of mass political choices in matters affecting war and peace. Should such structural constraints develop within China, it is possible that Beijing would see its great power interests in broader terms, that is, in terms of maintaining a stable international order in concert with other democratic great powers rather than as a competitive struggle for securing certain narrow self-interests.

This possibility of a cooperative China would be reinforced if the structural factors identified above were complemented by other more normative factors. These include, at root, the enshrinement of a *liberal* tradition that centers on a transcendentally grounded "respect for persons." This tradition, which recognizes all individuals as "subjects" rather than as "objects" of social action, results in a universalistic tolerance of all human beings, their preferences, and their choices. As such, it makes the possibility of a cooperative China more robust, since the democratic peace that ensues is grounded not simply in the presence of institutional and legal constraints but in a fundamental reordering of the values held by all entities within the zone of peace. The enshrinement of normative factors thus avoids the problems that may be caused by the presence of *illiberal democracies* (i.e., polities with popular institutions and popular rule but not liberal beliefs and orientations), thereby ensuring that a cooperative China becomes possible by reason of inner necessity and belief rather than simply by accident or external constraint.[80] The presence of this condition during a previous power transition—involving Great Britain and the United States early in this century—is often believed to have contributed to peaceful change in the leadership of the international system and, assuming that China becomes as democratic as Great Britain and the United States currently are, advocates of democratic peace would expect a similarly peaceful power transition to occur sometime in the first half of the 21st century.

The Tyranny of Power: An Assertive China?

Although China could emerge from its calculative strategy as a cooperative power because it is steadily transformed into a liberal polity over time, it is equally possible that it could emerge as an assertive state fully cognizant of, and demanding, its prerogatives in interna-

---

[80]Moreover, a liberal democratic China would presumably provide a form of state legitimacy grounded in democratic institutions, popular participation, and liberal views that would reduce the temptation for elites to maintain state power through appeals to chauvinistic forms of nationalism or to engage in foreign adventures.

tional politics. Such a turn toward assertiveness could arise because of factors peculiar to the Chinese experience: its historical memory of past greatness and the desire to restore previous eminence; its determination to erase the painful legacy of a century of national humiliation; its desire to recreate the traditional sinocentric world order as a means of regulating the political and economic structures of super- and subordination; its belief that China's external security in the past was primarily assured by a strong state able to dominate or at the very least neutralize the strategic periphery; and so on.[81] But, it could also arise as a result of the normal competition in world politics that compels every state to continually seek increases in national power in an effort to preserve security. Since this competition takes place against the backdrop of "the uneven growth of power among states,"[82] it should not be surprising to find that rising powers often adopt assertive political postures as they struggle to restructure the existing international system to better support their own interests and claims.

Irrespective of which mechanism (or combination thereof) propels China's assertiveness, the shift toward a more assertive strategy—after the current calculative phase runs its course—remains more than just an academic possibility. It has in fact been the normal outcome where most rising powers in the past are concerned and today there is a broad consensus in realist international relations theory on why such assertive behavior occurs. Robert Gilpin summarized the explanation succinctly when he argued that the assertiveness of rising powers derives fundamentally from the

> increasing disjuncture between the existing governance of the system and the redistribution of power in the system. Although the hierarchy of prestige, the distribution of territory, the rules of the system, and the international distribution of labor continue to favor the traditional dominant power or powers, the power base on which the governance of the system ultimately rests has eroded because of differential growth and development among states. This disjunc-

---

[81]These factors, as well as other more specific historical features of China's security behavior discussed in Chapter Three, strongly suggest that the characterization of Chinese behavior summarized in footnote number 78 represents a significant distortion of the historical record.

[82]Gilpin (1988), p. 591.

ture among components of the international system creates challenges for the dominant states and opportunities for the rising
states in the system.[83]

Gilpin's argument, in effect, suggests that rising powers become assertive because assertion remains the principal means by which they
can reconfigure the existing international system—which hitherto
was configured and sustained by the interests of the extant dominant
power—to suit their own demands and preferences. Such assertiveness may in fact become necessary because both the extant dominant power and its allies—states that profit most from the prevailing
systemic arrangements—may decline to surrender their privileges
meekly and without resistance. Consequently, rising states often feel
compelled to engage in an assertive exercise of power because they
conclude that it is unlikely that they would receive the authority con-
sonant with their newfound capabilities as a simple matter of course.
The propensity for such assertiveness is usually reinforced by the
phenomenon of uncertainty in international politics, which leads
states to seek to accumulate power merely as a hedge against contingencies arising in an unknowable future. Assertive policies, therefore, are likely to be initiated and these policies would continue so
long as the marginal costs of change do not exceed or equal the
benefits accruing to the new rising power.

Accepting these arguments—that assertive behavior on the part of
the rising state is inevitable because the latter seeks to restructure the
rules and arrangements by which international relations are
conducted to reflect its own preferences—does *not* require adopting
Gilpin's larger (and more contestable) thesis that hegemonic war
inexorably arises as a result of the disequilibrium between the
"hierarchy of prestige" and the "hierarchy of power." Rather, the
assertiveness of rising powers can be explained entirely by material
causes, that is, by the desire to have the established structures of
global governance reflect their own interests, *irrespective of what
outcomes obtain at the level of status-distribution in international
politics.* If status considerations are important to the rising power
(and, in the case of China, the historical record suggests that they
are), the tendency toward assertiveness may be further magnified,

---

[83]Gilpin (1981), p. 186.

but arguments hinging on status acquisition are not essential to deriving assertiveness on the part of rising states.[84]

Given these considerations, what would the Weberian "ideal type" of an assertive China look like? To begin with, an assertive China would be one that exhibited a consistently "self-regarding" posture on all major international issues. This means that no significant question in the realm of regional and global politics could be addressed, much less resolved, without reference to the interests, preferences, and desires of Beijing. Such assertiveness would be oriented toward ensuring that the evolving regional and global order contributes to, if not enhances, China's growing power and prestige; at the very least, it cannot be allowed to detract from, or undercut, Beijing's enduring interests. In all matters then, whether economic, political, or strategic, their effect on the preservation, if not the improvement, of Chinese power would become the key consideration governing Beijing's responses and behavior.

China's first priority in this regard would consist of securing unilateral gains that give it an advantage in the ongoing security competition among states; in most instances, the attainment of high relative gains would be accorded priority over securing high absolute or high joint gains, especially in those issue-areas considered to be strategically important to China. This does not imply that the pursuit of absolute or joint gains would be neglected, only that these gains would not be pursued if they came at the cost of important Chinese interests or if they required significant compromise or concessions at a time when China could well afford to be disdainful of cooperation with both the few powerful, but declining, states and the more numerous, but weaker, entities in international politics.

Such an orientation would no doubt become troubling to many of China's neighbors, but most particularly to the United States, because all its principal power-political interests (if examples drawn from current concerns are still relevant during a future power transition), such as the fate of the U.S. military presence in East Asia, the viability of the global nonproliferation regime, the protection of

---

[84]This point suggests that for historical or other reasons, whether China desires great power status and prestige in the international system is not a decisive determinant of the propensity for a strong Chinese state to adopt assertive behavior.

international property rights, and the expansion of the open trading system, would be realized if they did not clash with China's own preferences in each of these issue-areas.

Apart from such specific issues that directly affect the United States, the self-regarding behavior associated with an assertive China would manifest itself along three dimensions. First, Beijing would seek sinocentric solutions to most, if not all, of its territorial disputes (assuming that they still existed during a future power transition). This implies that the current strategy of either making minor concessions or postponing resolution of outstanding disputes would atrophy irrevocably. China would expect its regional competitors to either acquiesce to its claims or face the prospect of armed diplomacy, if not outright applications of military force. Since by this point it can be presumed that China would have consequential military capabilities, it would not be unreasonable for Beijing to hope that its steadily accumulating coercive power would actually yield some favorable returns where resolving its territorial claims is concerned. This would be particularly true with respect to important territorial claims, including the ideationally driven claims involving Taiwan, the strategically driven claims involving India in Aksai Chin, and the economically driven claims involving the Spratly Islands and the South China Sea in general. An assertive China would have an advantage over each of these local competitors in the balance of resolve because, assuming its interests in these disputed territories to be unwavering, Beijing's new power, including its military strength, would tip the balance of capabilities enough to make local opposition to China either irrelevant or relatively costly for most of its antagonists.

Second, Beijing would exhibit a readiness to use or threaten to use military instruments relatively freely for securing various political ends. In contrast to both the present posture, which is characterized by a general reluctance to use force except in self-defense or to ward off serious threats or losses, and the posture associated with a cooperative China, which is characterized by the subordination of military tools to the institutions and practices of collective security, the use of military force under an assertive strategy would be more unilateral, frequent, and closely oriented toward the pursuit of extended power-political goals. To be sure, all use of force is relatively costly and the readiness to use military instruments more freely does not imply that a powerful Beijing would automatically become mindlessly trigger-happy. It does imply, however, that whereas under previous conditions of weakness China might have shied away from actively using force, or the threat of force, to secure supernumerary goals, it would be less reticent about behaving similarly in circumstances when it was actually strong and capable in military terms *and* less dependent on the goodwill of external actors for the continued expansion of its national power. Under such circumstances, not only would the costs of using force actually decrease but the range of circumstances amenable to the successful use of force also increases.[85] Equally significant, military instruments can be usefully employed in less-conventional ways: They will continue to defend China and mitigate its losses but they can also be used for more acquisitive purposes—as they traditionally did during some strong-state periods—such as appropriating new territory or resources or as useful instruments of diplomacy, for subtly coercing adversaries; or as visible manifestations of China's power in the open commons; or as symbols of reassurance offered to others, as, for example, when military instruments become the embodied promises of extended deterrence. An assertive China, faced with more opportunities for the profitable use of its military instruments, would then find itself less restrained in using these instruments to secure objectives other than simply national survival.

Third, Beijing would seek to secure and sustain geopolitical preeminence on a global scale. Although the search for such preeminence may be rooted in the fact that China enjoyed for extended periods over many centuries throughout the imperial era a superior political, economic, and cultural position relative to its periphery in Asia, an ascendant China in the 21st century would arguably seek geopolitical preeminence on a global scale. In part, this would simply become a product of necessity as technology and the diffusion of power more generally result in dramatic increases in the range of political control. Further, the extant dominant power—the United States—already possesses political influence on a massive scale unparalleled in history and any suppression of this dominance,

---

[85]As Gilpin succinctly argued, "the critical significance of the differential growth of power among states is that it alters the cost of changing the international system and therefore the incentives for changing the international system [itself]" (1981), p. 95.

therefore, almost by definition must involve a substitution of control on a similar scale. Recognizing this, however, does not imply that China would be able to effortlessly control global outcomes, even if it were to become an assertive state. The constraints imposed by the power gradient, meaning the loss of power as a function of distance, would still apply: China would find it easier to control outcomes nearer to home than farther away. All imperial powers, historically, have been confronted by this phenomenon and it is unlikely that China would turn out to be the first successful exception to the rule. This implies that Beijing's principal objective would be to secure its hinterland first—meaning, as in the past, its Asian periphery along both its landward and oceanic borders—precisely to obtain those resources that would give it an advantage in its efforts to control the larger outcomes unfolding over the larger regional and global canvas. Control over the hinterland would inevitably require the close integration of client states, the acquisition of veto rights over the policies of neutral states, and the explicit or implicit containment, if not outright neutralization, of all local adversaries.

The search for global preeminence, therefore, implies that China would seek to enforce a structure of super- and subordination among the powers along its periphery as the first, and likely necessary, step toward reproducing, however loosely, a similar structure of super- and subordination at the core of the larger regional and global system. Indeed, because the Asian region represents a GNP even greater than that of NATO Europe, the attainment of such a position of regional preeminence would greatly facilitate, if not ensure, the attainment of China's larger objective of global preeminence—assuming that Asia's overall importance to global stability and prosperity continues to increase, as it has during the past several decades.

As mentioned above, this depiction of an assertive China remains a Weberian "ideal type." It delineates a stark vision of what an egotistical, "self-regarding" entity would look like. The purpose of this analytical image is, first, to present a clear conception of what an assertive Chinese posture would entail in theory, even if it never materializes with such clarity in practice. The second purpose is to draw as clear a distinction as possible between an assertive and a cooperative China. Each of these ideal types represents radically different approaches to international politics and understanding their distinctiveness conceptually is essential to assessing the broad underlying direction of any future Chinese grand strategy, a direction that would otherwise be hidden by the complexity and confusion that always surround the vast mass of political behaviors in reality. The clarity embodied by the ideal type is therefore essential precisely because it serves as the template that enables an observer to interpret the general orientation—cooperation or assertion—that Chinese grand strategy may follow over the long term. This is particularly important because any future assertiveness on the part of China will not be unadorned, raw, and clearly manifest. Rather, it will be clouded by various cooperative trappings and much complexity as far as "process"—understood as "the ways in which units relate to each other"[86]—is concerned. Yet, despite these complexities, an assertive orientation would reveal itself through certain basic attitudes adopted by China: the pervasive emphasis on securing sinocentric solutions to outstanding problems; the singular pursuit of its national aims by all means necessary, largely irrespective of the contending interests of others; the emphasis on developing potent military instruments and the ready willingness, in many instances, to use these as part of national policy; and, finally, the possible development of an ideology that legitimizes Chinese national interests in terms of some universal values.

If an assertive China were to materialize in some such form in the distant future, what factors would produce it? Or, framed differently, why would one expect China to behave as an assertive power when there are in fact several good reasons for believing in the possibility of a cooperative China? The summary answer to this latter question is that the good reasons enumerated above for believing that a cooperative China will emerge under the assumed conditions of high capacity and low external dependence are simply not good enough.

To begin with, the claim that China's current reliance on economic interdependence would socialize it into pursuing the benefits of cooperation (arising from the quest for joint gains) even after it becomes a great power is contestable on both empirical and conceptual grounds. There is little evidence historically that high levels of economic interdependence have retarded the assertive behavior and

---

[86]Keohane and Nye (1987).

the war-proneness of states when control of the international system was at issue, including those that were locked in very tight circles of economic interdependence with one another. The classic example of such high interdependence coinciding with assertive political behaviors remains Britain and Germany on the eve of World War I, when "economic ties were more extensive and significant than at any time before or since."[87] Yet this interdependence failed to prevent Germany from pursuing an expansionist policy that eventually led to war. One study in fact concludes that the relationship between "interdependence and conflict appears to be curvilinear, where low to moderate degrees of interdependence reduce the likelihood of dyadic disputes, and extensive economic linkages increase the probability of militarized disputes."[88] Most realists, reading the historical evidence, affirm this conclusion by arguing that high economic interdependence would actually increase the prospects of assertive behavior because states, faced with the increased vulnerability associated with high interdependence, will embark on predatory or preemptive responses to minimize their national exposure. Although this claim has been corroborated by the quantitative study cited above, it is still unclear—at a theoretical level—what the relationship between economic interdependence and assertive international behaviors actually is. In large part, this is because the established theories have not yet been able to satisfactorily integrate how the specific issue of interdependence affects the more general problem about decisionmaking choices relating to war or peace. Absent such an explanation, it is difficult to assess the precise causal mechanisms underlying the empirical claims about high trade coinciding with a lower incidence of conflict.

What makes matters more difficult analytically is that most established theories about interdependence and conflict are fairly general formulations: They do not incorporate variables such as domestic economic interests, the strength of the state relative to its society, and the role of future expectations about the value of interdependence, all of which arguably would bear upon the traditional liberal claim that high interdependence inevitably leads to cooperative as opposed to assertive behaviors. Research that incorporates such

---

[87]Papayoanou (1996), p. 42.

[88]Barbieri (1996).

variables has only just begun; findings are still not extensively corroborated but, unfortunately, they do not reinforce the liberal opti-
mism that high interdependence inevitably and unconditionally
leads to peace.[89] By demonstrating a more contingent relationship
between these two variables, this new research only serves to suggest
that dense economic interconnectivity may not be sufficient to prevent a great-power China in the future from embarking on assertive
policies. Even more pessimistically, the degree of interdependence
required to sustain a cooperative China may simply not exist in the
future to begin with. If China's economic growth over the long term
is sustained through an exploitation of its internal markets as opposed to its current export-led trading strategies, all the discussion
about the pacifying effects of interdependence may simply become
academic. The presence of autarkic growth would simply eliminate
all the constraints imposed by economic interdependence (assuming
that these were efficacious to begin with), thereby allowing other
variables such as the pursuit of security, power, gain, or glory to become the determinants beneath an assertive strategy. Since it is very
possible that China's level of interdependence will actually drop as it
continues to grow in both economic and in power-political terms,
the hypothesized cooperation that ostensibly arises from participating in a liberal economic regime will also steadily diminish over time.

If the benefits of economic interdependence turn out to be less
salient than is usually expected, the claims for cooperation deriving
from beliefs about the changing nature of power are even more misguided. The ultimate nature of power in international politics has
remained largely unchanged since the beginning of time; what has
changed are simply the sources that generate that power. Power in
international politics, at least in the realist reading, has always been
ultimately a function of a state's capability to coerce other states:
What contributes toward the making of such capabilities, however,
has changed as a result of new technologies and new social
arrangements. Whereas in a previous age, for example, industrial
expertise and nationalized or state-directed production may have
contributed to building effective sinews of war, information-
intensive technologies produced by profit-driven private enterprises

---

[89]See, for example, Copeland (1996); Rowe (1999); and Papayoanou (1999).

today arguably constitute the new sources of power.[90] These changes alter the means by which a state acquires national power while transforming how this power may be harnessed on the battlefield. But, in a structural sense, these changes are trivial when compared to the permanence exhibited by the essential nature of power itself. All great powers—yesterday and today—have been defined by their possession of superior coercive capabilities relative to the rest of the international system and a transformation of this key attribute cannot occur unless the "deep structure"[91] of international politics is itself altered. No such alteration, however, is in sight: International politics still remains the arena of egoist competition among states *par excellence*; it still subsists as a realm of self-help; and it still continues to be defined by the preferences of the great powers populating the system. In such an environment, no "candidate" great-power is likely to eschew acquiring the best and most sophisticated military capabilities it can afford; to do so would both imperil its security and undercut its claims to superior recognition, status, and control.

Germany and Japan today simply do not constitute examples of the changing nature of power. Rather, they remain illustrations of how defeat at the hands of other great powers can constrain and condition national preferences in certain unnatural directions for a while. Both Germany and Japan are models not of great powers but of client states whose fundamental autonomy—the ability to independently choose one's national direction—was compromised through defeat in war and whose subsequent direction as "trading states" was sustained only because they were compelled, thanks to common threats, to operate within an alliance framework managed by one great power, the United States, which found itself in competition with another great power, the Soviet Union, for global dominance. Thus, their "trading state" profile is testimony more to the dominant power of the United States and its ability to regulate the direction adopted by its clients than it is to any alleged changes in the nature of power in international politics. In fact, this profile will be sustained only so long as the United States can continue to protect Germany and Japan while simultaneously sustaining the global eco-

---

[90]These issues are further discussed in Tellis et al. (forthcoming).

[91]On the realist reading of deep structure, see Ruggie (1986).

nomic regime that allows both countries a peaceful outlet for their national energies; should U.S. capabilities in these two arenas atrophy, the trading state profiles of both countries would also quickly atrophy and be replaced by the "territorial state" forms common to all other countries in the international system. If anything, Germany and Japan are also examples of another less-recognized reality in international politics: Although both countries may have been great powers in an age when control of their local periphery afforded them a claim over the larger commons, the economies of scale associated with efficiently acquiring the attributes of modern military and economic powers today give advantage mostly to continental powers whose great size, vast natural resources, and large populations become incredible assets so long as they can resolve their power "transformation" problems with minimal efficiency.[92]

The implications of these judgments for possible Chinese assertiveness should be clear. Not only is there little evidence that coercion is becoming less central to the structure, organization, and administration of international politics, there is even less evidence that China believes such a transformation is presently under way. As one Chinese politics specialist put it, "China may well be the high church of realpolitik in the post-Cold War world."[93] If so, Beijing would—quite justifiably—presume that acquiring superior coercive capabilities is fundamentally necessary to sustaining its great power claims among other things because it perceives—quite rightly again—that there is little evidence for the belief that the nature of power is in fact changing. When China's desire to redress past humiliations is added to its strong (and possibly growing) suspicion that the United States, in concert with its regional allies, is stealthily contemplating responses aimed at the "constrainment" of Beijing, the expectation that a strong China would eschew acquiring the military attributes of a great nation and behave cooperatively in accordance with the changing nature of power thesis only becomes more untenable. For a variety of reasons, some unique to China and some common to all rising states, Beijing is likely to view claims about the changing nature of power as little other than a ruse fostered by the established states in the system to change the extant "rules of the game" just

---

[92]Kennedy (1983).

[93]Christensen (1996a), p. 37.

when it appeared as if China would be—finally—successful when measured by the predicates of those "rules." Not surprisingly, a strong China is likely to resist all such efforts at redefinition because they promise only to denature what is most attractive about power-political greatness—the ability to use superior coercive power to reshape the international system to comport with one's own interests—at exactly the time when China seeks to enjoy those hard-earned fruits accruing to its growing eminence.[94]

One partial caveat to the above assessment of the influence of Chinese history should be kept in mind, however. Although both structural factors associated with China's ascent to power within the international system and certain Chinese attitudes about state power suggest that Beijing will become more assertive, both militarily and otherwise, in protecting its expanding interests, the historical record also suggests that domestic leadership factors could seriously reduce the extent to which a strong Chinese state employs military force under certain circumstances. As Chapter Three indicates, considerable elite opposition to prolonged and particularly intense levels of force was evident even during strong-state periods in Chinese imperial history. Such opposition reflected the influence of both pragmatic bureaucratic calculations and more normative beliefs, including a long-standing, deep-seated notion that successful and just regimes attain their objectives, whenever possible, through a reliance on "benevolent" behavior and the force of example. In the modern era, such a belief continues to exert some influence on both elite and popular attitudes in China, despite the collapse of state Confucianism. Moreover, this notion has to some extent been reinforced by the belief that China should not act unilaterally to enforce its will on the regional or global system, derived from a modern-day Chinese aversion to the allegedly "predatory hegemonic behavior" of imperialist nation-states. This certainly does not mean that a strong Chinese state would employ force only in extremis, or would *never* employ high levels of force over a prolonged period. But it does suggest that the willingness of a strong and assertive China to unilaterally

---

[94]This argument thus suggests that the current emphasis placed by many Chinese observers on the importance of economic and technological over military factors in the definition of a state's "comprehensive national strength" is probably more indicative of the workings of the present-day calculative strategy than an indication of a fundamental disbelief in the continued vital relevance of military attributes to state power.

employ force in such a manner *might* be decisively restrained by the domestic leadership context.[95]

The claims for cooperation deriving from expectations based on the nuclear revolution are also misguided. Nuclear weapons no doubt can serve as fairly formidable deterrents: Assuming that all their possessors are rational and that the threats of accidents and catalytic use are ruled out, nuclear weapons can *reduce, though not entirely eliminate,* the risks of premeditated attack on the homeland and on the central assets cherished by a great power.[96] Such an outcome, however, is not automatic. It involves many political decisions to develop and acquire the secure retaliatory capabilities that can immunize against destruction. Until that point is reached, a fairly hostile competition can in fact ensue as each side attempts to preserve its nuclear capabilities against any damage-limiting technologies or strategies that may be adopted by an adversary. This interaction can involve highly assertive and visible actions in the realm of competitive nuclear modernization—an issue that becomes particularly relevant in the case of China because its currently small and fairly vulnerable arsenal appeared adequate only in the context of the positive externalities generated by the mutual deterrence relationship between the United States and the Soviet Union. Today, when neither Russian nor U.S. weapons provide any spillover benefits that can be exploited by Beijing, the imperative to modernize its arsenal—in the face of growing U.S. efforts to both deemphasize nuclear weapons and develop various technologies, such as national and theater missile defense systems, that could degrade hostile nuclear capabilities in general—may only result in new forms of arms racing and potential instability.

---

[95]It should be added that domestic leadership factors could at times also prompt both weak and strong Chinese regimes to employ a *greater* level of force than might be deemed prudent or "rational" from a structural perspective.

[96]This weaker conclusion holds because the nuclear era has provided numerous examples when established nuclear powers were attacked by conventional means, thus raising serious questions about the reliability of nuclear deterrence. These examples include China's attack on U.S. forces in Korea (1950), China's attack on the Soviet Union (1969), and Argentina's attack on Great Britain (1981). In at least one instance (1969), the conflict included an attack by one nuclear power on the territory of the other, leading Organski and Kugler to exclaim that to believe that nuclear weapons deter all conflicts is "to believe in magic" (1980), p. 179.

Even if this process is completed without mishap, with China acquiring comprehensive and highly secure nuclear retaliatory capabilities over time, it implies only that both Chinese and U.S. homelands would be further immunized against the prospect of comprehensive societal destruction (thanks to the dynamics of mutual deterrence). That, in turn, however, would push any on-going political competition "below" the strategic realm and into the arenas of extended deterrence and conventional and low-intensity conflicts occurring in peripheral areas. This phenomenon, brought about by the "stability-instability" paradox, could translate into severe threats being mounted by China to important U.S. strategic interests, including those involving the safety of U.S. possessions or forces abroad as well as the security of overseas allies. The presence of robust strategic nuclear capabilities would, then, serve mainly to channel active security competition into areas other than direct attacks on the homeland, which nonetheless would continue to remain vulnerable thanks to the complications of escalation, even if it could otherwise avoid the dangers inherent in straightforward premeditated attack.

The growing threat to extended U.S interests, which would inevitably occur as China grew in national capabilities (including both strategic nuclear weaponry and conventional power-projection capabilities), cannot provide any significant consolation to the United States whose global position is inextricably linked to its ability to defend numerous allies, some quite close to China but all quite far removed from its own home territory.[97] It was precisely this concern that dominated U.S. defense policy throughout the Cold War and this period abundantly illustrates the fact that even though the direct threat to the U.S. homeland was more or less "managed," thanks to the constraints of mutual assured destruction after about 1964, the United States was still engaged in an arduous struggle to contain Soviet assertiveness directed both at its extended allies in Europe and the Far East and on peripheral battlegrounds such as Central America, Africa, and South Asia.

---

[97]For this reason, among many others, the United States cannot contemplate the acceptance of a "no-first-use" nuclear strategy just as certainly as China will continue to insist on such a pledge for both geopolitical and propaganda purposes.

The presence of nuclear weapons, then, did not either reassure the Soviets or incapacitate the United States as both countries sought to grapple with the demands imposed by mutual threats. The challenges of security competition simply assumed new forms and Soviet assertiveness focused not so much on multiplying the threats to the continental United States (though these continued as well) but rather on altering the "global correlation of forces" by threatening U.S. extended deterrence relationships and capabilities, intimidating U.S. allies, and coopting, if not directly menacing, important neutral states.

A future global power transition involving China should in principle be no different. The risk to the homelands of both countries may be mitigated by the extreme destructiveness of their nuclear arsenals but the competitive attempts at assertion and counterassertion, which have traditionally been a feature of all active great-power rivalry, would endure inescapably. This "cold war" would not become any the less challenging simply because nuclear weapons imposed limits on the upper bounds of military assertiveness; rather, it would remain quite hostile because it involves a struggle over who governs the international system and consequently would result in both sides pursuing all methods short of direct, all-out war to increase their own national power while enervating that of the other. Although this outcome may offer modest relief when measured against the consequence of systemic war—clearly the distinguishing characteristic of every systemic transition before the nuclear age—it is still a far cry from the "peaceful competition, persuasion and compromise"[98] that supposedly characterizes the rivalry in a cooperative universe of international politics.

It is in the above context that other expectations about highly cooperative levels of Chinese behavior deriving from the democratic peace are less than convincing, although this hypothesis may fare better than other competitors in explaining the prospects of a peaceful power transition. To be sure, many skeptics argue that the democratic peace is simply irrelevant to China either because China is undemocratic or because it is unlikely to make major advances toward democracy so long as its current communist structures of gov-

---

[98]Layne (1994), p. 10.

ernance remain intact. Consequently, an assertive China should not prove surprising because it represents "a flawed regime"[99] that could assault democratic polities, including the United States, through any means including war. Other theorists might argue, as suggested above, that China, though flawed, is evolving toward democracy and the prospects of assertiveness increase not because of its benighted nature but because of its democratic immaturity.[100] To assess the prospect of an assertive China in the context of a systemic power transition many decades hence, both these arguments may be set aside, however. Even if it is assumed that China successfully democratizes, and that it avoids all the perils associated with a democratic transition in the interim, it is still unlikely that this democratic China would prove to be highly cooperative in the Weberian "ideal typical" sense described above, not because of any peculiarities relating to China per se, but because the notion of the democratic peace is less-than-entirely robust to begin with.

Although it has been argued that the "absence of war between democracies comes as close as anything we have to an empirical law in international relations,"[101] the fact remains that the substantive claims underlying this generalization are at least controversial if not problematic. For starters, the assertion that democracies never fight each other appears to be highly sensitive both to the way in which the terms "democracy" and "war" are viewed and to the statistical methods used to make the overarching generalization plausible.[102] Even if these problems are overlooked, however, the issue of whether the absence of war between democratic states is a statistically significant result remains an open question and at least one scholar has quite convincingly argued that the zero instances of war between democratic states is simply "predicted by random chance," which implies that if the "explanation we know to be untrue—random chance—predicts the absence of war between democracies better than liberal theories of international relations," then "the absence of

---

[99]Goldstein (1997/98), p. 66.

[100]See Mansfield and Snyder (1995) for an elaboration of such an argument.

[101]Levy (1989), p. 270.

[102]See the discussion in Thompson and Tucker (1997).

war should not be considered as confirming evidence of those theories."[103]

Moving on to more substantive grounds, other scholars have noted that "democracies have been few in number over the past two centuries" and hence, it should not be surprising to find that "there have not been many cases where two democracies were in a position to fight each other."[104] This argument also applies to the absence of war among democracies in the post-1945 period where the strong threats mounted by the Soviet Union, coupled with the stability provided by the United States as the dominant superpower, more than amply accounts for the pacificity among democratic states, especially in Europe. In fact, even one defender of the democratic peace argument has quite cogently argued that

> the creation of zones of peace or areas in which states are much less likely to go to war with one another has as much, and perhaps more, to do with the settlement of, or restraints imposed on, regional primacy questions as it does the type of political system. In essence, most of the states that became (and remained) democratic in the nineteenth and early twentieth centuries had created or found themselves in relatively cooperative niches that insulated them from extremely competitive, regional international politics. The various ways in which these niches were established had important and positive implications for the likelihood of domestic democratization processes. Usually the niches preceded substantial progress in democratization and, short of outright invasion, the geopolitical circumstances leading to the evolution of the niches seem most responsible for peace between democracies.[105]

Perhaps the most damning argument against democratic peace, however, has come from a close scrutiny of those instances when democratic powers went to the brink of war without going over it: One scholar was able to demonstrate that in every one of four major episodes examined, the claims of democratic peace theory were completely unable to account for the pacific outcomes eventually obtained, all of which in fact were better explained by power-

---

[103]Spiro (1994), p. 51.

[104]Mearsheimer (1994/95), pp. 50–51.

[105]Thompson (1996).

political considerations such as differences in national interests, the international distribution of capabilities, and the positional location of the competing states in the global system.[106]

Not surprisingly, one comprehensive survey of the relationship between democracy and peace concluded that "on the basis of the historical record, it is not clear that the spread of democracy in and of itself will exert much influence on the incidence of serious interstate conflict."[107] Given such conclusions, it is difficult to affirm that a democratic China would ipso facto resist the assertiveness that could possibly lead to war. If the realists are correct, even an international system populated entirely by democratic states would experience assertive behaviors and possibly even wars because the many shades of democracy would intersect with differing national interests to create conflicts in much the same way as competing national interests intersect with differences in domestic regimes today to produce occasional altercations and war. The democratic revolution per se may simply not be sufficient to prevent China from assertively reaching out for those great power privileges it believes are rightfully its own: It did not prevent the United States, a democratic power, from asserting its prerogatives against Great Britain, the previous dominant power and a democratic state to boot, in such a way during the last power transition at the turn of the century that one magisterial analysis concluded that "there was every strategic, economic and psychological justification for England to see in the United States the successor to Imperial Germany, Napoleonic and Bourbon France and Philip II's Spain as an overwhelming super-power dangerous to English prosperity and independence, even if armed aggression itself was hardly to be expected."[108] *Mutatis mutandis*, U.S.

---

[106]See Layne (1994).

[107]Farber and Gowa (1995), p. 146. This conclusion too has been contested mainly on methodological grounds. See Thompson and Tucker (1997); Gochman (1996/97); and Farber and Gowa's rejoinder in the same issue. For Gowa's definitive statement about the untenability of the democratic peace argument, see Gowa (1999).

[108]Barnett (1972), p. 257. Lest the last clause in this quotation cause any misunderstanding, it should be noted that the absence of "armed aggression" in the Anglo-American power transition referred to here had little to do with the democratic character of the two protagonists. Rather, Barnett convincingly argues that pacificity in this instance was clearly a product of a sentimental English disposition that resulted in the "British display[ing] towards the United States the forgiveness, [and] the blindness towards blemishes of character and conduct, commonly found in a man

attitudes toward China may one day be described in similar terms, their presumed common democratic structures notwithstanding.

The debate and the evidence for democratic peace, therefore, do not provide any uncontestable assurance of a cooperative China. Yet, it is possible that the spread of democracy remains the best hope for avoiding major conflicts leading to war if one believes that the universal egoism of human nature so clearly described by Thomas Hobbes in the *Leviathan* could in fact evolve in the direction of that greater moral awareness implicit in the conditions necessary for the success of Kant's prescriptions in *Perpetual Peace*. In other words, if a gradual growth of moral sensibilities is assumed to characterize the evolution of political order, it is possible that a strong, democratic China, although increasingly assertive in many respects, might rely less on military force to resolve major disputes with other democratic states, including the United States, than would a strong, authoritarian, China.

Overall, then, the expectation that China would increasingly pursue an assertive course, as (and if) its power grows to the point where a systemic power transition is feasible, derives in the first instance from an assessment that all the arguments offered for the pursuit of a contrary trajectory are either limited, contested, flawed, or irrelevant. Economic interdependence either may not be a salient restraining condition for China at this time or it may not create the cooperative posture even if dense economic interconnectivity obtains. Further, the nature of power in international politics has not been transformed as far as the fundamentals are concerned, thus leaving China with little choice but to pursue the strategies associated traditionally with "territorial states." Although nuclear weapons may provide security for the homeland—if they are not substantially denatured in the interim by new technologies created to counter them—they do so only at the cost of shifting the locus of assertive behavior toward conventional warfighting, targeting the extended deterrence relationships held by the adversary, and controlling important neutral

---

infatuated. For the British governing classes *were* infatuated with America—or, rather, with a mythical America conjured up by their own romantic vision" (p. 258).

states in the international system. And, finally, the spread of democracy, however perfect, also does not provide any clear assurance against the pursuit of an assertive posture, although, in the final analysis, the spread of democracy offers perhaps the best hope for mitigating the worst outcomes associated with power transitions at the core of the international system if some metaphysical conception of progress is held to be operative in the human world of politics.

In addition to all these arguments, which are derived primarily from the weaknesses of the claims for expected cooperation, there are other simple but extremely powerful reasons for arguing that Chinese assertiveness is to be expected for all the time-honored reasons associated with power-politics. First, "fear": As rising states grow in relative power, they seek to protect their steadily growing assets against the possible depredations of others by all means necessary, including assertive acts involving military force. Second, "anticipation": As rising states grow in relative power, they often feel compelled to act preemptively against potential rivals if they perceive that preclusive strategies would better safeguard their interests in the face of those inevitable counterresponses that will be mounted by other states as a reaction to their expanding power. Third, "status": As rising states grow in relative power, they inevitably seek to advance their standing in the international system as a way to secure both the psychic rewards of eminence and the more material benefits that arise from an ability to control the rules and arrangements governing the distribution of resources and rewards in international politics. Fourth, "greed": As rising states grow in relative power, they acquire the resources necessary to appropriate those objects they may have long desired but could not secure before their growth in power. Fifth, "irredentism": As rising states grow in relative power, they sometimes use their new capabilities to reacquire goods they once possessed (or believe are rightfully theirs) before the ownership of these goods changed hands either because of the mendacity or the superior power of others. Sixth, "cooptation": As rising states grow in relative power, their political leadership may occasionally use assertive international policies as payoffs for critical domestic constituencies whose support is essential for the continued survival and dominance of such elites at home.

These motivations, in various combinations, usually drive rising states toward assertive behaviors that often take the form of expanded military capabilities, increasingly muscular overseas presence, and greatly enlarged foreign security commitments. Together, they serve to exacerbate the "security dilemma"[109] that arises because of the difficulty in distinguishing between the measures states take to defend themselves and the measures that increase their capacity for aggression. Thanks to such difficulties, other powers—especially the existing dominant power and the neighbors of the rising state—tend to react to the rising state by military or political counter-responses of their own; these, in turn, serve only to increase the rising state's sense of threat and results in even more accelerated efforts at power accumulation as the latter prepares to stave off any potential "preventive war" that may be waged by the declining dominant power. The interactive nature of this dynamic can produce extended "crisis slides" during an incipient power transition when "relatively trivial incidents or a string of seemingly minor crises"[110] may suffice to transform what is usually a precarious structural transformation into major war.

The historical record, in fact, seems to corroborate the theoretical expectations delineated above and it suggests that, despite the different reasons in every case, rising powers invariably turn out to be assertive—an assertiveness that has usually led to war in the past. It is useful, therefore, to briefly scrutinize the historical record because it provides many insights that bear on the prospects for future assertiveness by China over the long term. The record, summarized in Table 1 is drawn from Modelski and Thompson's early work on the "long cycles of world politics," and this chronology is used, despite the problems attributed to Modelski and Thompson in particular and to narratives centered on hegemonic theories in general, primarily as a heuristic that illuminates the dynamics associated with systemic transitions rather than as an endorsement of long-cycle theory in all

---

[109]Jervis (1978).

[110]Thompson (1983a), p. 100.

Table 1

Hegemonic Cycles in Modern History

Hegemon	Rising Power	Rising Power's Actions	Opposition to Rising Power	Outcome	Structural Consequences
Venice (Middle Ages–1494)	Spain, France	Spain and France at war over Italy	England, Ottoman Turkey, Italian city-states	1494–1517 (Italian Wars)	Spanish victory; demise of Venetian hegemony; rise of Portuguese hegemony
Portugal (1517–1580)	Spain	Spain absorbs Portugal (1580), attacks Portuguese ally, the United Provinces	England, France	1585–1608 (Spanish Wars)	Demise of Spanish challenge; rise of Dutch hegemony
Netherlands (1609–1713)	France, Great Britain	France attacks the United Provinces, Germany, and Spain	Great Britain	1689–1713 (Wars of Louis XIV)	Demise of French challenge; demise of Dutch hegemony; rise of British hegemony
Great Britain (1714–1815)	France	Napoleonic France wars against rest of Europe	Great Britain, Austria, Prussia, Russia	1793–1815 (Napoleonic Wars)	Demise of Napoleonic challenge; continued British hegemony
Great Britain (1816–1918)	Germany, United States, Russia	Germany attempts to dominate Europe	Great Britain, United States, Russia	1914–1918 (First World War)	Demise of German challenge; continued British hegemony
Great Britain (1918–1945)	Germany, Japan, USSR, United States	Germany and Japan attempt to dominate Europe and the Pacific	Great Britain, United States, USSR	1939–1945 (Second World War)	Demise of German and Japanese challenge and of British hegemony; rise of U.S. hegemony
United States (1945–1992)	USSR, China (after 1978)	Soviets attempt to dominate Europe and the globe	United States, Western Europe, Japan, China (after ~1960)	1950–1992 (Cold War)	Collapse of the Soviet Union; continuation of U.S. hegemony
United States (1992–)	China (?)	(?)	United States (?)	(?)	(?)

its details.[111] The analysis below does not attempt to describe the various hegemonic cycles at length, as these descriptions are available elsewhere. Instead, it concentrates on uncovering the insights offered by such a reconstruction with respect to the propensity for, and patterns of, assertiveness on the part of competing great (including rising) powers and the effects of such competition in the context of the power transitions that have previously taken place in international politics.

The historical reconstruction represented by Table 1 obviously represents a view of international politics as a succession of hegemonic cycles. In an analytic tradition going back to Quincy Wright's work at the University of Chicago in the 1940s and incorporating the views of others such as Arnold Toynbee, Ludwig Dehio, and A.F.K. Organski, the hegemonic cycle is based on the idea that one country rises to the pinnacle of the international system as the result of a hegemonic war and it subsists there until the uneven growth of power creates new challengers who, through political actions aimed at either the existing dominant power or other states, precipitate new global wars that start a new hegemonic cycle.

Viewed in this perspective, the reconstruction begins with Venice as the first dominant power in the modern period, since before about 1500 "the global system was a dispersed one."[112] The Venetian hegemony arose gradually as a result of Venice's maritime victories over its other Italian competitors, mainly Genoa, in the late 14th century, and it was steadily consolidated thanks to its maritime location which allowed it to control the long distance trade between China, India, Persia, and Western Europe. As Venetian hegemony was being consolidated, however, an internal transformation was occurring in

---

[111]One difficulty associated with the hegemonic cycles conceptualized by long-cycle theories is the criterion for hegemony. By defining hegemony primarily in terms of sea power, these hegemonic cycles underplay the importance of continental states that, despite their lack of sea power assets, nonetheless dominated the political affairs of large continental areas. For a good discussion of the substantive and methodological limits of various conceptions of hegemony, see Nye (1991), pp. 1–48. Fortunately, none of these difficulties handicap this analysis unduly, since all alternative constructions of hegemonic cycles, as for example those detailed in Goldstein (1988), support the primary conclusion advanced in the following paragraphs: that systemic power transitions historically have usually been accompanied by war.

[112]Modelski (1978), p. 218.

Spain in the form of the marriage between Ferdinand II of Aragon and Isabella of Castile—an event that would create a new "united and revitalized country [and] lead Spain to a pre-eminent global position of power and wealth."[113] A similar transformation was occurring in France with the rise of the Valois monarchy and before long the two rising powers—the French Valois and the Spanish Hapsburgs—were engaged in the Italian wars, a lengthy series of struggles for dominance over the Italian city states. The eventual Spanish victory over France, assisted in great measure by assistance from England, Ottoman Turkey, and most of the Italian city-states, including Venice, did not suffice to prevent the slow demise of Venetian hegemony as a result of the painfully high costs borne during the Italian wars.

As the Italian wars were occurring along the south European periphery, the Portuguese monarchs, determined to replace the lucrative Venetian control over the eastern trade east with their own, began a series of overseas expeditions and "in the series of swift naval campaigns that followed, a string of naval bases was established and rival fleets were wiped off the oceans."[114] By 1515, Portugal, hitherto merely a rising aspirant, became a global power on the strength of her naval fleet which, incorporating new long-range sailing technologies such as the galleon and the caravel, allowed it to secure an Eastern empire, monopolize the spice trade, and mount explorations as far off as Brazil. The rise of Portuguese hegemony, however, was to be short lived: "feeling the strain of maintaining this far-flung system on a rather slender home base,"[115] Portugal succumbed to its still-growing landward neighbor, Spain, which, fresh from its victories in the Italian Wars, seized Portugal in 1580. On the strength of this conquest, the newly enlarged Spain attempted to incorporate previous Portuguese territories and allies by force and in particular focused on the wealthy Dutch United Provinces "which derived much of their income from trade with Lisbon" and until a short time ago had "served as the banking and distribution center of the Por-

---

[113]Dupuy and Dupuy (1986), p. 430.

[114]Modelski (1978), p. 218

[115]Modelski (1978), p. 219

tuguese system."[116] This assertive Spanish behavior was opposed by England and Spain's old but not entirely eliminated competitor, France. The resulting Spanish wars that followed resulted in the defeat of Spanish assertiveness and the rise of Dutch hegemony.

The Dutch hegemony which probably could be dated as beginning in 1609 was consolidated by 1660, when the Dutch navy established its superiority over the Spanish fleet and controlled three-quarters of all European merchant shipping. As the Dutch slowly replaced first the Venetian and then the Portuguese and Spanish control over the eastern trade with their own "firm hold over the spice trade of the Indies" combined with "substantial interests in Africa and the Americas,"[117] another rising European power was emerging on the horizon. This power, France, had profited greatly from English assistance in the previous struggles with Spain and thanks to its new growth in internal power under the Bourbon monarchy, launched another round of assertive behaviors through attacks on the Dutch United Provinces, Germany, and Spain for mastery in Europe. The great French pressure on the Dutch in particular resulted in a new alliance between the Dutch United Provinces and Great Britain—an alliance which continued throughout the wars of Louis XIV. Although the Dutch managed to hold their own against France, the costs of resistance turned out to be extremely high "as the Netherlands were as slender a platform for [sustaining] a global system as Portugal had been [before]."[118] As a result, even though French assertiveness was beaten back, Dutch hegemony declined as well and there occurred an "effective transfer of global power to what had just become Great Britain."[119]

The rise of Great Britain, which resulted both from internal consolidation occurring within the British Isles and the successful defeat of successive challenges emanating from Spain and France over a couple of centuries, would over time produce the most significant imperium in modern times. During this period, however, it would face three important rising powers, each of which launched formidably

---

[116]Modelski (1978), p. 220.

[117]Modelski (1978), p. 220.

[118]Modelski (1978), p. 220.

[119]Modelski (1978), p. 221.

assertive campaigns aimed at restructuring the existing patterns of governance in the global system. During the first phase of British hegemony (1714–1815), Great Britain, mostly alone, faced a rising France in the person of Napoleon whose exercise of assertion involved simply a war against all of Europe. This challenge, which resulted in the Napoleonic wars between 1793–1815, was settled by the defeat of the Napoleonic challenge and a continuation of Britain's hegemony. During the second phase (1816–1918), Great Britain faced a rising Germany which, after its unification in 1870, grew rapidly in power and eventually engaged in an exercise of assertion that would embroil all of Europe in the First World War. Aided by the United States, Britain beat back the German challenge momentarily but was greatly enervated in the process. Thanks to internal changes during the 1930s, Germany returned once again—in tandem with another rising power, Japan—to confront Great Britain during the third phase of its hegemony (1918–1945) in an even more demanding exercise of assertiveness, which eventually became the Second World War. Aided now by the recently consolidated Soviet Union and the mature but hitherto uninvolved United States, Britain checkmated the German and Japanese challenges but at the cost of its own hegemony which, like the transfer to the Dutch United Provinces many centuries earlier, was now similarly transferred to the United States through the crucible of war.

The affirmation of U.S. hegemony in 1945 was immediately confronted by the assertive attempts made by the Soviet Union which, as one of the victors in the war against Germany and Japan, experienced a rapid distension in its power after the Second World War. From 1950–1992, the United States spent enormous resources, effort, and energy in checkmating various assertive behaviors on the part of the Soviet Union in a fashion quite closely analogous to the British efforts directed against Napoleon between 1793–1815. These efforts, collectively termed the Cold War, ended only in 1992 with the internal collapse of the Soviet Union and the triumphant continuation of U.S. hegemony, at least until the next serious assertive challenge is mounted by some other rising challenger in the future. The relatively peaceful systemic transition that occurred in 1992 was the first such example in over 500 years of modern history and has been attributed in large part to the presence of nuclear weaponry possessed by both the existing hegemon and the declining challenger. The extreme destructiveness embodied by these weapons is supposed to have prevented the latter from resorting to war even in the face of an unprecedented internal political failure and subsequent collapse.

This brief reconstruction of international political history since 1494 embodies several critical insights that bear on the question of future Chinese behavior over the long term. Before this extrapolation is explicitly addressed however, it may be useful to simply summarize the major insights gleaned from the historical record.

First, rising challengers have materialized throughout history for various reasons. These include internal political consolidation, as occurred in Spain during 1479–1504; revolutionary technological changes as, for example, those occurring in the realm in seafaring, which underwrote Portugal's rise in power from 1517–1580; external economic and political changes, primarily the acquisition of a stable overseas empire which was responsible for Britain's maintenance of global hegemony during the years 1714–1945; and, finally, the experience of rapid domestic economic growth, as occurred in Germany after its reunification in 1870 and continuing until the onset of the First World War in 1914.

Second, *no* rising state thus far has accepted the prevailing international political order and peacefully integrated itself into it. Given the theoretical arguments elucidated above, this is not at all surprising, since accepting the extant arrangements of governance would imply that the rising state has chosen not to reconfigure the existing order to suit its own interests. It is theoretically possible that the existing order perfectly suits the interests of the new rising state and hence demands no restructuring, but it is highly unlikely that such a condition would ever obtain in practice. This is because each international order usually reflects, however imperfectly, the preferences of the reigning hegemon and, in the competitive world of egoist international politics, it is highly unlikely that what suits the existing hegemon also suits the rising challenger just as well. Not surprisingly, then, every major rising power thus far—Spain, France, Germany, Japan, the United States, and the Soviet Union—has mounted challenges in different ways to the established order when they were in their ascending phase, and even those rising powers that appear not to have mounted any military challenges leading to systemic war—such as the United States—were spared the burdens of doing so because other rising powers—by challenging the preexisting hegemonies—provided an opportunity for challengers such as the United States to temporarily defend the preexisting hegemonic order but ultimately replace it with their own.[120]

Third, geopolitics conditions the character and targets of a rising state's assertiveness, not the fact of it. The evidence seems to suggest that geographical considerations—that is, whether a country is a continental or a maritime entity—affect how its assertiveness would be manifested, especially with respect to the range and identity of its targets, but it does not seem to make a major difference as far as the presence or absence of assertiveness is concerned. In general, rising states that have a continental character appear to focus on nearby targets, whereas maritime states can range more widely, dominating territories at a much greater range from the homeland. Although these differences, therefore, both affect who the "victims" of a rising state might be and condition the intensity of opposition emerging as a result of a given state's assertiveness—with continental powers precipitating greater immediate opposition in comparison to maritime powers—the geophysical location of the rising state itself does not seem to make any difference to the fact of assertiveness: Thus, maritime powers such as Portugal, the Netherlands, Great Britain, Japan, and the United States proceeded to acquire great formal or informal empires at some distance from their political frontiers (even as they attempted to manipulate strategic outcomes in other areas), whereas Spain, France, Germany, Russia, and the Soviet Union were, thanks to geography, condemned to manifest their assertive strategies much closer to home and often in the face of immediate and more intense opposition.

Fourth, *all* rising states, save one, have been involved in systemic wars at the time of a global power transition. As noted above, the principal exception to the rule involves the collapse of the Soviet Union, an exception usually attributed to the presence of nuclear weapons. Whether this attribution is accurate is hard to say given that Soviet collapse occurred outside of the context of defeat in war

---

[120]It is worth noting that before its defense of the preexisting hegemonic order, first in 1914–1918 and later in 1939–1945, the United States itself mounted a series of challenges to British hegemony, mainly in the Western Hemisphere. See, Barnett (1972) and Thompson (1996), for a good review of the details.

and principally as a result of internal political choices. If the latter cause, in fact, was responsible for the absence of war, then the peacefulness of this systemic transition was a product of mainly idiosyncratic causes. Very often, though, another example of a peaceful transition is offered—that involving the United States and Great Britain. It is difficult to accept this as a good example of a peaceful systemic transition because the transfer of power from Britain to the United States came about explicitly through war—a war that did not pit the United States against Great Britain because, among other things, German actions guaranteed that such a conflict was in fact unnecessary. During the Second World War, two rising states, Germany and Japan, attacked the existing hegemon, Great Britain, forcing the hegemon-in-waiting, the United States, to rush to the assistance of the latter because it too would soon be attacked by the rising challengers. Whether a peaceful systemic transition would have occurred between Britain and the United States, if Germany and Japan had not been present on the global scene, remains an issue for counterfactual history, but the empirical record does not warrant labeling this systemic transition peaceful except in a narrow Pickwickian sense.[121]

Fifth, the systemic wars that do occur as part of hegemonic transitions have multiple causes and diverse origins. Some of these wars occur because rising challengers may choose to attack the existing hegemon *directly*. Although there is an impression that such wars are frequent, an impression that may be fostered in part by cursory readings of Organski's and Gilpin's work on hegemonic wars, the fact remains that direct attacks on a hegemon by rising challengers are rare and infrequent in modern times. The best examples of such a

---

[121]This confusion about the peacefulness of the U.S.-British transition often arises on methodological grounds because systemic power transitions are often viewed as purely dyadic events, an impression unfortunately fostered by Organski and Kugler's early work on power transition theory. If systemic transitions, however, are viewed—as they should be—as involving more than two actors (which include the existing hegemon, several rising powers, and some bystanders), then the fact that some rising powers may not initiate systemic wars because other rising powers either attack them or attack the preexisting hegemon can be properly appreciated. The fact that some of these rising challengers do not initiate wars, then, does not make the systemic transition peaceful: Rather, the transition is always conflictual whether it is brought about by the actions of some or of all rising powers or even because of preventative war decisions made by the declining hegemon.

war from Modelski's narrative remains the French attack on the Dutch United Provinces under Louis XIV. Most systemic wars in fact occur because (a) some rising states attack other rising states to consolidate their power but nonetheless manage to precipitate systemic war because the existing hegemon enters the fray on behalf of the weaker side to preempt a future challenge that may be mounted by the stronger rising power (the Italian wars); or, (b) some rising states attack key allies of the existing hegemon or important neutrals in a search for regional gains, which nonetheless precipitates systemic war because the existing hegemon enters the fray on behalf of the ally or the neutral to prevent a shift in the future balance of power (the Spanish wars, the Napoleonic wars, and the First and Second World Wars). Most systemic wars, therefore, come about as a result of catalytic interventions by the existing hegemon on behalf of some other victims—interventions undertaken mainly for balance of power considerations—and rarely because the rising state directly attacks the existing hegemon to begin with.[122]

Sixth, and finally, systemic power transitions often occur because *successes* in systemic wars can irreparably weaken existing hegemonies. In fact, *no* rising challenger has thus far succeeded in supplanting any prevailing hegemony by war. Spain, France, Germany, Japan, and the Soviet Union all tried in different ways but failed. This fact notwithstanding, hegemonic transitions still occurred and this points to two critical insights about the succession process in world politics. First, struggles for hegemony are rarely dyadic encounters between two powers. Although these struggles involve the existing hegemon and the rising challenger as the preeminent antagonists, the entire cast of characters and the nature of their involvement become relevant to the succession process. Second, who wins is as important as by how much. This is particularly true because the strongest surviving state in the winning coalition usually turns out to be the new hegemon after a systemic war. Both Great Britain and the United States secured their hegemony in this way, the former

---

[122]As Thompson (1983a) succinctly phrased it, it is "*the threat of transition, and not its accomplishment, that creates a crisis for the global political system,*" as assertive behaviors on the part of rising powers, which may be inherently "relatively insignificant, or seemingly so" create conflagration because they occur at about the time when a structural transition is exactly at stake in the system and looks all but inevitable (cf., p. 112) [emphasis added].

through the wreckage of the wars with Louis XIV and with Napoleon, the latter through the wreckage of the wars with Hitler and Hirohito. Thus, "while fundamental structural changes are indeed associated with world or global wars, the changes [eventually] brought about are as much in spite of the challengers' efforts as they are due to them."[123]

What does this comparative historical narrative suggest about China's future behavior? Expressed briefly in propositional form, it suggests the following:

- If China does materialize as a rising power, it will be because a domestic economic transformation converts it into a potential challenger at the core of the international system.

- As a rising state, it is unlikely to simply accept the prevailing U.S.-dominated international political order and peacefully integrate itself into it.

- As a continental state (though with local maritime aspirations), China is more likely to display assertiveness closer to home rather than in the "distant abroad" (at least in the early stages of its growing power) though such behavior—if it occurs—is likely to precipitate counterbalancing coalitions involving its immediate landward and offshore neighbors in concert with more distant powers.

- This exercise of assertiveness could generate a range of political, economic, and military conflicts and, in the limiting case, even a major regional war which involves the existing hegemon, the United States.

- The participation of the United States in such a conflict on behalf of, or in concert with, other local states threatened by China may be intended initially merely as a limited engagement but it could mutate ultimately into a consequential struggle over control of the international system.

These five propositions drawn from the analysis of the past power transitions in international politics illustrated in Table 1 may be

---

[123]Thompson (1983b), p. 353.

summed up in the deceptively simple conclusion that the weight of global history suggests that China as a rising power will exhibit increasingly assertive behaviors over time, especially during the phase surrounding a systemic power transition, but that the triumph of the United States would be truly evanescent if, in the process of successfully combating such assertiveness, it enervated itself to the point where another rising power assumes global leadership simply because the victorious but now exhausted hegemon has no further capacity to resist.

Chapter Six

CONCLUSIONS

The expectation that China eventually would pursue an assertive grand strategic policy—in the aftermath of successfully attaining comprehensive national strength—will not be surprising to most students of international politics, since such behavior would be fairly consistent with the conduct of previous great powers historically.

Assertive policies in the case of China may be more likely for two other reasons. First, the unique and long-standing Chinese experience of geopolitical primacy and the association of that primacy with good order, civilization, virtue, and justice, may make the pursuit of geopolitical centrality through assertive behavior once again attractive, even in the absence of a hierarchical Confucian world view.[1] Moreover, the record presented in Chapter Three suggests that the use and exploitation of force was by no means exceptional in Chinese history, many official protestations today notwithstanding,[2] even though the application of intense levels of force for prolonged periods was often resisted by some Chinese political elites and even though strong Chinese regimes would at times eschew the use of force when it was shown to be ineffective and inferior to appeasement. In general, it is unlikely that imperial China behaved significantly differently from Republican Rome where defense of the periphery was concerned and at least one authority has argued that

---

[1]As suggested in Chapters Two and Three, the Chinese emphasis on geopolitical primacy derives as much from China's general historical experience as the predominant political, economic, cultural, and military power of East Asia as it does on the specific belief system of the Chinese state at any particular time.

[2]For one such example, see Li (1997).

Neither Chinese nor Romans, retreating in the face of aggressive barbarians, dug in on a fortified line to save civilization. On the contrary, Chinese and Romans, each exploiting a geographical environment that had recognizable characteristics, built up the highest civilizations of their times. They expanded to take in all the terrain that could be profitably exploited by the techniques they already had, until they reached a zone—the depths of Mongolia, the depths of Germany—which because of costs of transportation and distances from metropolitan markets could not be further integrated with the urban-rural *oikumene*. Further expansion would mean diminishing returns—too much military expenditure, too little additional revenue. That was where they dug in and why they dug in. Their "defense lines" were in fact the limits which they themselves set on their own expansion.[3]

As also shown in Chapter Three, within this general dynamic, the Chinese, like the Romans, pursued a variety of stratagems—punitive expeditions in some cases, coopting adversaries in others, and multiple forms of bribery in still some other instances—but the overarching objective still remained at the very least the neutralization of, or at best control over, the strategic periphery and, more important, the defense of a hegemony that was initially created by force, when possible, and ultimately legitimized and maintained by the claim of virtue and superior order and a related demand for deference from neighboring powers. *If* China fulfills its expected potential, there is no reason to believe that it will *not* eventually seek to "establish some sort of hegemony to protect and promote its interests."[4] Thanks to the changing circumstances of the age and at least some of the lessons provided by Chinese history, this hegemony may not "necessarily involve the physical conquest and occupation of neighboring countries[5] . . . but [it] would mean the use of various types of coercion to maintain an environment favorable to China's interests, and not necessarily to anyone else's."[6]

At the very least, therefore, growing Chinese power would at some point in the future likely result in a search for "hegemony" under-

---

[3]Lattimore (1979), p. 274.

[4]Roy (1996), p. 762.

[5]Nor, we should add, prolonged or major conflicts with other powers.

[6]Roy (1996).

stood as a quest for universal acceptance of its increased power, status, and influence as a legitimate right. Toward that end, if history is a reasonably accurate guide, an assertive China could reasonably be expected to augment its military capabilities in a manner commensurate with its increased power; develop a sphere of influence by acquiring new allies and underwriting the protection of others; acquire new or reclaim old territory for their resources or for symbolic reasons by penalizing, if necessary, any opponents or bystanders who resist such claims; prepare to redress past wrongs it believes it may have suffered; attempt to rewrite the prevailing international "rules of the game" to reflect its own interests; and, in the most extreme policy choice imaginable, even ready itself to thwart preventive war or to launch predatory attacks on its foes. Although it is unlikely that the last choice would be attractive in the nuclear age and might be made less likely if China were to become a democracy, the fact remains that any combination of these policies, though natural from the perspective of a powerful state, would stir the suspicion of its rivals and precipitate an action-reaction spiral that reinforces the temptation to embark on assertive stratagems even more strongly.

Second, an assertive China is likely to appear over the long haul, under the assumptions discussed above (including continued high growth, domestic political and social stability, etc.) precisely because the United States, the established hegemon, will—if the historical record pertaining to previous declining hegemonies holds—prepare to arrest its own gradual loss of relative power and influence. This behavior may, of course, not be oriented explicitly and solely to coping with an emerging Chinese threat, but it will nonetheless take place "under the shadow" of steadily increasing Chinese power. As a result, the attempts at regeneration will most likely provide numerous opportunities for various domestic constituencies within the United States to cast the process in explicitly anti-Chinese terms. Some of this rhetoric may be intended to shape the national consensus in pursuit of a robust containment strategy directed against the new rival, whereas other constituencies may be content simply to use the rhetoric to obscure their own private pursuit of some narrow rent-seeking opportunities that may arise as a result of growing Chinese power.

Even apart from such efforts at exploiting the China threat (which might materialize at the societal level), the U.S. state itself, for purely prudent reasons, would most likely be inclined at some point to accelerate its efforts at national renewal merely to immunize itself against the worst consequences imaginable as a result of greatly increased Chinese power. Consistent with this objective, the United States, for fully understandable reasons, would eventually seek to further improve its military capabilities in the face of significant increases in Chinese military power to ensure an effective defense of itself and its allies; restructure its economy and society to reverse unfavorable growth trends, increase technological innovation, or absorb or counter innovations that may be emerging elsewhere; preserve the extant international "rules of the game" with minimal changes in an effort to accommodate the rising challenger at the lowest minimal cost; maintain the existing political order by renewing its existing alliances, perhaps by altering the existing division of labor, reapportioning prevailing burdens, or recruiting new allies; develop new alliances by offering protection to states potentially threatened by the new rising power; and, in the most extreme response imaginable, contemplate preventive war or at least anticipate and prepare for military challenges mounted at itself and its allies.

Although it is unlikely that extreme variants of the last ingredient would form part of responsible U.S. policymaking, the fact remains that even the other policy responses would be interpreted by Beijing as little other than a covert attempt to contain China. Suspicions of this sort are already strong in Beijing, but they are likely to become even more corrosive—probably more justifiably—*if and when China approaches the status of a true global peer of the United States.* If China, in fact, continues to be governed by a nonliberal regime at that point, the traditional U.S. crusading impulse may only reinforce those imperatives flowing from the desire to maintain a balance of power into an even more aggressive attempt at containment. In any event, and irrespective of the precise dynamics involved, the intersection of diffidence on the part of the declining power—and all the efforts at arresting decline that those give rise to—and confidence on the part of the rising power—with all the assertiveness occasioned by that assurance—is likely to result in a rivalry that can only be managed but not avoided or wished away.

If such a rivalry can be anticipated, even if only over the long term, the question of how the United States should respond becomes a critical issue.[7] Many political realists argue that so long as the rise of China is assessed to be inevitable, there is no strategic alternative, in essence, to containing China—assuming that weakening, or undermining, or destroying it in some risk-free way is impossible. Machiavelli, writing at a different point in history, in fact provided the first systematic baseline for such a policy when he described the contours of Roman imperial strategy toward the Greeks. As Machiavelli approvingly described, Rome was compelled to conquer Greece to preempt Antiochus of Syria from securing Greece for himself. Clearly, neither Greece nor Syria threatened Roman security in any immediate sense but,

> the Romans, seeing inconveniences from afar, always found remedies for them and never allowed them to continue so as to escape a war, because they knew that war may not be avoided but [only] deferred to the advantage of others.[8]

The realism of Machiavelli, therefore, concludes that security can be preserved only by prudential action and that prudence in the face of potential changes in the international power structure can only take the form of continual preemptive conquest.[9] Since it is unlikely that the U.S. polity would find the Machiavellian solution very appetizing, preemptive conquest, which may be costly, unsuccessful, and perhaps even unethical in the modern age, may have to be replaced, in the view of some observers, by more conservative strategies such as preemptive containment or "polite containment,"[10] since weakening or undermining China is both costly to the current U.S. desire for high absolute gains and is fraught with great risks. One of the most insightful analyses of U.S. foreign policy has claimed, however,

---

[7]The best discussion of how alternative theoretical formulations like realism and liberalism in their various forms generate different policy responses can be found in Betts (1993/94). For a more recent discussion of U.S. policy responses, see Khalilzad et al. (1999).

[8]Machiavelli, XII–XIII.

[9]On Machiavelli's realism and its prescriptions for effective politics, see Tellis (1995/96), pp. 25–39.

[10]Betts (1993/94), p. 54.

that preemptive containment, even if desirable and effective, is not possible. Quoting John Quincy Adams who remarked that "America does not go abroad in search of monsters to destroy," the historian Walter McDougall has argued that the U.S. national temperament, which favors late and reluctant entrance into warfare (perhaps, after having absorbed the first blow), could not countenance preemptive strategies of any kind, no matter how efficacious those might have been in retrospect.[11]   Other scholars have argued that even if preemptive containment of China were possible, it is simply undesirable because "if you insist on treating another country like an enemy, it is likely to become one."[12] In other words, U.S. efforts to contain China would almost certainly provoke the emergence of an assertive, and more militant, China far sooner and to a much greater degree than might have otherwise occurred and, by implication, would likely preclude the emergence of a more cooperative China through any means short of internal collapse or conquest in war. For a variety of reasons, therefore, a containment strategy configured as an anticipatory response to the potential growth in Chinese power, is not feasible or desirable as a U.S. grand strategic policy.

If preemptive containment is inappropriate, the opposite strategy of preemptive appeasement is certainly premature and probably untenable as well. The notion of appeasement has acquired a certain odium in the vocabulary of modern politics because of its association with the failure of British policies toward Hitler in the 1930s and at least one scholar has argued that because of its loaded connotations, it ought to be banished from the political lexicon altogether.[13] If these nominalistic considerations are disregarded for the moment in favor of a more analytic approach, the fact remains that appeasement has been a time-honored strategy employed by many states, often with effective results. In the most general sense, appeasement consists of meeting a claimant's demands without asking for any reciprocal advantages. Such a strategy has often been thought to be self-defeating because of the inherently altruistic premises built into

---

[11]McDougall (1997), p. 25.

[12]Harries (1997), p. 35.

[13]Medlicott (1969).

its logic.[14] Yet, successful instances of appeasement in the past have had little to do with altruism. Rather, they arose because the appeaser often could do nothing other than appease in the specific situation at hand; or because the claimant's objectives were limited, justified, and legitimate; or because the appeaser simply elected to respond conciliatorily to initiate a process of diffuse reciprocity that would eventually result in higher joint gains for both sides.

The principal problem with preemptive appeasement as a grand strategic response to China, however, may not be its potential ineffectiveness but rather its prematurity. This is because China's rise to greatness is yet to be assured.[15] As argued in Chapter Five, many obstacles could still undermine its acquisition of comprehensive national strength and result in the failure of China to become a global peer competitor of the United States, or delay the attainment of that status beyond even the lengthy time period identified in this study. Because China's success is not yet assured, a general strategy of preemptively appeasing China may turn out to be a case of giving away too much, too early. Consequently, so long as China is not a true superpower, that is, a state that "enjoys relatively low sensitivity, vulnerability, and security interdependence because of massive resources and skill differentials and relative economic self-sufficiency,"[16] it ought not be treated as a peer competitor whose goodwill must be procured at any cost, including unilateral conciliation on important strategic issues, by the United States.

This of course does not mean that the United States should never undertake unilateral initiatives to encourage a more cooperative China, or to reassure a fearful China, or even to catalyze a cooperative relationship with a powerful China. Those decisions should depend, as Morgenthau put it, on whether the Chinese claim or concern in question embodies "rationally limited objectives which must be disposed of either on their intrinsic merits or by way of compromise."[17] If this claim is not part of a "chain at the end of which

---

[14]Middlemas (1972).

[15]In a somewhat hyperbolic vein, one commentator has even argued that China may not even matter very much today. See Segal (1999).

[16]Kim (1997), p. 24.

[17]Morgenthau (1985), p. 78.

stands the overthrow of the status quo,"[18] U.S. appeasement may be worthwhile at some future point in time. But U.S. grand strategy today is simply confronted by the *possibility* of a rising China, not the assurance of a global rival, and consequently a significant preemptive appeasement strategy that results both in the continued accretion of Chinese power and in the bolstering of Chinese status without concern for the implications such improvements pose for U.S. power and status cannot be in U.S. interests.

If both preemptive containment and preemptive appeasement of China are then judged to be premature as basic strategies, the only broad surviving policy option for the United States remains some form of realistic engagement. It may seem ironic that an analytic assessment that prognosticates the rise of Chinese power and argues that such power would eventually become assertive finally concludes that there may be no alternative to engaging China, at least in the policy-relevant future. Yet, the presumed irony rapidly disappears when it is understood that the analysis emphatically affirms the inherently high level of uncertainty afflicting all projections relating to China's future growth in power-political capacity, and the *possibility* that an assertive, strong China might become more moderate toward the use of force under some circumstances if its political system were to become democratic. If the growth in Chinese power and the resulting application of that power to external policy-related areas is a much more contingent phenomenon than is usually realized, then the mere possibility of this growth occurring cannot be reason enough for engaging in a preemptive strategy of any kind. This is especially true so long as there exists some small chance of avoiding the worst outcomes that would almost certainly result from the pursuit of a preemptive strategy.

Thus, so long as there is some chance that Chinese assertiveness may not occur for various reasons, U.S. strategy ought neither create the preconditions for its occurrence nor retreat in the expectation that its occurrence is inevitable. Further, if there is some hope that the worst ravages of future security competition between the United States and a strong China can be avoided, U.S. grand strategists are bound by

---

[18]Morgenthau (1985).

both the dictates of prudence and moral sensibility to explore every possibility that reduces the prospects of future international turmoil.

Even if the rise of Chinese power and its associated assertiveness were an absolute certainty—in terms of the "systemic" predictions deduced by some theory of world politics—the sheer length of time it would take this process to unfold allows the United States an opportunity to condition both the form and the intensity of the resulting competition. Among the first things the United States ought to do in preparing for this potential competition is to jettison the use of rhetorical labels such as "containment," "appeasement," and "constrainment" to define all or part of its strategic orientation toward China. It is worth remembering that an effective policy toward rising Chinese power will include various operational elements associated with each of these very different, and in many respects antagonistic, concepts. Consequently, it is more productive for U.S. security managers to focus on the *content* of desirable policies to be pursued in various issue-areas than on iconic and in some cases potentially inflammatory labels that are supposed to exhaustively describe the nature of U.S. strategic orientation.[19]

Unfortunately, discussing the precise content of these desirable policies would take this document too far afield[20] and, hence, subsequent discussion will be restricted simply to identifying the basic components that any realistic engagement of China ought to encompass. First, the process of engagement ought to include three related strands or objectives of policy: (1) to *pursue*, whenever feasible, the possibilities of cooperation aimed at attaining deeper levels of encounter, stronger degrees of mutual trust and confidence, more clearly defined notions of reciprocity or equity, and greater levels of integration into the international system, and to use the resulting expanded level of cooperation and integration to encourage movement by China toward a democratic form of government; (2) to discourage or, if ultimately necessary, *prevent* acquisition by China

---

[19]Even the term "engagement" itself can be highly misleading in this context, if it is taken to mean some form of appeasement or unqualified search for amicable relations with China at any cost. As is made clear below, the authors do not ascribe to such a flawed definition of "engagement."

[20]However, such an effort is currently under way, as part of a more detailed examination by the authors of China's calculative strategy and its implications for U.S. policy.

of capabilities that could unambiguously threaten the most fundamental core national security interests of the United States in Asia and beyond; and (3) to remain *prepared*, if necessary, to cope with—by means of diplomacy, economic relations, and military instruments—the consequences of a more assertive and militant China with greater capabilities in a variety of political, strategic, and economic issue-areas.

All three of these policy strands are arguably implicit in existing U.S. strategy toward China. Yet they are rarely recognized as such; nor are they espoused, much less implemented, in a coordinated and integrated fashion across various issue areas by the multiple bureaucracies within the U.S. government. On the contrary, many observers, and some government officials, often emphasize only one strand, often at the expense of one or both of the other two.

Second, engagement should identify and maintain a clear set of operational objectives, preferably centered on China's external security behavior, given the critical significance of such behavior to core U.S. national security interests. In particular, these objectives should relate most directly to key issue-areas of interest to the United States, including the U.S. presence, access, and alliance structure in Asia, the open international economic order, and the proliferation of weapons of mass destruction.

Third, engagement should be based upon a clear assessment of the multiple instruments available to support its three central strands and the tradeoffs inherent in the use of these instruments. This should include an evaluation of the range and types of hedging strategies required of the United States together with an assessment of how the pursuit of some hedging strategies could either undermine or enhance the success of engagement to begin with. Further, it should be recognized that even if engagement experiences great success in the interim, the policy may not survive unscathed over the longer term, when the superiority in Chinese power may make the necessity of accommodating the United States less pressing. Consequently, prudent forethought about what is necessary should or when engagement fails, both in the near and far term, is critical.

Finally, the overall development of a more effective engagement policy requires a better understanding of how China's calculative strategy might evolve over time as China's capabilities change, to influence the form and intensity of both China's cooperative and its assertive behavior.

Even as this sharper reassessment of engagement is developed, however, it is important to clarify U.S. grand strategy and the objectives to which it aspires: The engagement of China should not be a policy prescription designed to assist the growth of Chinese power so that it may eventually eclipse the United States, even if peacefully. Rather, engagement must be oriented toward encouraging a more cooperative China, whether strong or weak, while also preserving U.S. primacy in geopolitical terms, including in critical military and economic arenas, given the fact that such primacy has provided the conditions for both regional and global order and economic prosperity. Together, the predicates of engagement should also focus on eliciting Beijing's recognition that challenging existing U.S. leadership would be both arduous and costly and, hence, not in China's long-term interest.

The U.S. effort in this regard will arguably be facilitated if China becomes a democratic state that is more fully integrated into the international order and less inclined to employ military means. In general, so long as Beijing eschews the use of force and works peacefully to both adjust to and shape the future international system, the most destabilizing consequences of growing Chinese power will be minimized and, if the advocates of the democratic peace are correct, a U.S.-led international order of democratic states of which China is a part might even be able to avoid the worst ravages of security competition. Yet one must also keep in mind that the historical record suggests that the challenges to the attainment of this goal are likely to prove enormous because the structural constraints imposed by competitive international politics will interact with the chaotic domestic processes in both the United States and China to most likely produce an antagonistic interaction between these entities at the core of the global system.

BIBLIOGRAPHY

"Agreement Between the Government of the Union of Soviet Social-ist Republics and the Government of the People's Republic of China on the Guidelines of Mutual Reduction of Forces and Con-fidence Building in the Military Field in the Area of the Soviet-Chi-nese Border," April 24, 1990.

"Agreement Between the Russian Federation, the Republic of Ka-zakhstan, the Kyrgyz Republic, the Republic of Tajikistan and the People's Republic of China on Confidence Building in the Military Field in the Border Area," 1996.

Anderson, Jennifer, "The Limits of Sino-Russian Strategic Partner-ship," *Adelphi Paper*, No. 315, December 1997.

Armstrong, J. D., *Revolutionary Diplomacy: Chinese Foreign Policy and the United Front Doctrine*, University of California Press, Berkeley, California, 1977.

Austin, Greg, "The Strategic Implications of China's Public Order Crisis," *Survival*, Vol. 37, No. 2, Summer 1995.

Austin, Greg, *China's Ocean Frontier: International Law, Military Force and National Development*, Allen & Unwin Australia Pty Ltd., Canberra, Australia, 1998.

Bachman, David, "The Limits to Leadership in China," in "The Fu-ture of China," *NBR Analysis*, Vol. 3, No. 3, August 1992.

Bachman, David, "Domestic Sources of Chinese Foreign Policy," in Samuel S. Kim, ed., *China and the World: Chinese Foreign*

Relations in the Post-Cold War Era, Westview Press, Boulder, Colorado, 1994.

Backus, Charles, *The Nan-chao Kingdom and T'ang China's Southwestern Frontier,* Cambridge University Press, Cambridge, 1981.

Baldwin, David, "Power Analysis and World Politics," *World Politics,* Vol. 31, January 1979.

Ball, Desmond, "Arms and Affluence: Military Acquisitions in the Asia-Pacific Region," *International Security,* Vol. 18, No. 3, Winter 1993/94.

Barbieri, Katherine, "Economic Interdependence: A Path to Peace or a Source of Interstate Conflict?" *Journal of Peace Research,* Vol. 33, No. 1, 1996.

Barfield, Thomas J., *The Perilous Frontier: Nomadic Empires and China,* Blackwell Publishers, Inc., Cambridge, Massachusetts, 1989.

Barnett, A. Doak, *China and the Major Powers in East Asia,* The Brookings Institution, Washington, D.C., 1977.

Barnett, A. Doak, *The Making of Foreign Policy in China: Structure and Process,* Westview Press, Boulder, Colorado, 1985.

Barnett, Correlli, *The Collapse of British Power,* William Morrow, New York, 1972.

Barraclough, Geoffrey, ed., *The Times Atlas of World History,* Times Books, London, England, 1993.

Bartlett, Beatrice, *Monarchs and Ministers: The Grand Council in Mid-Ch'ing China, 1723–1820,* University of California Press, Berkeley, California, 1991.

Beckwith, Christopher I., *The Tibetan Empire in Central Asia; A History of the Struggle for Great Power Among Tibetans, Turks, Arabs, and Chinese During the Middle Ages,* Princeton University Press, Princeton, New Jersey, 1987.

Bernstein, Richard, and Ross Munro, *The Coming Conflict with China,* A. A. Knopf, New York, 1997.

Bert, Wayne, "Chinese Policies and U.S. Interests in Southeast Asia," *Asian Survey*, Vol. 33, No. 3, March 1993.

Betts, Richard K., "Wealth, Power, and Instability: East Asia and the United States after the Cold War," *International Security*, Vol. 18, No. 3, Winter 1993/94.

Blank, Stephen J., *The Dynamic of Russian Arms Sales to China*, Strategic Studies Institute, Carlisle Barracks, U.S. Army War College, 1996.

Blasko, Dennis, Philip Klapakis, and John Corbett, "Training Tomorrow's PLA: A Mixed Bag of Tricks," *The China Quarterly*, Vol. 146, June 1996.

Boylan, Edward S., "The Chinese Cultural Style of Warfare," *Comparative Strategy*, Vol. 3, No. 4, Crane, Russack, and Company, Inc., 1982.

Brecher, Michael, Jonathan Wilkenfeld, and Sheila Moser, *Crises in the Twentieth Century, Vol. 2: Handbook of Foreign Policy Crises*, Pergamon Press, Oxford, England, 1988.

Brown, Lester, *Who Will Feed China?* W. W. Norton and Company, Inc., New York, 1995.

Burles, Mark, *Chinese Policy Towards Russia and the Central Asian Republics*, RAND, Santa Monica, California, 1999.

Buzan, Barry, and Gerald Segal, "The Rise of "Lite" Powers: A Strategy for the Postmodern States," *World Policy Journal*, Vol. 13, No. 3, Fall 1996.

Caldwell, John, and Alexander T. Lennon, "China's Nuclear Modernization Program," *Strategic Review*, Vol. 23, Fall 1995.

"Can a Bear Love a Dragon?" *The Economist*, April 26, 1997.

Chen, Bingfu, "An Economic Analysis of the Changes in China's Military Expenditures in the Last Ten Years," *Junshi jingji yanjui* [Military economic studies], No. 6, June 1990.

Chen, Feng, "Order and Stability in Social Transition: Neoconservative Political Thought in Post-1989 China," *The China Quarterly*, Vol. 151, September 1997.

Chen, Jian, *China's Road to the Korean War, The Making of the Sino-American Confrontation*, Columbia University Press, New York, 1994.

Chen, King C., *Vietnam and China, 1938–1954*, Princeton University Press, Princeton, New Jersey, 1969.

Chen, Qimao, "New Approaches in China's Foreign Policy: The Post-Cold War Era," *Asian Survey*, Vol. 33, No. 3, March 1993.

Cheung, Tai Ming, "China-Taiwan Relations," *Kim Eng Securities Bulletin*, May 1996.

Chiang Kai-shek, *China's Destiny*, 1943 (English edition, 1947).

A Chinese-English Dictionary, Commercial Press, Beijing, 1992.

Christensen, Thomas J., "Chinese Realpolitik," *Foreign Affairs*, Vol. 75, No. 5, September/October 1996a.

Christensen, Thomas J., *Useful Adversaries: Grand Strategy, Domestic Mobilization, and Sino-American Conflict, 1947–1958*, Princeton University Press, Princeton, New Jersey, 1996b.

Chu, Shulong, "The PRC Girds for Limited, High-Tech War," *Orbis*, Vol. 38, No. 2, Spring 1994.

Clarke, Christopher M., "China's Transition to the Post-Deng Era," in *China's Economic Dilemmas in the 1990's: The Problems of Reforms, Modernization, and Interdependence*, study papers submitted to the Joint Economic Committee, Congress of the United States, U.S. Government Printing Office, Washington, D.C., 1991.

Cohen, Joel E., *How Many People Can the Earth Support?* W. W. Norton and Company, Inc., New York, 1995.

Cohen, Paul A., "Ch'ing China: Confrontation with the West," *Modern East Asia: Essays in Interpretation*, Harcourt, Brace & World, New York, 1970.

Copeland, Dale C., "Economic Interdependence and War: A Theory of Trade Expectations," *International Security*, Vol. 20, No. 4, Spring 1996.

Dardess, John W., *Confucianism and Autocracy: Professional Elites in the Founding of the Ming Dynasty*, University of California Press, Berkeley, California, 1983.

Davis, Zachary S., "China's Nonproliferation and Export Control Policies," *Asian Survey*, Vol. XXXV, No. 6, June 1995.

De Crespigny, Rafe, "Tradition and Chinese Foreign Policy," in Stuart Harris and Gary Klintworth, eds., *China as a Great Power, Myths, Realities and Challenges in the Asia-Pacific Region*, St. Martin's Press, New York, 1995.

Dibb, Paul, *Towards a New Balance of Power in Asia*, Adelphi Paper 295 IISS, London, 1995.

Dittmer, Lowell, "Bases of Power in Chinese Politics: A Theory and an Analysis of the Fall of the 'Gang of Four,'" *World Politics*, Vol. 31, No. 1, October 1978.

Dittmer, Lowell, and Samuel S. Kim, eds., *China's Quest for National Identity*, Cornell University Press, Ithaca and London, 1993.

Downs, Erica Strecker, "China's Quest for Energy Security: Catalyst for Conflict?" RAND, Santa Monica, California, unpublished.

Doyle, Michael, "Kant, Liberal Legacies and Foreign Affairs, Part I," *Philosophy and Public Affairs*, Vol. 12, No. 3, Summer 1983.

Dreyer, Edward L., *Early Ming China*, Stanford University Press, Stanford, California, 1982.

Dreyer, June Teufel, and Ilpyong J. Kim, eds., *Chinese Defense and Foreign Policy*, Paragon House, New York, 1988.

Dupuy, Ernest R., and Trevor N. Dupuy, *The Encyclopedia of Military History from 3500 B.C. to the Present*, 2nd ed., Harper & Row, New York, 1986.

Economy, Elizabeth, "China's Environmental Diplomacy," in Samuel S. Kim, ed., *China and the World: Chinese Foreign Policy Faces the*

New Millennium, 4th ed., Westview Press, Boulder, Colorado, 1998.

Economy, Elizabeth, and Michel Oksenberg, eds., *China Joins the World: Progress and Prospects,* Council on Foreign Relations Press, New York, 1999.

"Envoy Comments on Declaration on Human Rights Defenders," Xinhua, 4 March 1998.

Fairbank, John K., *Trade and Diplomacy on the China Coast,* Stanford, Palo Alto, California, 1964.

Fairbank, John King, "A Preliminary Framework," in John K. Fairbank, ed., *The Chinese World Order: Traditional China's Foreign Relations,* Harvard University Press, Cambridge, Massachusetts, 1968a.

Fairbank, John King, ed., *The Chinese World Order: Traditional China's Foreign Relations,* Harvard University Press, Cambridge, Massachusetts, 1968b.

Fairbank, John King, "Introduction: Varieties of the Chinese Military Experience," in Frank A. Kierman, Jr., and John K. Fairbank, eds., *Chinese Ways in Warfare,* Harvard University Press, Cambridge, Massachusetts, 1974.

Fairbank, John King, "Introduction: The Old Order," in Denis Twitchett and John F. Fairbank, eds., *The Cambridge History of China, Volume 10, Late Ch'ing, 1800–1911, Part 1,* Cambridge University Press, London, England, 1978a.

Fairbank, John King, "The Creation of the Treaty System," in Denis Twitchett and John F. Fairbank, eds., *The Cambridge History of China, Volume 10, Late Ch'ing, 1800–1911, Part 1,* Cambridge University Press, London, England, 1978b.

Fairbank, John King, *China, A New History,* Harvard University Press, Cambridge, Massachusetts, 1992.

Farber, Henry S., and Joanne Gowa, "Politics and Peace," *International Security,* Vol. 20, No. 2, Fall 1995.

Fitzgerald, C. P., *The Southern Expansion of the Chinese People,* Praeger, New York, 1972.

Fletcher, Joseph, "Ch'ing Inner Asia, c.1800," in Denis Twitchett and John F. Fairbank, eds., *The Cambridge History of China, Volume 10, Late Ch'ing, 1800–1911, Part 1,* Cambridge University Press, London, England, 1978.

Foot, Rosemary, "China in the ASEAN Regional Forum: Organization Processes and Domestic Modes of Thought," *Asian Survey,* Vol. 38, No. 5, May 1998.

Forbes, Andrew D. W., *Warlords and Muslims in Chinese Central Asia: A Political History of Republican Sinkiang,* Cambridge University Press, London, England, 1986.

Freeman, Chas. W., Jr., "Managing U.S. Relations with China," paper presented at Asia/Pacific Research Center, Stanford University, April 1996.

Freeman, Chas. W., Jr., *Arts of Power: Statecraft and Diplomacy,* United States Institute of Peace Press, Washington D.C., 1997.

Freris, Andrew F., ed., *The Economy of the PRC: Analysis and Forecasts,* Salomon Brothers, Inc., New York, November 1995.

Friedberg, Aaron, "Ripe for Rivalry: Prospects for Peace in a Multipolar Asia," *International Security,* Vol. 18, No. 3, Winter 1993/94.

Friedman, Edward, *The Politics of Democratization: Generalizing East Asian Experiences,* Westview Press, Boulder, Colorado, 1994.

Frieman, Wendy, "New Members of the Club: Chinese Participation in Arms Control Regimes 1980–1995," *The Nonproliferation Review,* Vol. 3, No. 3, Summer 1996.

Frolov, Viacheslav A., "China's Armed Forces Prepare for High-Tech Warfare," *Defense & Foreign Affairs Strategic Policy,* January 1998.

Garrett, Banning N., and Bonnie S. Glazer, "Chinese Perspectives on Nuclear Arms Control," *International Security,* Vol. 20, No. 3, Winter 1995/96.

Garver, John, "Sino-Russian Relations," in Samuel S. Kim, ed., *China and the World: Chinese Foreign Policy Faces the New Millennium*, Westview Press, Boulder, Colorado, 1998.

Gill, Bates, and Taeho Kim, *China's Arms Acquisitions from Abroad: A Quest for "Superb and Secret Weapons,"* Oxford University Press, New York, 1995.

Gilpin, Robert, *War and Change in World Politics,* Cambridge University Press, Cambridge, 1981.

Gilpin, Robert, "The Theory of Hegemonic War," *Journal of Interdisciplinary History,* Vol. XVIII, No. 4, Spring 1988.

Gittings, John, *The Role of the Chinese Army,* Oxford University Press, New York, 1967.

Gittings, John, *The World and China, 1922–1972,* Harper & Row, New York, 1974.

Gladney, Dru C., *Muslim Chinese: Ethnic Nationalism in the People's Republic,* Harvard University Press, Cambridge, Massachusetts, 1991.

Glaser, Bonnie S., "China's Security Perceptions: Interests and Ambitions," *Asian Survey,* Vol. 33, No. 3, March 1993.

Gochman, Charles S., "Correspondence," *International Security,* Vol. 21, No. 3, Winter 1996/97.

Godwin, Paul H. B., "Changing Concepts of Doctrine, Strategy, and Operations in the People's Liberation Army 1978–87," *The China Quarterly,* No. 112, December 1987.

Godwin, Paul H. B., "Chinese Military Strategy Revised: Local and Limited War," *The Annals of the AAPSS,* Vol. 519, January 1992.

Godwin, Paul H. B., "From Continent to Periphery: PLA Doctrine, Strategy and Capabilities Towards 2000," in David Shambaugh and Richard H. Yang, eds., *China's Military in Transition,* Clarendon Press, Oxford, England, 1997.

Goldstein, Avery, "Robust and Affordable Security: Some Lessons from the Second-Ranking Powers During the Cold War," *Journal of Strategic Studies,* Vol. 15, No. 4, December 1992.

Goldstein, Avery, "Great Expectations: Interpreting China's Arrival," *International Security,* Vol. 22, No. 3, Winter 1997/98.

Goldstein, Joshua S., *Long Cycles,* Yale University Press, New Haven, Connecticut, 1988.

Goldstein, Melvyn C., *A History of Modern Tibet, 1913–1951: The Demise of the Lamaist State,* University of California Press, Berkeley, California, 1989.

Goldstein, Steven M., "Nationalism and Internationalism: Sino-Soviet Relations," in Thomas W. Robinson and David Shambaugh, eds., *Chinese Foreign Policy: Theory and Practice,* Clarendon Press, Oxford, England, 1994.

Goldstone, Jack A., "The Coming Chinese Collapse," *Foreign Policy,* Summer 1995.

Gowa, Joanne, *Ballots and Bullets,* Princeton University Press, Princeton, New Jersey, 1999.

Grieco, Joseph M., "Anarchy and the Limits of Cooperation," *International Organization,* Vol. 42, No. 3, Summer 1988.

Grunfeld, A. Tom, *The Making of Modern Tibet,* M. E. Sharpe, Inc., New York, July 1996.

Gunter, Lt. Col. F. R., "China in 2020: Three Scenarios," briefing presented to the Army After Next (AAN) China Revolution in Military Affairs (RMA) Workshop, February 6, 1998.

Gurtov, Mel, and Byong-Moo Hwang, *China's Security: The New Roles of the Military,* Lynne Rienner Publishers, Inc., Boulder, Colorado, 1998.

Hamrin, Carol Lee, *China and the Challenge of the Future: Changing Political Patterns,* Westview Press, Boulder, Colorado, 1990.

Hamrin, Carol Lee, "The Party Leadership System," in Kenneth G. Lieberthal and David M. Lampton, eds., *Bureaucracy, Politics, and Decision Making in Post-Mao China*, University of California Press, Berkeley, California, 1992.

Hamrin, Carol Lee, "Elite Politics and the Development of China's Foreign Relations," in Thomas W. Robinson and David Shambaugh, eds., *Chinese Foreign Policy: Theory and Practice*, Clarendon Press, Oxford, England, 1994.

Han, Nianlong, *Diplomacy of Contemporary China*, New Horizon Press, Hong Kong, 1990.

Hao, Chang, "Intellectual Change and the Reform Movement, 1890–8," in Denis Twitchett and John K. Fairbank, eds., *The Cambridge History of China, Volume 11, Late Ch'ing 1800–1911, Part 2,* Cambridge University Press, London, England, 1980.

Hao, Yen-p'ing, and Erh-min Wang, "Changing Chinese Views of Western Relations, 1840–95," in Denis Twitchett and John K. Fairbank, eds., *The Cambridge History of China, Volume 11, Late Ch'ing 1800–1911, Part 2,* Cambridge University Press, London, England, 1980.

Harding, Harry, ed., *China's Foreign Relations in the 1980s,* Yale University Press, New Haven, Connecticut, 1984.

Harding, Harry, *China's Second Revolution, Reform after Mao,* The Brookings Institution, Washington, D.C., 1987.

Harding, Harry, *A Fragile Relationship: The United States and China Since 1972,* The Brookings Institution, Washington, D.C., 1992.

Harding, Harry, "China's Cooperative Behavior," in Thomas W. Robinson and David Shambaugh, eds., *Chinese Foreign Policy: Theory and Practice,* Clarendon Press, Oxford, England, 1994a.

Harding, Harry, "'On the Four Great Relationships': The Prospects for China," *Survival,* Vol. 36, No. 2, Summer 1994b.

Harries, Owen, "How Not to Handle China," *The National Review,* May 5, 1997.

Harris, Stuart, and Gary Klintworth, eds., *China As a Great Power, Myths, Realities and Challenges in the Asia-Pacific Region*, St. Martin's Press, New York, 1995.

Hinton, Harold C., *China's Turbulent Quest: An Analysis of China's Foreign Relations Since 1949*, Indiana University Press, Bloomington, Indiana, 1970.

Hsiung, James C., "China's Omni-Directional Diplomacy," *Asian Survey*, Vol. XXXV, No. 6, June 1995.

Hsu, Immanuel C. Y., *The Rise of Modern China*, Oxford University Press, New York, 1970.

Hsu, Immanuel C. Y., "Late Ch'ing Foreign Relations, 1866–1905," in Denis Twitchett and John K. Fairbank, eds., *The Cambridge History of China, Volume 11, Part 2*, Cambridge University Press, London, England, 1980.

Hu, Weixing, "Beijing's New Thinking on Security Strategy," *The Journal of Contemporary China*, No. 3, Summer 1993.

Huang, Alexander, "The Chinese Navy's Offshore Active Defense Strategy: Conceptualization and Implications," *Naval War College Review*, Vol. XLVII, No. 3, Summer 1994.

Huang, Ray, *China: A Macro History*, M. E. Sharpe, Inc., New York, New York, 1997.

Huck, Arthur, *The Security of China: Chinese Approaches to Problems of War and Strategy*, Columbia University Press, New York, 1970.

Hucker, Charles O., *China to 1850: A Short History*, Stanford University Press, Stanford, California, 1975.

Hunt, Michael H., "Chinese Foreign Relations in Historical Perspective," in Harry Harding, ed., *China's Foreign Relations in the 1980s*, Yale University Press, New Haven, Connecticut, 1984.

Hunt, Michael H., "Chinese National Identity and the Strong State: The Late Qing-Republican Crisis," in Lowell Dittmer and Samuel S. Kim, eds., *China's Quest for National Identity*, Cornell University Press, Ithaca, New York, and London, 1993.

Hunt, Michael H., *The Genesis of Chinese Communist Foreign Policy*, Columbia University Press, New York, 1996.

Jacobs, J. Bruce, and Lijian Hong, "China's Relationship with Taiwan," in Stuart Harris and Gary Klintworth, eds., *China as a Great Power, Myths, Realities and Challenges in the Asia-Pacific Region*, St. Martin's Press, New York, 1995.

Jagchid, Sechin, and Van Jay Symons, *Peace, War, and Trade Along the Great Wall: Nomadic-Chinese Interaction Through Two Millennia*, Indiana University Press, Bloomington, Indiana, 1989.

Jencks, Harlan, "Wild Speculations on the Military Balance in the Taiwan Straits," in James Lilley, ed., *Crisis in the Taiwan Strait*, National Defense University Press, Washington, D.C., 1997.

Jervis, Robert, "Cooperation Under the Security Dilemma," *World Politics*, Vol. 30, No. 2, 1978.

Jervis, Robert, *The Meaning of the Nuclear Revolution*, Cornell University Press, Ithaca, New York, 1989.

Jiang Zemin, "China's Policy Toward East Asia," *Heping*, 36-37, March 1995.

Joffe, Ellis, "Party-Army Relations in China: Retrospect and Prospect," *The China Quarterly*, Vol. 146, June 1996.

Johnston, Alastair Iain, *Cultural Realism: Strategic Culture and Grand Strategy in Chinese History*, Princeton University Press, Princeton, New Jersey, 1995.

Johnston, Alastair Iain, "China's New 'Old Thinking': The Concept of Limited Deterrence," *International Security*, Vol. 20, No. 3, Winter 1995/96.

Johnston, Alastair Iain, "Learning versus Adaptation: Explaining Change in Chinese Arms Control Policy in the 1980s and 1990s," *The China Journal*, Vol. 35, January 1996a.

Johnston, Alastair Iain, "Prospects for Chinese Nuclear Force Modernization: Limited Deterrence Versus Multilateral Arms Control," *The China Quarterly*, Vol. 146, June 1996b.

Johnston, Alastair Iain, "China's Militarized Interstate Dispute Behaviour: 1949–1992: A First Cut at the Data," *The China Quarterly*, No. 153, March 1998.

Kaye, Lincoln, "The Grip Slips," *Far Eastern Economic Review*, Vol. 158, May 11, 1995a.

Kaye, Lincoln, "Fragile China: Affluent Regions Go Their Own Way," *Far Eastern Economic Review*, Vol. 158, pp. 18–21, May 11, 1995b.

Kennedy, Paul M., *Strategy and Diplomacy, 1870–1945: Eight Studies*, Allen & Unwin, London and Boston, 1983.

Kennedy, Paul M., *The Rise and Fall of the Great Powers*, Random House, New York, 1987.

Keohane, Robert O., and Joseph S. Nye, Jr., "Power and Interdependence Revisited," *International Organization*, Vol. 41, Autumn 1987.

Kessler, Lawrence D., *K'ang-Hsi and the Consolidation of Ch'ing Rule 1661–1684*, The University of Chicago Press, Chicago, Illinois, 1976.

Khalilzad, Zalmay, and Ian Lesser, eds., *Sources of Conflict in the 21st Century*, RAND, Santa Monica, California, 1998.

Khalilzad, Zalmay, et al., *The United States and a Rising China*, RAND, Santa Monica, California, 1999.

Kierman, Frank A., Jr., and John K. Fairbank, eds., *Chinese Ways in Warfare*, Harvard University Press, Cambridge, Massachusetts, 1974.

Kim, Samuel S., ed., *China and the World: Chinese Foreign Policy in the Post-Mao Era*, Westview Press, Boulder, Colorado, 1984.

Kim, Samuel S., *China In and Out of the Changing World Order*, Center for International Studies, Princeton, New Jersey, 1991.

Kim, Samuel S., "China as a Regional Power," *Current History*, Vol. 91, No. 566, September 1992.

Kim, Samuel S., ed., *China and the World: Chinese Foreign Relations in the Post-Cold War Era*, Westview Press, Boulder, Colorado, 1994.

Kim, Samuel S., "China in the Post-Cold War World," in Stuart Harris and Gary Klintworth, eds., *China as a Great Power, Myths, Realities and Challenges in the Asia-Pacific Region*, St. Martin's Press, New York, 1995.

Kim, Samuel S., *China's Quest for Security in the Post-Cold War World*, Strategic Studies Institute, Carlisle Barracks, U.S. Army War College, 1996.

Kim, Samuel S., "China as a Great Power," *Current History*, September 1997.

Kim, Samuel S., ed., *China and the World: Chinese Foreign Policy Faces the New Millennium*, Westview Press, Boulder, Colorado, 1998.

Kim, Samuel S., "China and the United Nations," in Elizabeth Economy and Michel Oksenberg, eds., *China Joins the World: Progress and Prospects*, Council on Foreign Relations Press, New York, 1999.

Kirby, William C., "Traditions of Centrality, Authority, and Management of Modern China's Foreign Relations," in Thomas W. Robinson and David Shambaugh, eds., *Chinese Foreign Policy: Theory and Practice*, Clarendon Press, Oxford, England, 1994.

Kirby, William C., "The Internationalization of China: Foreign Relations at Home and Abroad in the Republican Era," *The China Quarterly*, No. 150, Wace Journals, Oxfordshire, England, June 1997.

Klintworth, Gary, "South East Asia—China Relations Evolve," *Asia Pacific Defence Reporter*, February–March 1997.

Klintworth, Gary, and Des Ball, "China's Arms Buildup and Regional Security," in Stuart Harris and Gary Klintworth, eds., *China as a Great Power, Myths, Realities and Challenges in the Asia-Pacific Region*, St. Martin's Press, New York, 1995.

Knorr, Klaus, *Power and Wealth*, Basic Books, New York, 1973.

Krauthammer, Charles, "Why We Must Contain China," *Time*, July 31, 1995.

Kupchan, Charles A., and Clifford A. Kupchan, "The Promise of Collective Security, *International Security*, Vol. 20, No. 1, Summer 1995.

Lam, Truong Buu, "Intervention Versus Tribute in Sino-Vietnamese Relations, 1788–1790," in John K. Fairbank, ed., *The Chinese World Order*, Harvard University Press, Cambridge, Massachusetts, 1968.

Lampton, David M., *Paths to Power: Elite Mobility in Contemporary China*, Center for Chinese Studies, University of Michigan, Ann Arbor, 1989.

Lardy, Nicholas R., "China's Growing Economic Role in Asia," in "The Future of China," *NBR Analysis*, Vol. 3, No. 3, August 1992.

Lardy, Nicholas R., "The Challenge of Economic Reform and Social Stability," paper prepared for the conference "The PRC After the Fifteenth CCP Party Congress," organized by the Institute for National Policy Research, Taipei, Taiwan, February 19–20, 1998.

Lattimore, Owen, *Studies in Frontier History: Collected Papers, 1928–1958*, Oxford University Press, London, 1962.

Lattimore, Owen, "Great Wall and Jungle: China's Historical Hegemony," *The Nation*, Vol. 228, No. 10, 1979.

Layne, Christopher, "Kant or Cant: The Myth of the Democratic Peace," *International Security*, Vol. 19, No. 2, Fall 1994.

Lee, Chae-jin, *China and Korea*, Hoover Press, Stanford, California, 1996.

Lee, Choon Kun, *War in the Confucian International Order*, Doctoral Dissertation, The University of Texas at Austin, August 1988.

Levathes, Louise, *When China Ruled the Seas*, Simon and Schuster, New York, 1994.

Levy, Jack S., "The Causes of War: A Review of Theories and Evidence," in Philip E. Tetlock et al., eds., *Behavior, Society, and National War*, Vol. 1, Oxford University Press, New York, 1989.

Li, Jijun, Lieutenant General, "On Strategic Culture," *Zhongguo Junshi Kexue*, No. 1, February 1997, pp. 8–15, in FBIS-CHI-97-092, May 15, 1997.

Li, Tianran, "On the Question of Comprehensive National Strength," *Journal of International Studies*, Vol. 2, April 1990.

Liang, Liangxing, ed., *China's Foreign Relations: A Chronology of Events (1948–1988)*, Foreign Languages Press, Beijing, China, 1989.

Liao, Kuang-sheng, "Linkage Politics in China: Internal Mobilization and Articulated External Hostility in the Cultural Revolution, 1967–1969," *World Politics*, Vol. 28, No. 4, 1976.

Liao, Kuang-sheng, *Antiforeignism and Modernization in China, 1860–1980: Linkage Between Domestic Politics and Foreign Policy*, The Chinese University Press, Hong Kong, 1984.

Lieberthal, Kenneth, "Domestic Politics and Foreign Policy," in Harry Harding, ed., *China's Foreign Relations in the 1980s*, Yale University Press, New Haven, Connecticut, 1984.

Lieberthal, Kenneth G., "China in the Year 2000: Politics and International Security," in "The Future of China," *NBR Analysis*, Vol. 3, No. 3, August 1992.

Lieberthal, Kenneth G., *Governing China: From Revolution Through Reform*, W. W. Norton and Company, Inc., New York, 1995.

Lieberthal, Kenneth G., and Michael Lampton, eds., *Bureaucracy, Politics, and Decision Making in Post-Mao China*, University of California Press, Berkeley, California, 1992.

Lilley, James, ed., *Crisis in the Taiwan Strait*, National Defense University Press, Washington, D.C., 1997.

Liska, George, *Quest for Equilibrium*, Johns Hopkins, Baltimore, Maryland, 1977.

Liu, Drew, "Questioning the Prospect of Political Reform in China," *China Strategic Review,* Vol. II, No. 5, The China Strategic Institute, Washington, D.C., September/October 1997.

Liu, F. F., *A Military History of Modern China 1924–1949,* Princeton University Press, Princeton, New Jersey, 1956.

Liu, Kwang-Ching, and Richard J. Smith, "The Military Challenge: The North-West and the Coast," in Denis Twitchett and John K. Fairbank, eds., *The Cambridge History of China, Volume 11, Late Ch'ing 1800–1911, Part 2,* Cambridge University Press, London, England, 1980.

Lu, Ning, *The Dynamics of Foreign Policy Decision-making in China,* Westview Press, Boulder, Colorado, 1997.

Luard, Evan, *The Blunted Sword: The Erosion of Military Power in Modern World Politics,* New Amsterdam, New York, 1988.

Machiavelli, Niccolò, *Discorsi sopra la prima deca di Tito Livio (Discourses on Livy),* Harvey C. Mansfield and Nathan Tarcov, trans., University of Chicago Press, Chicago, 1996.

Malik, J. Mohan, ed., *Asian Defence Policies,* Deakin University Press, Geelong, Victoria, Australia, 1993.

Mansfield, Edward D., and Jack Snyder, "Democratization and the Danger of War," *International Security,* Vol. 20, No. 1, Summer 1995.

Mansfield, Edward D., and Jack Snyder, "Democratization and the Danger of War," in Michael Brown et al., eds., *Debating the Democratic Peace,* MIT Press, Cambridge, Massachusetts, 1996a.

Mansfield, Edward D., and Jack Snyder, "The Effects of Democratization on War," *International Security,* Vol. 20, 1996b.

Mao, Zhenfa, ed., *Bianfang Lun (On Frontier Defense),* Junshi Kexue Chubanshe, Beijing, 1996.

McCormick, Barrett L., *Political Reform in Post-Mao China: Democracy and Bureaucracy in a Leninist State,* University of California Press, Berkeley, California, 1990.

McCormick, Barrett L., "Democracy or Dictatorship? A Response to Gordon White," in *The Australian Journal of Chinese Affairs*, No. 31, Canberra, Australia, January 1994.

McDougall, Walter, "Foreign Monsters, False Alarms," *The New York Times*, April 15, 1997, Section A.

Mearsheimer, John, "Back to the Future: Instability in Europe After the Cold War, *International Security*, Vol. 19, No. 3, Winter 1994/95.

Medlicott, William N., *Britain and Germany*, St. Martin's Press, New York, 1969.

Middlemas, Keith, *The Diplomacy of Illusion*, Wiedenfield and Nicholson, London, England, 1972.

Modelski, George, "The Long Cycle of Global Politics and the Nation-State," *Comparative Studies in Society and History*, April 1978.

Modelski, George, and William R. Thompson, *Leading Sectors and World Powers*, University of South Carolina Press, Columbia, South Carolina, 1996.

Molander, Roger C., and Peter A. Wilson, *The Nuclear Asymptote*, RAND, Santa Monica, California, 1993.

Morgenthau, Hans, *Politics Among Nations*, Alfred K. Knopf, New York, 1968.

Morgenthau, Hans, *Politics Among Nations*, 6th ed., Alfred K. Knopf, New York, 1985.

Morse, H. B., *The International Relations of the Chinese Empire*, Cheng Wen Publishing Company, Taipei, Taiwan, 1960.

Mueller, John, *Retreat from Doomsday: The Obsolescence of Major War*, Basic Books, New York, 1989.

Muller, David G., Jr., *China as a Maritime Power*, Westview Press, Boulder, Colorado, 1983.

Mulvenon, James, *Professionalization of the Senior Chinese Officer Corps: Trends and Implications*, RAND, Santa Monica, California, 1997a.

Mulvenon, James, ed., *China Facts and Figures Annual Handbook 21*, Academic International Press, Gulf Breeze, Florida, 1997b.

Mulvenon, James C., "Soldiers of Fortune: The Rise of the Military-Business Complex in the Chinese People's Liberation Army," Ph.D. Dissertation, University of California at Los Angeles, September 1998.

Munro, Ross H., "Eavesdropping on the Chinese Military: Where It Expects War—Where It Doesn't," *Orbis*, Vol. 38, No. 3, Summer 1994.

Munro, Ross H., "China, India, and Central Asia," in Jed C. Snyder, ed., *After Empire: The Emerging Geopolitics of Central Asia*, NDU Press, Washington, D.C., 1995.

Nan, Li, "The PLA's Evolving Warfighting Doctrine, Strategy and Tactics, 1985–95: A Chinese Perspective," in David Shambaugh and Richard H. Yang, eds., *China's Military in Transition*, Clarendon Press, Oxford, England, 1997.

Nathan, Andrew J., *China's Crisis: Dilemmas of Reform and Prospects for Democracy*, Columbia University Press, New York, 1990.

Nathan, Andrew, "Human Rights in Chinese Foreign Policy," *The China Quarterly*, Vol. 139, September 1994.

Nathan, Andrew, "China and the International Human Rights Regime," in Elizabeth Economy and Michel Oksenberg, eds., *China Joins the World: Progress and Prospects*, Council on Foreign Relations Press, New York, 1999.

Nye, Joseph, Jr., *Bound to Lead*, Basic Books, New York, 1991.

Nye, Joseph, "China and the Future of the Asia-Pacific Region," paper presented to the 39th Annual IISS Conference in Singapore, 11–14 September, 1997.

"Official Meets Japanese Envoy Over Defense Guidelines," *Xinhua Domestic Service*, 29 May 1998, in FBIS-CHI-98-149, 29 May 1998.

Ogarkov, Marshal N. V., *Always in Readiness to Defend the Homeland,* 25 March 1982.

Oksenberg, Michel C., Michael D. Swaine, and Daniel C. Lynch, "The Chinese Future," report prepared for Study Group by Pacific Council on International Policy and RAND Center for Asia-Pacific Policy.

O'Neill, Hugh B., *Companion to Chinese History, Facts on File Publications,* New York, 1987.

Organski, A.F.K., and Jacek Kugler, *The War Ledger,* Basic Books, University of Chicago Press, Chicago, Illinois, 1980.

Orme, John, "The Utility of Force in a World of Scarcity," *International Security,* Vol. 22, No. 3, Winter 1997/98.

Oxnam, Robert B., *Ruling From Horseback: Manchu Politics in the Oboi Regency, 1661–1669,* University of Chicago Press, Chicago, Illinois, 1975.

Paine, S.C.M., *Imperial Rivals: China, Russia, and Their Disputed Frontier,* M. E. Sharpe, Inc., New York, 1996.

Paltiel, Jeremy, "PLA Allegiance on Parade: Civil-Military Relations in Transition," *The China Quarterly,* Vol. 143, September 1995.

Papayoanou, Paul A., "Interdependence, Institutions, and the Balance of Power: Britain, Germany, and World War I," *International Security,* Vol. 20, No. 4, Spring 1996.

Papayoanou, Paul A., *Power Ties,* University of Michigan Press, Ann Arbor, Michigan, 1999.

Pearson, Margaret M., "China's Integration into the International Trade and Investment Regime," in Elizabeth Economy and Michel Oksenberg, eds., *China Joins the World: Progress and Prospects,* Council on Foreign Relations Press, New York, 1999.

Pei, Minxin, "Is China Democratizing?" *Foreign Affairs,* January/February 1998.

Pillsbury, Michael, *Salt on the Dragon: Chinese Views of the Soviet-American Strategic Balance*, P-5374, RAND, Santa Monica, California, 1975.

Pollack, Jonathan D., "Chinese Attitudes Towards Nuclear Weapons, 1964–69," *The China Quarterly*, No. 50, London, April–June 1972.

Pollack, Jonathan D., "The Logic of Chinese Military Strategy," *Bulletin of Atomic Scientists*, Vol. 35, No. 1, January 1979.

Pollack, Jonathan D., "China and the Global Strategic Balance," in Harry Harding, ed., *China's Foreign Relations in the 1980s*, Yale University Press, New Haven, Connecticut, 1984.

Pollack, Jonathan D., "The Cox Reports' 'Dirty Little Secret,'" *Arms Control Today*, The Arms Control Association, Washington, D.C., April/May 1999.

Pollack, Jonathan D., and Hyun-Dong Kim, eds., *East Asia's Potential for Instability and Crisis*, RAND CAPP/The Sejong Institute, Santa Monica, California, 1995.

Power, Mary, "China and GATT: Implications of China's Negotiations to Join GATT," *Asian Studies Review*, Vol. 18, No. 2, 1994.

Pye, Lucian W., *The Dynamics of Chinese Politics*, Oelgeschlager, Gunn & Hain, Cambridge, 1981.

Pye, Lucian W., "China: Erratic State, Frustrated Society," *Foreign Affairs*, Vol. 69, No. 4, Fall 1990.

Pye, Lucian W., "How China's Nationalism Was Shanghaied," *Australian Journal of Chinese Affairs*, No. 29, January 1993.

Pye, Lucian W., "Chinese Politics in the Late Deng Era," *The China Quarterly*, No. 142, June 1995.

Qian Qichen, speech to the 49th UN General Assembly, 28 September 1994.

Reiss, Hans, "Introduction," in Hans Reiss, ed., *Kant: Political Writings*, Cambridge University Press, Cambridge, 1995.

Robinson, Thomas W., and David Shambaugh, eds., *Chinese Foreign Policy: Theory and Practice,* Clarendon Press, Oxford, England, 1994.

Rohwer, Jim, "Asia: A Billion Consumers," *The Economist,* October 30, 1993.

Rosecrance, Richard N., *The Rise of the Trading State: Commerce and Conquest in the Modern World,* Basic Books, New York, 1986.

Rosen, Jeremy Brooks, "China, Emerging Economies, and the World Trade Order," *Duke Law Journal,* Vol. 46, No. 6, 1997.

Rossabi, Morris, ed., *China Among Equals,* University of California Press, Berkeley, California, 1983.

Rowe, David M., "World Economic Expansion and National Security in Pre-World War I Europe," *International Organization,* Vol. 53, No. 2, Spring 1999.

Roy, Denny, "The 'China Threat' Issue," *Asian Survey,* Vol. XXXVI, No. 8, August 1996.

Ruggie, John G., "Continuity and Transformation in the World Polity: Toward a Neorealist Synthesis," in Robert O. Keohane, ed., *Neorealism and Its Critics,* Columbia University Press, New York, 1986.

Russett, Bruce, *International Relations and the International System,* Rand McNally, Chicago, Illinois, 1967.

Sanger, David E., "China Faces Test of Resolve to Join Global Economy," *The New York Times,* March 2, 1997.

SarDesai, D. R., *Vietnam: Past and Present,* Westview Press, Boulder, Colorado, 1998.

Schell, Orville, *Discos and Democracy: China in the Throes of Reform,* Pantheon, New York, 1988.

Schlesinger, J. R., *European Security and the Nuclear Threat Since 1945,* RAND, Santa Monica, California, 1967.

Segal, Gerald, "Does China Matter?" *Foreign Affairs,* Vol. 78, No. 5, September/October 1999.

Segal, Gerald, and William T. Tow, eds., *Chinese Defence Policy,* University of Illinois Press, Chicago, Illinois, 1984.

Sha, Zukang, "A Chinese View of the World Situation and the New International Order," in Stuart Harris and Gary Klintworth, eds., *China as a Great Power, Myths, Realities and Challenges in the Asia-Pacific Region,* St. Martin's Press, New York, 1995.

Shambaugh, David, "China's Security Strategy in Post-Cold War Era," *Survival,* Vol. 34, No. 2, Summer 1992.

Shambaugh, David, "Containment or Engagement of China? Calculating Beijing's Responses," *International Security,* Vol. 21, No. 2, Fall 1996a.

Shambaugh, David, "Taiwan's Security: Maintaining Deterrence Amid Political Accountability," *The China Quarterly,* Vol. 148, December 1996.

Shambaugh, David, and Richard H. Yang, eds., *China's Military in Transition,* Clarendon Press, Oxford, England, 1997.

Sheperd, John Robert, *Statecraft and Political Economy on the Taiwan Frontier, 1600–1800,* Stanford University Press, Stanford, California, 1993.

Shiba, Toshinobu, "Sung Foreign Trade: Its Scope and Organization," in Morris Rossabi, ed., *China Among Equals,* University of California Press, Berkeley, California, 1983.

Shirk, Susan, *The Political Logic of Economic Reform in China,* University of California Press, Berkeley, California, 1993.

Simon, Sheldon W., *The Economic Crisis and ASEAN States' Security,* U.S. Army War College, Carlisle Barracks, 1998.

Sims, Holly, "The Unsheltering Sky: China, India, and the Montreal Protocol," *Policy Studies Journal,* Vol. 24, No. 2, 1996.

Smith, Warren W., Jr., *Tibetan Nation: A History of Tibetan Nationalism and Sino-Tibetan Relations,* Westview Press, New York, 1998.

Snyder, Jed C., ed., *After Empire: The Emerging Geopolitics of Central Asia*, NDU Press, Washington, D.C., 1995.

So, Kwan-wai, *Japanese Piracy in Ming China During the 16th Century*, Michigan State University Press, East Lansing, Michigan, 1975.

Song, Yimin, *On China's Concept of Security*, UNDIR, Geneva, Switzerland, 1986.

Spence, Jonathan D., *The Search for Modern China*, W. W. Norton and Company, Inc., New York, 1990.

Spero, Joan E., *The Politics of International Economic Relations*, St. Martin's Press, New York, 1985.

Spiro, David E., "The Insignificance of the Liberal Peace," *International Security*, Vol. 19, No. 2, Fall 1994.

State Council Information Office, *China's National Defense*, Beijing, July 1998.

Stokes, Mark, *China's Strategic Modernization*, Strategic Studies Institute, U.S. Army War College, Carlisle Barracks, 1999.

Struve, Lynn A., *The Southern Ming 1644–1662*, Yale University Press, New Haven, Connecticut, and London, 1984.

Sutter, Robert G., Shirley Kan, and Kerry Dumbaugh, "China in Transition: Changing Conditions and Implications for U.S. Interests," CRS Report for Congress, Congressional Research Service, Library of Congress, Washington, D.C., December 20, 1993.

Suzuki, Chusei, "China's Relations with Inner Asia: The Hsiung-nu, Tibet," in John K. Fairbank, ed., *The Chinese World Order*, Harvard University Press, Cambridge, Massachusetts, 1968.

Swaine, Michael D., "Leadership Succession in China: Implications for Domestic and Regional Stability," paper prepared for the RAND-Sejong Project on East Asia's Potential for Instability and Crisis, February 1995a.

Swaine, Michael D., *China: Domestic Change and Foreign Policy*, RAND, Santa Monica, California, 1995b.

Swaine, Michael D., "China," in Zalmay Khalilzad, ed., *Strategic Appraisal 1996*, RAND, Santa Monica, California, 1996a.

Swaine, Michael D., "Chinese Military Modernization: Motives, Objectives, and Requirements," in *China's Economic Future: Challenges to U.S. Policy (Study Papers)*, submitted to the Joint Economic Committee, 104th Congress of the United States, 2d Session, U.S. Government Printing Office, Washington, D.C., August 1996b.

Swaine, Michael D., *The Role of the Chinese Military in National Security Policymaking*, RAND, Santa Monica, California, revised edition, 1998a.

Swaine, Michael, "Chinese Military Modernization and Asian Security," Asia/Pacific Research Center of the Institute for International Studies, Stanford University, Palo Alto, California, August 1998b.

Swaine, Michael D., and Alastair I. Johnston, "China and Arms Control Institutions," in Elizabeth Economy and Michel Oksenberg, eds., *China Joins the World: Progress and Prospects*, Council on Foreign Relations Press, New York, 1999.

Swanson, Bruce, *Eighth Voyage of the Dragon: A History of China's Quest for Seapower*, Naval Institute Press, Annapolis, Maryland, 1982.

Tarling, Nicholas, *The Cambridge History of Southeast Asia: Volume 1; From Early Times to c. 1800*, Cambridge University Press, Cambridge, Massachusetts, 1992.

Taylor, Keith W., "The Early Kingdoms," in Nicholas Tarling, ed., *The Cambridge History of Southeast Asia: Volume 1; From Early Times to c. 1800*, Cambridge University Press, Cambridge, Massachusetts, 1992.

Tellis, Ashley J., "Military Technology Acquisition and Regional Stability in East Asia," in Jonathan D. Pollack and Hyun-Dong Kim eds., *East Asia's Potential for Instability and Crisis*, RAND CAPP/The Sejong Institute, Santa Monica, California, 1995.

Tellis, Ashley J., "Reconstructing Political Realism: The Long March to Scientific Theory," *Security Studies,* Vol. 2, 1995/96.

Tellis, Ashley J., et al., "Sources of Conflict in Asia" in Zalmay Khalilzad and Ian Lesser, eds., *Sources of Conflict in the 21st Century,* RAND, Santa Monica, California, 1998.

Tellis, Ashley J., et al., "Measuring National Power in the Post-Industrial Age," RAND, Santa Monica, California, 1999, forthcoming.

Thompson, William R., "Succession Crises in the Global Political System," in Albert L. Bergesen, ed., *Crises in the World-System,* Sage Publications, Beverly Hills, California, 1983a.

Thompson, William R., "Uneven Economic Growth, Systemic Challenges and Global Wars," *International Studies Quarterly,* Vol. 27, No. 3, September 1983b.

Thompson, William R., *On Global War,* University of South Carolina Press, Columbia, South Carolina, 1988.

Thompson, William R., "Democracy and Peace: Putting the Cart Before the Horse?" *International Organization,* Vol. 50, No. 1, Winter 1996.

Thompson, William, and Richard Tucker, "A Tale of Two Democratic Peace Critiques," *Journal of Conflict Resolution,* Vol. 41, No. 3, June 1997.

Tien, Hung-mao, and Yun-han Chu, "Building Democracy in Taiwan," *The China Quarterly,* Vol. 148, December 1996.

Tow, William T., "China and the International Strategic System," in Thomas W. Robinson and David Shambaugh, eds., *Chinese Foreign Policy: Theory and Practice,* Clarendon Press, Oxford, England, 1994.

Townsend, James, "Chinese Nationalism," *Australian Journal of Chinese Affairs,* January 1992.

Twitchett, Denis, and John F. Fairbank, eds., *The Cambridge History of China, Volume 10, Late Ch'ing, 1800–1911, Part 1,* Cambridge University Press, London, England, 1978.

Twitchett, Denis, and John K. Fairbank, eds., *The Cambridge History of China, Volume 11, Part 2,* Cambridge University Press, London, England, 1980.

Twitchett, Denis, and Arthur F. Wright, "Introduction," in Arthur F. Wright and Denis Twitchett, eds., *Perspectives on the T'ang,* Yale University Press, New Haven, Connecticut, 1973.

U.S. Congress, *China's Economic Dilemmas in the 1990's: The Problems of Reforms, Modernization, and Interdependence, Vol. 1,* study papers submitted to the Joint Economic Committee, U.S. Government Printing Office, Washington, D.C., 1991.

U.S. Senate Committee on Governmental Affairs, *The Proliferation Primer,* Washington, D.C., January 1998.

Vatikiotis, Michael, "Friends and Fears," *Far Eastern Economic Review,* Vol. 160, 8 May 1997.

Wakeman, Frederic, Jr., *Strangers at the Gate: Social Disorder in South China 1839–1861,* University of California Press, Berkeley, California, 1966.

Wakeman, Frederic, Jr., *The Fall of Imperial China,* The Free Press, New York, 1975.

Wakeman, Frederic, Jr., "The Canton Trade and the Opium War," in Denis Twitchett and John F. Fairbank, eds., *The Cambridge History of China, Volume 10, Late Ch'ing, 1800–1911, Part 1,* Cambridge University Press, London, England, 1978.

Waldron, Arthur, *The Great Wall of China: From History to Myth,* Cambridge University Press, Cambridge, Massachusetts, 1990.

Waldron, Arthur, *From War to Nationalism: China's Turning Point, 1924–1925,* Cambridge University Press, Cambridge, Massachusetts, 1995a.

Waldron, Arthur, "After Deng the Deluge," *Foreign Affairs,* September/October 1995b.

Waltz, Kenneth, *Theory of International Politics,* Random House, New York, 1979.

Wanandi, Jusuf, *Southeast Asia-China Relations,* Chinese Council of Advanced Policy Studies, Taipei, December 1996.

Wang, Gungwu, "Early Ming Relations with Southeast Asia: A Background Essay," in John K. Fairbank, ed., *The Chinese World Order: Traditional China's Foreign Relations*, Harvard University Press, Cambridge, Massachusetts, 1968.

Wang, James C. F., *Contemporary Chinese Politics: An Introduction,* Prentice Hall, Englewood Cliffs, New Jersey, 1995.

Wang, Jisi, "Comparing Chinese and American Conceptions of Security," draft of paper presented at the NPCSD Workshop on History, Culture and the Prospects of Multilateralism, Beijing, people's Republic of China, 7–9 June 1992.

Wang, Jisi, "International Relations Theory and the Study of Chinese Foreign Policy: A Chinese Perspective," in Thomas W. Robinson and David Shambaugh, eds., *Chinese Foreign Policy: Theory and Practice,* Clarendon Press, Oxford, England, 1994a.

Wang, Jisi, "Pragmatic Nationalism: China Seeks a New Role in World Affairs," *Oxford International Review,* Winter 1994b.

Weede, Erich, "Correspondence," *International Security,* Vol. 20, Spring 1996.

Weidenbaum, Murray, and Harvey Sicherman, eds., *The Chinese Economy: A New Scenario,* FPRI, Philadelphia, Pennsylvania, 1999.

White, Gordon, "Democratization and Economic Reform in China," *The Australian Journal of Chinese Affairs,* No. 31, Canberra, Australia, January 1994.

Whiting, Allen, "Assertive Nationalism in Chinese Foreign Policy," *Asian Survey,* Vol. 23, August 1993.

Whiting, Allen S., "Chinese Nationalism and Foreign Policy After Deng," *The China Quarterly,* Vol. 142, June 1995.

Whitson, William W., ed., *The Military and Political Power in China in the 1970s,* Praeger, New York, 1972.

Wills, John E., Jr., "Ch'ing Relations with the Dutch, 1662–1690," in John Fairbank, ed., *The Chinese World Order: Traditional China's Foreign Relations*, 1968.

Wilson, Ian, "Sino-Japanese Relations in the Post-Cold War World," in Stuart Harris and Gary Klintworth, eds., *China as a Great Power, Myths, Realities and Challenges in the Asia-Pacific Region*, St. Martin's Press, New York, 1955.

Wolf, Charles, Jr., "Three Systems Surrounded by Crisis," in Murray Weidenbaum and Harvey Sicherman, eds., *The Chinese Economy: A New Scenario*, FPRI, Philadelphia, Pennsylvania, 1999.

Wolf, Charles, Jr., et al., *Long-Term Economic and Military Trends 1994–2015: The United States and Asia*, RAND, Santa Monica, California, 1995.

Wolf, Reinhold, "Correspondence," *International Security*, Vol. 20, Spring 1996.

Wolters, O. W., *The Fall of Srivijaya in Malay History*, Lund Humphries Pub., Ltd., London, 1970.

Womack, Brantly, ed., *Contemporary Chinese Politics in Historical Perspective*, Cambridge University Press, Cambridge, Massachusetts, 1991.

Wong, John, "China and the WTO," *Asian Economic Journal*, Vol. 10, No. 3, 1996.

The World Bank, *The East Asian Miracle: Economic Growth and Public Policy*, Oxford University Press, New York, 1993.

The World Bank, *China 2020: Development Challenges in the New Century*, The World Bank, Washington, D.C., 1997a.

The World Bank, *Sharing Rising Incomes: Disparities in China*, The World Bank, Washington, D.C., 1997b.

Wright, Mary, *The Last Stand of Chinese Conservatism: The T'ung-Chih Restoration, 1862–1874*, Stanford University Press, Stanford, California, 1962.

Yahuda, Michael B., *China's Role in World Affairs,* St. Martin's Press, New York, 1978.

Yahuda, Michael B., "China and Europe: The Significance of a Secondary Relationship," in Thomas W. Robinson and David Shambaugh, eds., *Chinese Foreign Policy: Theory and Practice,* Clarendon Press, Oxford, England, 1994.

Yao, Yunzhu, "Differences Between Western and Chinese Deterrence Theories," paper prepared for Academy of Military Science, People's Liberation Army, China.

Yi Xiaoxiong, "China's U.S. Policy Conundrum in the 1990s," *Asian Survey,* Vol. XXXIV, No. 8, August 1994.

Yu, Yiguo, "Watch Out for Revival of Japanese Militarism in New Guise," *Xinhua,* 15 August 1997, in FBIS-CHI-97-227, 15 August 1997.

Yue, Ren, "China's Dilemma in Cross-Strait Crisis Management," *Asian Affairs,* Fall 1997.

Zakaria, Fareed, "Culture Is Destiny: A Conversation with Lee Kuan Yew," *Foreign Affairs,* Vol. 73, March/April 1994.

Zang, Xiaowei, "Elite Formation and the Bureaucratic-Technocracy in Post-Mao China," *Studies in Comparative Communism,* Vol. 24, No. 1, March 1991.

Zhao, Suisheng, "Chinese Intellectuals' Quest for National Greatness and Nationalistic Writing in the 1990s," *The China Quarterly,* Vol. 152, December 1997.

Strategic interests. *See* Security
    problems
Success, irony of in a chaotic China,
    xi–xii, 183–187
Sui Dynasty, 34, 52, 61, 62
Sun Yat Sen, 86
Sunzi, view of use of violence, 45–46
Surface-to-surface missiles (SSMs),
    168
Survival space, concept of, 105
Suzerainty relations, 36, 130;
    establishment of by superior
    military force, x, 19
Suzhou urban center, 27

Taiwan, 78, 93, 167; Chinese claims to,
    4, 61, 78, 102, 146–147, 181, 201;
    declining U.S. military assistance
    to, 110; as a future maritime
    adversary, 124–125; incorporated
    into China, 35, 60; independence
    of, 100–101; links with U.S.
    Congress, 116; military
    capabilities of, 166–167; as
    prefecture of Fujian Province, 35;
    present-day relations with, 119–
    120, 131–132, 142; as a threat to
    China, 11, 37–38, 126–127
Tajikstan, 131
Tang Dynasty, 11, 24, 36, 47, 51, 52,
    54, 55, 71, 89, 130; demise of, 52;
    maps of, 42
Tang Taizong, Emperor, 34, 56, 89
Tangut, Chinese campaign against, 48
Tax considerations, 28; reforms
    needed, 99, 185
Technological advances, impact on
    industrialized states' lethality, 103
Technological reform, benefits and
    challenges of, 98–100
Ten Kingdoms, era of, 39
Territorial claims, policies toward,
    129–133
Territorial disputes, xii, 129–130
Thompson, William R., 180, 218
Threats to China, 9–11; to the
    heartland, 27–29; lowering of
    external, 110–111. *See also*
    individual powers
Tibet: attempts to absorb, 60; border
    with China, 57; Chinese behavior
    toward, 64; Chinese campaign
    against, 48; incorporated into
    China, 27, 36, 61, 75, 101, 181;

possible breakaway of, 186; as a
    threat to China, 11, 29
Tibetan Empire, 29
Tibetan peoples, 28, 45. *See also*
    Proto-Tibetan tribes
Tibeto-Burman Nan-chao Kingdom,
    36, 54
Toynbee, Arnold, 220
Toyotomi Hideyoshi, 51
Trade, 2–3, 14–15, 30; for
    appeasement, 66–67; exploitative
    practices, 117, 170, 181; further
    liberalization needed, 99; U.S.-led
    process of privatized, 102–103
Tributary relationships, 58, 67, 69–71,
    89–90
Turkestan, semi-nomadic peoples, 29.
    See also Xinjiang
Turkic peoples, 28, 51, 56
Tyranny of power, in an assertive
    China, xii, 197–229

Uighurs, 55
UN. *See* United Nations
United Nations Development
    Program, 139
United Nations (UN), 135
United States, xii–xiv, 76, 78, 123, 140,
    211; British attitude toward, 215;
    challenge to British hegemony,
    225; China's policies toward, 4,
    114–121, 239; concern over
    China's nuclear weapons
    modification, 3; Congress, 116; as
    a future maritime adversary, 124;
    future rivalry with China, 234–235;
    grand strategy toward China, xii–
    xiv, 154, 241; hedging strategies
    required of, xiii; hegemony
    established by, 219, 223–224, 233;
    influence over China, 76, 78;
    involvement in Southeast Asia,
    110; likelihood of Chinese
    confrontation with, xi; Mutual
    Defense Treaty with Japan, 116;
    pluralist society of, 117; policy of
    detente toward China, 110; policy
    of nuclear deterrence, 87;
    presence and alliance structure in
    Asia, xiii, 76; preservation of
    primacy of, xiii–xiv, 5; as primary
    provider of order-maintenance for
    international system, 2, 202–203;
    relationship with Japan, 116, 119;